B-MOVIE GOTHIC

Traditions in World Cinema

General Editors
Linda Badley (Middle Tennessee State University)
R. Barton Palmer (Clemson University)

Founding Editor
Steven Jay Schneider (New York University)

Titles in the series include:

Traditions in World Cinema
Linda Badley, R. Barton Palmer, and Steven Jay Schneider (eds)

Japanese Horror Cinema
Jay McRoy (ed.)

New Punk Cinema
Nicholas Rombes (ed.)

African Filmmaking
Roy Armes

Palestinian Cinema
Nurith Gertz and George Khleifi

Czech and Slovak Cinema
Peter Hames

The New Neapolitan Cinema
Alex Marlow-Mann

American Smart Cinema
Claire Perkins

The International Film Musical
Corey Creekmur and Linda Mokdad (eds)

Italian Neorealist Cinema
Torunn Haaland

Magic Realist Cinema in East Central Europe
Aga Skrodzka

Italian Post-Neorealist Cinema
Luca Barattoni

Spanish Horror Film
Antonio Lázaro-Reboll

Post-beur Cinema
Will Higbee

New Taiwanese Cinema in Focus
Flannery Wilson

International Noir
Homer B. Pettey and R. Barton Palmer (eds)

Films on Ice
Scott MacKenzie and Anna Westerståhl Stenport (eds)

Nordic Genre Film
Tommy Gustafsson and Pietari Kääpä (eds)

Contemporary Japanese Cinema Since Hana-Bi
Adam Bingham

Chinese Martial Arts Cinema (2nd edition)
Stephen Teo

Slow Cinema
Tiago de Luca and Nuno Barradas Jorge

Expressionism in Cinema
Olaf Brill and Gary D. Rhodes (eds)

French Language Road Cinema
Michael Gott

Transnational Film Remakes
Iain Robert Smith and Constantine Verevis

Coming-of-age Cinema in New Zealand
Alistair Fox

New Transnationalisms in Contemporary Latin American Cinemas
Dolores Tierney

Celluloid Cinema
Edna Lim

Short Films from a Small Nation
C. Claire Thomson

B-Movie Gothic
Justin D. Edwards and Johan Höglund (eds)

edinburghuniversitypress.com/series/tiwc

B-MOVIE GOTHIC

International Perspectives

Edited by Justin D. Edwards and Johan Höglund

EDINBURGH
University Press

Edinburgh University Press is one of the leading university presses in the UK. We publish academic books and journals in our selected subject areas across the humanities and social sciences, combining cutting-edge scholarship with high editorial and production values to produce academic works of lasting importance. For more information visit our website: edinburghuniversitypress.com

© editorial matter and organisation Justin D. Edwards and Johan Höglund, 2018
© the chapters their several authors, 2018

Edinburgh University Press Ltd
The Tun – Holyrood Road
12 (2f) Jackson's Entry
Edinburgh EH8 8PJ

Typeset in 10/12.5 pt Sabon by
Servis Filmsetting Ltd, Stockport, Cheshire

A CIP record for this book is available from the British Library

ISBN 978 1 4744 2344 1 (hardback)
ISBN 978 1 4744 2345 8 (webready PDF)
ISBN 978 1 4744 2346 5 (epub)

The right of the contributors to be identified as authors of this work has been asserted in accordance with the Copyright, Designs and Patents Act 1988 and the Copyright and Related Rights Regulations 2003 (SI No. 2498).

CONTENTS

List of Figures — vii
Acknowledgements — x
Traditions in World Cinema — xi

    Introduction: International B-Movie Gothic — 1
    Justin D. Edwards and Johan Höglund

PART I AMERICA

1. Its, Blobs and Things: Gothic Beings Out of Time — 17
   Justin D. Edwards

2. Re-scripting Blaxploitation Horror: *Ganja and Hess* and the Gothic Mode — 32
   Maisha Wester

3. Alucardas and Alucardos: Vampiric Obsessions, Gothic and Mexican Cult Horror Cinema — 50
   Enrique Ajuria Ibarra

4. Gothic Forests and Mangroves: Ecological Disasters in *Zombio* and *Mangue Negro* — 64
   Daniel Serravalle de Sá

PART II EUROPE

5. Mummies, Vampires and Doppelgängers: Hammer's B-Movies and Classic Gothic Fiction 83
   John Edgar Browning

6. Fantaterror: Gothic Monsters in the Golden Age of Spanish B-Movie Horror, 1968–80 95
   Xavier Aldana Reyes

7. Austro-trash, Class and the Urban Environment: The Politics of *Das Ding aus der Mur* and its Prequel 108
   Michael Fuchs

8. Wither the Present, Wither the Past: The Low-budget Gothic Horror of Stockholm Syndrome Films 122
   Johan Höglund

9. Turkish B-Movie Gothic: Making the Undead Turkish in *Ölüler Konuşmaz Ki* 139
   Tuğçe Bıçakçı Syed

PART III AFRICA AND ASIA

10. *Filamu ya kutisha*: Tanzanian Horror Films and B-Movie Gothic 157
    Claudia Böhme

11. Psychopaths and Gothic Lolitas: Japanese B-Movie Gothic in Gen Takahashi's *Goth: Love and Death* and Go Ohara's *Gothic & Lolita Psycho* 172
    Jay McRoy

12. Hong Kong Gothic: Category III Films as Gothic Cinema 186
    Katarzyna Ancuta

13. B is for Bhayanak: Past, Present and Pulp in Bollywood Gothic 209
    Tabish Khair

Notes on the Contributors 221
Index 225

FIGURES

1.1	Carrington grows alien pods in *The Thing from Another World*	20
1.2	The blob outside the movie theatre in *The Blob*	28
2.1	Meda and Hess discuss suicide, betrayal, racial isolation and racial violence in a scene evoking Jim Crow violence	35
2.2	Crumbling black statue at elite private school reflects Hess's cultural and spiritual state	37
3.1	Justine is tortured by the executioner in *Alucarda*	53
3.2	Manuel and Eduardo pose next to an altar made of merchandise from the film *Alucarda* in *Alucardos*	60
4.1	Night shot of zombies walking in the forest	69
4.2	Evisceration special effects	70
4.3	Priestess morphs into a bestial monster	71
4.4	A POV shot of Luís shooting a zombie in the back of the head	74
4.5	A flooded tropical mangrove and a tide-out mangrove with its aerial roots	75
4.6	Old *candomblé* priestess and night shot of a zombie in the mangrove	77
5.1	A rocket crashes into England's countryside in *The Quatermass Xperiment*	86
5.2	Christopher Lee dons his macabre make-up as the Monster in *Curse of Frankenstein*	87

5.3	Count Dracula embraces Mina, his not-unwilling victim, in *Horror of Dracula*	88
5.4	Mircalla/Carmilla Karnstein takes Amanda in a lesbian embrace in *Lust for a Vampire*	93
6.1	Christopher Lee reprised his emblematic Hammer role for Jess Franco's faithful yet financially compromised adaptation of Bram Stoker's novel, *El conde Drácula / Count Dracula*	97
6.2	Amando de Ossorio's Blind Dead, from the co-production *La noche del terror ciego / Tombs of the Blind Dead*, are a quintessential example of Spain's production of national Gothic myths	104
7.1	The Mur about two kilometres north of the old town/city centre of Graz	110
7.2	The Ding in all its glorious ridiculousness	111
7.3	The movies' amateurish special effects invite what Jeffrey Sconce has called 'paracinematic reading'	113
8.1	Promotional poster showing the Swedish villains of *Madness*	129
8.2	Poster for *Wither/Vittra*	133
9.1	The poster for *Çığlık*	143
9.2	Newspaper advert dating back to 24 April 1949 regarding the release of *Çığlık*	145
9.3	The poster for *Ölüler Konuşmaz Ki*	147
11.1	Yoru reclines in the stream where the serial killer's first victim was found in Gen Takahashi's *Goth: Love of Death*	177
11.2	Itsuki crouches over the unconscious Yoru in Gen Takahashi's *Goth: Love of Death*	179
11.3	The vengeful Yuki wields her deadly parasol in Gô Ohara's *Gothic & Lolita Psycho*	180
11.4	Yuki's mother crucified on the living room wall in Gô Ohara's *Gothic & Lolita Psycho*	181
11.5	Clothed in schoolgirl attire, the dangerous Lady Elle opens fire on Yuki in Gô Ohara's *Gothic & Lolita Psycho*	183
12.1	Poverty and cramped space contribute to the making of the murderer in *Dr. Lamb*	190
12.2	Anthony Wong as the Gothic villain: *Ebola Syndrome* and *The Untold Story*	192
12.3	The shadow of Hong Kong handover looms over the characters in *Run and Kill*	195
12.4	The mundane face of cannibalism *Human Pork Chop* and *The Untold Story*	198

12.5	The interplay of caged spaces and shadows in *The Rapist*	203
12.6	Evil lurking within the labyrinthine spaces of *Red to Kill*	204
12.7	Spaces of entrapment and separation: *The Underground Banker* and *Run and Kill*	206

ACKNOWLEDGEMENTS

The editors want to thank Edinburgh University Press for making this collection possible. In particular, Leslie Gillian, Linda Badley and Barton Palmer deserve our gratitude for their hard work on the manuscript during its various stages. Johan Höglund wishes to thank the Linnaeus University Centre for Concurrences in Colonial and Postcolonial Studies which sponsored research trips and provided a forum for discussion of the project, his wife Cecilia for her love and support, and his children David and Agnes for all the joy they give.

TRADITIONS IN WORLD CINEMA

General editors: **Linda Badley and R. Barton Palmer**
Founding editor: **Steven Jay Schneider**

Traditions in World Cinema is a series of textbooks and monographs devoted to the analysis of currently popular and previously underexamined or undervalued film movements from around the globe. Also intended for general interest readers, the textbooks in this series offer undergraduate- and graduate-level film students accessible and comprehensive introductions to diverse traditions in world cinema. The monographs open up for advanced academic study more specialised groups of films, including those that require theoretically oriented approaches. Both textbooks and monographs provide thorough examinations of the industrial, cultural and socio-historical conditions of production and reception.

The flagship textbook for the series includes chapters by noted scholars on traditions of acknowledged importance (the French New Wave, German Expressionism), recent and emergent traditions (New Iranian, post-Cinema Novo), and those whose rightful claim to recognition has yet to be established (the Israeli persecution film, global found footage cinema). Other volumes concentrate on individual national, regional or global cinema traditions. As the introductory chapter to each volume makes clear, the films under discussion form a coherent group on the basis of substantive and relatively transparent, if not always obvious, commonalities. These commonalities may be formal, stylistic or thematic, and the groupings may, although they need not, be popularly identified as genres, cycles or movements (Japanese horror, Chinese martial arts cinema, Italian Neorealism). Indeed, in cases in which a group of films is not already commonly identified as a tradition, one purpose of the volume is to establish its claim to importance and make it visible (East Central European Magical Realist cinema, Palestinian cinema).

Textbooks and monographs include:

- An introduction that clarifies the rationale for the grouping of films under examination
- A concise history of the regional, national or transnational cinema in question
- A summary of previous published work on the tradition
- Contextual analysis of industrial, cultural and socio-historical conditions of production and reception
- Textual analysis of specific and notable films, with clear and judicious application of relevant film theoretical approaches
- Bibliograph(ies)/filmograph(ies)

Monographs may additionally include:

- Discussion of the dynamics of cross-cultural exchange in light of current research and thinking about cultural imperialism and globalisation, as well as issues of regional/national cinema or political/aesthetic movements (such as new waves, postmodernism or identity politics)
- Interview(s) with key filmmakers working within the tradition.

INTRODUCTION: INTERNATIONAL B-MOVIE GOTHIC

Justin D. Edwards and Johan Höglund

International B-movie Gothic may well seem like a fraught category: Gothic was a Western European form that spread outwards (to the USA and beyond); B-movies were originally US productions that influenced filmmakers in Western Europe and elsewhere. Gothic began in novels such as Horace Walpole's *Castle of Otranto* (1764) and Mary Shelley's *Frankenstein* (1818); it was then translated into an American texts such as Charles Brockden Brown's *Wieland* (1798), William Faulkner's *Absalom, Absalom!* (1936) and Stephen King's '*Salem's Lot* (1975). B-movies such as Jacques Tourneur's *Cat People* (1942) and *I Walked with a Zombie* (1943) developed out of the Hollywood low-budgets of the 1930s and 1940s, but evolved in the post-War period with studio pictures such as *The Creature from the Black Lagoon* (1954) and *I Was a Teenage Werewolf* (1957) before moving across the Atlantic and morphing into, for instance, British Hammer Productions such as *The Curse of Frankenstein* (1957), *Horror of Dracula* (1958) and *The Mummy* (1959) (Davis 2012, 1–18). On the one hand, these transatlantic movements illustrate an international dimension to Gothic and B-movies; on the other, they illustrate how Anglophone North Atlantic cultures can be consolidated into hegemonic cultural forces that extend their reach beyond the region, gaining economic and cultural dominance in other geographical locations.

In this book, we do not seek to perpetuate a cultural form of North Atlantic empire by, for instance, imposing the terms of Gothic aesthetics on Tanzanian cinema or B-movie categorisation on Indian films. Indigenous movies must be recognised on their own terms and in their own contexts, but, as with American and British B-movie Gothic, they also develop as a result of reactions to and engagement with other film cultures. International B-movie Gothic arises out of shared cinematic technologies, techniques and budgetary limitations across cultures. It also gains traction in the latter part of the twentieth century and early in the twenty-first century through filmmakers from across the globe who have begun to explore their own traditions of strange and supernatural phenomena on film, sometimes independent of North Atlantic cinematic art and sometimes influenced by it. According to Glennis Byron (2013), there is 'increasing evidence of cross-cultural and transnational gothics that call out for attention and which suggest that, despite the emergence of so many national and regional forms, in the late twentieth and early twenty-first centuries gothic [is] actually progressing far beyond being fixed in terms of any one geographically circumscribed mode' (1). For Byron, this is not a one-way process; it has engendered transnational exchanges in Gothic wherein new forms are generated and old forms are reinvigorated. In this international environment, Gothic films are significant because movies can easily cross linguistic borders and 'they lend themselves to the marketing of a popular culture that can be easily commoditized, sold and consumed' (4). As a visual form of cultural production, Gothic in film has become more multidirectional than the mode in literary texts.

Gothic in B-Movies

Gothic film is simultaneously easy and difficult to categorise. In the broader context of the horror genre, the history of Gothic films began with the adaptation of Gothic literary works from the eighteenth and nineteenth centuries. In 1910, for instance, Edison Studios in the USA made a sixteen-minute film of Mary Shelley's *Frankenstein*; in 1913, Carl Laemmle, founder of Universal Studios, made an adaptation of Stevenson's *Jekyll and Hyde*, and in 1915 D. W. Griffith adapted Poe's 'Tell-Tale Heart' and 'Annabel Lee' into his film *Avenging Consciousness* (Prawer 1980, 9).

From a historical perspective, we can define a Gothic film as, quite literally, the cinematic adaptation of a Gothic novel or story. However, this definition would be too limited, for the aesthetics and sensibility of Gothic – a Gothic mode – are integrated into films such as Edward D. Wood's *Plan 9 from Outer Space* (1959), which includes vampire and zombie iconography alongside cheapo sci-fi images, and Alfred Hitchcock's *Psycho* (1960), with its eerie doppelgänger narrative and haunting visuals. For the critic Heidi Kaye (2015), Gothic films reflect contemporary anxieties through 'strong visuals' and an 'emphasis on audience response' by combining elements from Gothic literature, stage melodrama and German Expressionism (239–42). Other critics, such as Misha Kavka, see Gothic not as a cinematic genre, but as a mode that is woven into movie images, styles, plots and characters. This mode adapts Gothic literary spaces and figures – haunted houses, dark forests, vampires, ghosts – to the screen, thus tantalising the viewer with trepidation in its subject matter and affect. According to Kavka, fear in Gothic literature and film is generated not primarily through its characters, plots or language, but through its dynamics as spectacle (2002, 209–12).

As spectacle, Gothic films have a recognisable *mise-en-scène*. The visual signifiers and narrative codes are associated with the uncanny, and often include imagery associated with old dark houses, underground passages, secret places, dungeons and graveyards. Settings are often obscured by darkness, fog or even cobwebs to destabilise the viewer and convey a sense of seclusion and isolation. Shadows blur the action and soft lighting creates the sense of perpetual night while under-lighting distorts features. As in Gothic novels, dream and reality are blurred; irrationality is not overcome by rational explanation; transgressions and taboos are indulged, confounding ethical boundaries. Characters include sexual predators, doubles, deformed creatures, mad scientists, the insane, the animal within, as well as figures of the undead such as vampires, zombies and spectral forms. The audience responses of fear, shock, suspense and disorientation are engendered through breakdowns in the distinctions between life and death, the homely and unhomely, obedience and transgression.

This collection theorises the international development of low-budget cinema mainly through the concept of Gothic, but any discussion of movies that seek to frighten the audience must also consider the concept of horror. The two are often difficult to distinguish, partly because both lay claim to the same origin-texts, and partly because they seek to produce similar, although not necessarily identical, affect in their audience. Thus, H. P. Lovecraft claimed in 1927 that Walpole must be considered 'the actual founder of the literary horror-story as a permanent form' (Lovecraft 1927, 21). Horror scholar Noel Carroll agrees, arguing in *The Philosophy of Horror* (1990) that of 'greatest importance for the evolution of the horror genre proper was the supernatural gothic, in which the existence and cruel operations of unnatural forces are asserted graphically' (4). This conclusion allows Carroll to define late-Victorian Gothic narratives such as Oscar Wilde's *The Picture of Dorian Gray* (1891) and Bram Stoker's *Dracula* (1897) as '[c]lassic novels of horror' (6). From this perspective, horror can be described as a by-product and development of Gothic literature and film, but also as a potentially synonymous term that describes a very similar generic corpus. As a result, Gothic and horror share texts and also tropes and conventions such as the maiden in distress, the haunted house, the predatory, monstrous villain and, often, a deep sense of suspicion about rationality and modernity.

Horror arguably produces a different affective response from Gothic. Carroll argues that in horror texts, human protagonists encounter monsters that they perceive as 'abnormal, as disturbances of the natural order' (16). This encounter causes both the characters and, through a 'mirroring effect' (18), the audience reading or watching the horror text to experience shudders as well as 'nausea, shrinking, paralysis, screaming, and revulsion' (18). This has much in common with Fred Botting's definition of Gothic: he argues that while Gothic encourages an 'expansion of one's sense of self, horror describes the movement of contraction and recoil' so that 'terror marks the uplifting thrill where horror distinguishes a contraction at the imminence and unavoidablility of the threat' (10).

Horror is arguably more clearly centred on the visceral than Gothic. Horror is typically physically violent, often displaying the aftermath of brutality in the gory blood and guts that ooze out of mangled bodies that have been destroyed by an abject, monstrous force, person or presence. The terror, panic and dread experienced by the audience of horror arise out of anticipating and seeing the corporeal impact of violence on the body. Horror plays upon the fear of death and the nightmare of dismemberment or the repulsive acts of a psychopath or serial killer. Horror gets under our skin. Rather than a spectacle unfolding on the screen in front of us, horror subsumes the viewer, through the mirroring effect, into its own world of the anticipation of pain, torture, suffering. The real merges with the simulation. We do not leave horror at the cinema. Afterwards, it lurks behind the corner of our street, in the closets of our house, under our bed and behind our curtains. By contrast, the spectacle of Gothic film erects a boundary between audience and film, or between spectating subject and cinematic object. Conversely, the horror movies' affective power resides in its ability to infect the psyche of the viewer beyond the film as self-contained object.

But genres and other forms of cinematic categorisation are always fluid, not fixed. Horror films often overlap with, among other forms, thrillers, science fiction and fantasy. This permeability of modes gives rise to a hybrid form that Xavier Aldana Reyes (2014) refers to as the 'Gothic horror' film, which 'emphasizes the affective qualities of the horror genre' while also including 'recognizable Gothic settings and [conveying] disturbing moods that aim to create the unease or destabilization often ascribed to the reading experience of the Gothic novel' (388). For Reyes, the hybrid category of 'Gothic horror' is useful because it combines Gothic atmospheres and settings (the spectacle) with the 'grossing out' potential of horror (the corporeal). Some of the features of Gothic horror are the corporealisation of the ghost, the focus on forms of monstrosity and the body as a site of monstrous sexualities, as well as a 'marked move toward embodiment which has led to an opening up of the body and its transformation as the ultimate site of Gothic inscription' (388–9).

INTRODUCTION

B-MOVIES AND GOTHIC: INTERNATIONAL PERSPECTIVES

The expression 'B-movie' was originally used to describe Hollywood movies that were largely subordinate to and supportive of the Hollywood A-film. Made with modest budgets, the first B-movies of the 1930s and 1940s were made to generate healthy profits and satisfy a market-place that demanded more cinematic entertainment. While these films were originally designed for a specific means of distribution within the framework of the double bill, the production of B-movies pioneered new cinematic methods in order to overcome the fiscal restraints of the limited budgets. These innovations ensured that, even after improved economic conditions in the 1950s, the B-movie did not disappear. Instead, the expression 'B-movie' became used to describe any low-budget films made in the 1950s, including underground filmmaking, that were more concerned with artistic expression than with bottom-line profit motives (Taves 1993, 313–25).

As early as the 1930s, low-budget movies and Gothic cinematic productions went international. Inspired by Hollywood B-movies, the British Hammer Film Productions made a series of pictures based on the Gothic writings of Edgar Allan Poe, including cinematic adaptations of *The Black Cat* in 1934, *The Raven* in 1935, *The Fall of the House of Usher* in 1960 and *The Pit and the Pendulum* in 1961. There is a significant international dimension to Hammer's Gothic movies, for these B-movies are based on American Gothic texts and are highly influenced by the Hollywood Gothic productions released by Universal Pictures in the early 1930s, particularly Todd Browning's adaptation of Bram Stoker's *Dracula* and James Whale's adaptation of Mary Shelley's *Frankenstein* (both released in 1931). The success of these films – Whale went on to make the highly lucrative sequel *Bride of Frankenstein* in 1935 – disseminated many of the tropes associated with the undead and Gothic spaces used in the Hammer productions. The success of these films also inspired other filmmakers to adapt Gothic novels and stories to the screen. Alfred Hitchcock's 1940 adaptation of Daphne Du Maurier's Gothic novel *Rebecca* (1938) is a notable example.

As this book observes, Anglophone low-budget Gothic cinema was disseminated to an international audience and had a tremendous impact on the emergence and development of local cinematic traditions. Even in the early twentieth century, the cinemas and distribution systems needed to view these films were in place. The technology of cinema had travelled the globe very rapidly. The first cinematograph arrived in South America in 1896 (Barnard 2011, xiv) and in Japan in 1897 (Balmain 2008, 12). Before long, the movie theatres and distribution channels needed for receiving and disseminating films were present in most major parts of the world, and a number of national cinematic traditions had begun to appear. Inspired by Anglophone Gothic, filmmakers in countries as diverse as Italy and South Korea have produced their own Gothic narratives for the screen. These transnational influences have led to significant works such as Dario Argento's *Suspira* (1977) in Italy and Ki-hyeong Park's *Whispering Corridors* (*Yeogogoedam* 1998) in Korea.

The international and transnational territories of Gothic and horror have been neglected by scholarship. Cinematic Gothic and horror traditions, from Hollywood's golden age in the 1930s to the rise of J-horror in the late 1990s, have been studied from national perspectives and contexts. There are also several studies, including Steffen Hantke's *Horror Film: Creating and Marketing Fear* (2004) and Bruce Kawin's *Horror and the Horror Film* (2012), that discuss the general phenomena of horror film and occasionally wander into international territories. However, very few works have made a concerted attempt to explore the global field of Gothic and horror film. Jay Schneider's *Fear Without Frontiers: Horror Cinema Across the Globe* (2003) is an ambitious, strikingly illustrated and kaleidoscopic attempt at describing global horror films; it is useful as a comprehensive and fascinating inventory of various national traditions, but does not offer a careful scholarly exploration of international horror films. Jay Schneider and Tony William's *Horror International* (2005) takes a more academic approach and observes that the 'horror film traditions of other national and regional cinemas are engaged in a dynamic process of cross-cultural exchange with American mainstream, independent, and underground alike' (2). However, the concept of horror is used here only in its generic sense, a fact that makes it difficult for the book's excellent contributions to fully account for the affective and cultural work performed by the films and industries under scrutiny.

B-Movie Gothic: International Perspectives moves beyond previous scholarship by discussing the emergence of international cinema through the theoretical lenses supplied by Gothic, by horror, and by Gothic horror. This allows for a more complex reading of these films than the designation of them as simply 'horror'. In addition to this, this book highlights the B-movie or low-budget quality of international Gothic and horror film and observes how low-budget Gothic and horror film produced by independent filmmakers or independent companies has led to artistic innovations, new approaches to genre, and unique demographic patterns and screening practices. After the 1950s, major and minor film studios across the globe questioned the commercial viability of low-budget productions and, as a result, B-movies often exist in opposition to the big-budget studios in the USA, Britain, India and Japan, a legacy that has inspired many independent filmmakers to produce imaginative Gothic cinema.

This book also contributes to existing scholarship by further exploring the international horror traditions that texts such as *Horror International* have begun to investigate. A crucial point here is that the films studied in this volume are not just derivatives of Gothic narratives from North Atlantic

B-movies, but draw on stories that are intimately tied to local narratives. Italian filmmakers have, for instance, played a crucial role in the development of international low-budget Gothic horror movies. Dark and psychological horror thrillers such as Hitchcock's *Psycho* (1960) inspired what many film critics call Giallo, a low-budget mode that, like much Gothic fiction, focuses on young women who are stalked by faceless murderers. Giallo disturbs its audience by using a *mise-en-scène* that sometimes turns the viewer into the voyeur and, at times, includes the point of view of the violent male perpetrator. While these films include misogynist imagery, they also reflect a crisis in Italian culture and society during the period. From this perspective, they can be described, in the words of Mikel J. Koven (2006), as a form of subaltern 'vernacular cinema' (v), a tradition 'below most of our cultural radar' (vi) that refuses to be categorised in terms of good and bad, that speaks to itself, to its own genre and to its aficionados located firmly outside of 'mainstream, bourgeois cinema culture' (19). Importantly, the low budgets of these films make the vernacular cinematic realm possible. While mainstream cinema is typically tasked with recovering an often large financial investment by appealing to a vast mainstream audience and its critics, low-budget Giallo can afford to explore alternative intellectual and affective spaces.

At the same time, Giallo speaks clearly about its political present. The 1960s and 1970s were, in Italy as in many other places, times of rampant political and domestic violence as patriarchy and religion were being questioned. In this context, Catholicism can be understood as both a regional and a global influence that led to the production of new forms of Italian Gothic films. For instance, the director Lucio Fulci is said to draw from a distinctly patriarchal and Catholic universe, and in several of his films he depicts the bloody killing of wayward, independent women by a faceless patriarch; in other films, such as *Don't Torture a Duckling* (1972), the killer of young women is a Catholic priest.

Giallo was part of the reinvention of the low-budget Gothic film in the 1960s and had a profound impact on the emergence of low-budget slasher, splatter and gore movies in the USA, which often adapted Giallo's violent imagery to comment on teenage rebellion and teenage sexuality, two central concerns in North America at the time. Meanwhile, in Italy, directors such as Argento and Fulci used Giallo to test the limits of images depicting explicit sexuality and graphic violence. This resulted in another set of seminal and commercially successful Italian movies, including Fulci's *Zombi 2* (1979) (which he considered to be a sequel to Romero's 1978 film *Dawn of the Dead*) and Ruggero Deodato's *Cannibal Holocaust* (1980), the most notorious of the many cannibal exploitation films of late 1970s and early 1980s.

These ultra-violent films, most of which fit into Xavier Reyes's definition of Gothic horror, are not only a test of societal propriety, but also commentaries on contemporary society and culture. The director Ruggero Deodato explains that his film *Cannibal Holocaust* was conceived as a critique of the Italian media coverage of the political strife in Italy and in Europe in the late 1970s (DeVos 2010, 82). But the horrifically explicit violence of the movie can also be read as an indictment of the war in Vietnam (taking place in another jungle) and, more generally, of European and US imperialism. Thus, in *Cannibal Holocaust*, white European protagonists perish at the hands (and mouths) of those who have been colonised and who are on the edge of extinction. Like many nineteenth-century Gothic novels, though, the film also strips the indigenous people of humanity and commodifies the retributive violence that is projected onto the screen. A similar reading is appropriate for Fulci's *Zombie 2*, which takes place on a Caribbean island complete with a labyrinthine jungle and a Conquistador graveyard. On this island the white, American protagonists are attacked by black zombies, zombified Conquistadores and infected family members. As Simone Brioni observes, 'zombies cannot be strictly identified with the colonised subject, but the colonial overtones of their characterization bring back the memory of a past that seeks revenge in the present' (2013, 170). In this way, the Gothic horror B-movie of this era is both a vehicle of reactionary discourses and a way to critically comment on social and historical development.

If Italian low-budget Gothic cinema includes a critique of North Atlantic imperialism, we find something slightly different in B-movies from South Korea. South Korea is a nation troubled by recent conflict: Japanese occupation and the Soviet–Japanese War, as well as the Chinese Civil War. In this context, South Korea has been a colonised, rather than a colonising, nation, a situation that was further emphasised when the USA offered military aid to the nation in an attempt to limit the spread of communism via North Korea. These violent historical developments manifest in the B-movie Gothic produced in the nation; Hong-jin Na's film *The Wailing* (*Goksung* 2016) depicts the Japanese as triggering a zombie epidemic in the region while the opening scene of Joon-ho Bong's *The Host* (*Gwoemul* 2006) includes a US physician ordering his Korean assistant to pour toxic formaldehyde into the Han River, an act that spawns a monstrous creature.

Some critics of the rich tradition of South Korean Gothic cinema do not focus on historical contexts, but choose instead to examine how these films draw on local stories and folklore. Unlike North Atlantic Gothic cinema wherein the victim is often a young woman, *The Thousand Year-Old Fox* (*Cheonnyeon ho* 1969), instead represents this figure as a perpetrator by casting a young women as a demonic fox. Similarly, the *Ju-On* series (2000–16) (as well as the 1998 Japanese production *Ringu*) depict young women as often animalistic threats who inspire terror. In fact, this female Gothic character is present in the very first South Korean Gothic film, Kim Ki-young's *The Housemaid* (*Hanyeo*

1969), and it is widespread in the resurgence of South Korean Gothic cinema that began with Park Ki-hyung's *Whispering Corridors* (*Yeogogoedam*) in 1998, where a female ghost haunts the corridors of a local high school.

The female ghosts and the spirit demons in these films are tied to an East Asian folkloric tradition that centres on a malign female fox demon who seeks to shape-shift into a human form (Pierse and Byrne 2013, 35–6). In all these films, we witness the rupturing of traditional gender relations and women's rejection of patriarchy. Yet the representation of these women as vengeful ghosts or monstrous creatures also refers to the wide circulation of international Gothic cinema wherein women are depicted as threatening creatures who inspire anxiety and fear. Apart from the Japanese and Chinese cinema wherein this image is common, the trope of the ghostly or demonic woman sometimes appears in North Atlantic Gothic cinema such as *Carrie* (1976), *Ginger Snaps* (2000) and *Darkness Falls* (2003). Thus, Korean low-budget Gothic movies must be read with sensitivity to their local context, but also as part of the international circulation of cinematic Gothic. Another significant example of such circulation is the prevalence of the zombie. Korean filmmaker Sang-ho Yeon has added to the ubiquity of this genre through films such as *Seoul Station* (2016) and *Train to Busan* (*Busanghaeng* 2016). These include local Korean plots, but they are also influenced by Romero's early zombie flicks and Fulci's *Zombi 2*, as well as big-budget Gothic horror movies such as *28 Days Later* (2002) *Resident Evil* (2002) and *World War Z* (2013).

B-movie Gothic is, then, a form of transnational cinema that includes a complex matrix of local and global influences. On the one hand, these texts encourage a shift away from the focus on national brands and show the impact of the world and of global cinema, joined together through the new media and digital culture that can disseminate films in new ways. On the other hand, Gothic B-movies are often rooted in a sense of place, incorporating local stories (such as folklore) and local histories that include counter-hegemonic responses from former colonial and emerging countries. While the economic and cultural machine of Hollywood first unleashed Gothic B-movies on the world, the mode has haunted back: contemporary Gothic films from, for instance, Korea and Mexico have influenced US film directors, and filmmakers from those countries are just as likely to cite passages from work by Lucio Fulci, Jaume Balaguero or Hideo Nakata as they are to reference films by Tod Browning or George Romero.

The Chapters

The first part of this book focuses on B-movie Gothic and Gothic horror produced in America, the continent that spawned the concept of B-movies. The first chapter of this part reflects on 1950s American B-movies about the foreign body – the thing – that disrupts the homely place of the nation. Here, Justin D. Edwards explores the relationship between Gothic stories by Theodore Sturgeon and H. P. Lovecraft and B-movies such as *It Came from Outer Space* (1953), *It! The Terror from Beyond Space* (1958) and *The Blob* (1958), all of which include nameless creatures that resist the articulation and categorisation that would place them in the order of things. The liminality of these phenomena links them to Gothic literary and cinematic traditions that feature the 'undead', mysterious spectres and unexplainable supernatural presences. For Edwards, the arrival of the foreign body in these B-movies does not only confound the classifications of bodies and spaces, but also disturbs human conceptions of time and temporality. This is because 'the Thing' sparks an awareness of another history – a non-human time – that exists in an alien place. The spatial question 'where does it come from?' thus leads to a temporal question: 'what is its history?' The Thing is not just a Gothic being from outer space; it is also a Gothic being out of time.

Moving into the 1970s, the racial politics of B-movie Gothic are considered by Maisha Wester, who argues that an African-American low-budget film such as Bill Gunn's *Ganja and Hess* (1973) places the Gothic tradition of the vampire narrative alongside representations of racial turmoil, assimilation and fractured communities. For Wester, the claustrophobic framing techniques and eerie score of the film produce a Gothic spectacle that suggests violence rather than explicitly depicting its corporeal impact and aftermath. Wester also reflects on how *Ganja and Hess* is a model for Black filmmakers of the 1990s and 2000s. Gothic B-movies such as *Def By Temptation* (1990), *Crazy as Hell* (2002) and *A Vampire in Brooklyn* (1995) are, Wester maintains, part of a Gothic tradition that suppresses the depiction of the monster until the conclusions of the movies. Thus, they choose to focus on the construction of contemporary African American identity, the significance of history, and the tension between ancestral culture and modern American identity. Real terror arises out of attempts to negotiate a modern Black identity in the USA, not the depiction of a monstrous creature.

Similar forms of hybridity are explored by Enrique Ajuria Ibarra in his reading of Gothic B-movies from Mexico. He interrogates the intertextual, referential and Gothic aspects of Ulises Guzmán's film *Alucardos* (2010), a Mexican mockumentary movie that pays homage to the underground low-budget film director Juan López Moctezuma. For Ibarra, *Alucardos* presents the audience with a perverse and fantastic plot wherein the vampire is a key figure that addresses issues of sexuality, transgression, memory, spectrality, life and death. More importantly, though, this chapter analyses how the film is part of the process of mythification surrounding the Gothic B-movies of López Moctezuma, whose films continue to have a devoted cult following in Mexico.

The ubiquity of Gothic in twenty-first-century popular culture is also considered by Daniel Serravalle de Sá in his chapter on Brazilian low-budget zombie movies. Here, he considers the influence of comic books, TV series and videogames on Petter Baiestorf's *Zombio* (1999), David Pinheiro's *Porto dos mortos* (2008) and Rodrigo Aragão's *Mangue Negro* (2009). Within this cannibalisation of forms, de Sá argues that, in the Brazilian context, the cannibalism of the zombie needs to be theorised as a cultural metaphor for a creative aesthetic that is linked to hybridity and tropicalisation.

Part II of the book moves from the Americas to Europe and opens with a chapter by John Browning that describes the path-breaking Gothic produced by Hammer films in the middle of the twentieth century. Browning's chapter maps the rise of this studio and describes the creation of some of the revolutionary films that emerged from its Gothic premises. A point here is that the studio's use of explicit violence and sexuality had a tremendous impact on international Gothic cinema through the global dissemination of various dubbed versions.

Hammer's Gothic movies and Hollywood B-movie Gothic had a profound influence on the Turkish film industry. With this in mind, Tuğçe Bıçakçı analyses how Yavuz Yalınkılıç's film *Ölüler Konuşmaz Ki / The Dead Don't Talk* (1970) reinvents the classic Gothic tropes of the haunted house, the graveyard and the undead for a Turkish audience. Bıçakçı documents how the film focuses on the 'hortlak', a creature from Turkish folklore who returns from the dead to terrorise the living. In this process, the B-movie figure of the undead is Islamicised, thus making Gothic tropes relevant for local viewers.

In his chapter on Spanish Gothic B-movies, Xavier Aldana Reyes contextualises the rise and popularity of the form – called 'fantaterror' or fantastic terror in Spain – and examines its main characteristics and thematic concerns. Like other quick-cash-in genres, the horror industry in Spain was commercially driven. However, fantaterror cannot simply be dismissed as thrash culture, for these films thematically engage with power structures in Franco's Spain, particularly issues such as state-sanctioned tyranny and the impacts of the dictatorship. For Reyes, B-movies such as Enrique López Eguiluz's *La marca del hombre lobo / Frankenstein's Bloody Terror* (1967) and Narciso Ibáñez Serrador's *La Residencia / The House That Screamed* (1969) adapt the Gothic aesthetics of Hollywood Bs and Hammer Productions to explore the political environment of Spain between 1968 and 1980.

The other contributions in the European part discuss contemporary Gothic horror. In his chapter on Nordic Gothic B-movies, Johan Höglund identifies the production studio Stockholm Syndrome Film's movies *Madness* (2010), *Blood Runs Cold* (2011) and *Wither* (2012) as merging US Gothic horror aesthetics with Swedish social contexts. According to Höglund, these low-budget movies challenge the metanarratives of Swedish history, particularly canonical national stories about Swedish migration to the USA, colonisation and the egalitarian welfare state. SSF does this, Höglund argues, by replacing Swedish metanarratives with Gothic stories about violent rednecks, the return of the repressed and the haunting history of Swedish imperialist projects.

The political dimensions of B-movies are also explored by Michael Fuchs in his analyses of the Austrian ultra-low-budget movies *Das Ding aus der Mur* (2012) and *Das Ding aus der Mur: Zero* (2015). For Fuchs, the fake blood, super-cheap special effects and 'splatstick' aspects of these films combine with Gothic's ability to generate unease through corporeal instability. The monster of the films – a half-human, half-amphibian creature – encourages audiences to reflect on the political and economic issues of ecological sustainability. The homely place of the monster, the river Mur, is negatively impacted by economic 'progress' that threatens to destroy the environment and create a 'false' nature.

The third and final part of the book studies the emergence of African and Asian Gothic and Gothic horror cinema. The adaptation of North Atlantic B-movie Gothic aesthetics for local audiences is central to our considerations of the form. This global readiness to adapt is discussed by Tabish Khair in his chapter on Indian 'masala' pulp films, which investigates the concept of 'bhayanak'. This term loosely translates as 'horror', but is, in fact, derived from classical Sanskrit aesthetic theories of the seven (or nine) 'rasas' and is better translated into English as 'Gothic'. Drawing on examples of Hindi films from the 1950s to the 1990s, particularly *Jaani Dushman* (1979) and *Karz* (1980), Khair argues that the Bollywood productions that focus on horrific effects have historically resulted in critical and commercial failure. However, the low-budget Bollywood movies that invoke the sublime terrors of the Gothic fare much better among critics and at the box office.

This consideration of the financial success of B-movies is also an important consideration when reading Hong Kong's Category III films, which were introduced to the city in 1988 as part of the new ratings system. Katarzyna Ancuta's chapter on these films maps a dystopian side to Hong Kong's financial success in the Gothic aesthetics of films such as *Men Behind the Sun* (1988), *Daughter of Darkness* (1993) and *The Eight Immortals Restaurant* (1993). Here, Hong Kong is a place of violence and exploitation within its dark alleys, overpopulated estates and restaurants that serve dumplings made from human flesh. The urban Gothic flourishes in postcolonial Hong Kong.

In recent decades, Japanese fashion has embraced North Atlantic Gothic styles. Dozens of popular *anime* series and *manga* titles feature characters sporting attire that evokes American and European Gothic aesthetics; one can find young women dressed as 'Gothic Lolitas' and young men adorned in long black dusters and affecting carefully practised postures outside Harajuku Station. Jay McRoy surveys the presence of Gothic style in Japan and analyses two Japanese B-movies, Gen Takahashi's *Goth* (2008) and Go Ohara's *Psycho Gothic Lolita* (2011), to reflect on how Japanese popular culture has adopted and adapted Gothic styles and narratives.

In the book's closing chapter, Claudia Böhme takes the analysis from Asia to Africa through a study of the first Tanzanian low-budget Gothic movie, *filamu ya kutisha* (2003), directed by Mussa Banzi. The chapter illustrates how the film merges North Atlantic Gothic aesthetics with the local form of 'Nsyuka', a narrative based on the Tanzanian story of an evil ancestor spirit. For Böhme, Banzi's movie is a ground-breaking text that has inspired a generation of young filmmakers to merge the North Atlantic Gothic figures of ghosts, witches and zombies with stories from Tanzanian folklore.

In this way, *B-Movie Gothic* is the first major attempt to map B-movie Gothic horror from a global perspective. The ambition to study such a global body of culture means that the chapters comprise a similarly wide range of disciplines, including ethnology, anthropology, postcolonial studies, film studies, cultural studies and critical theory. Regardless of the theoretical and methodological approach, however, all the chapters in this book investigate the aesthetic desire to represent the uncanny dynamics of modernity and its psycho-social anxieties, its political dilemmas and dark sides, its creepiness, as well as its collapsing of the binaries of life and death, nature and culture, self and other. *B-Movie Gothic* maps, from its multiple geographical and theoretical perspectives, the remarkably complex results that this desire's engagement with modernity has produced in various parts of the globe. The results, we firmly believe, show that international B-movie Gothic cinema speaks eloquently about local and global relations, about past and present anxieties, and about Gothic as such. Using small to non-existent financial resources, off-the-shelf technology and often boundless enthusiasm, low-budget B-movie Gothic produces remarkable and at times deeply unsettling narratives grounded in local traditions, in horrific historical developments, in diverse and stratified social contexts, and in a willingness to explore and comment on the genre itself.

Bibliography

Balmain, Colette (2008), *Introduction to Japanese Horror Film* (Edinburgh: Edinburgh University Press).
Barnard, Timothy (2011), 'Preface', in Timothy Barnard and Peter Rist (eds), *South American Cinema: A Critical Filmography 1915–1994* (London: Routledge), ix–xix.
Brioni, Simone (2013), 'Zombies and the Post-colonial Italian Unconscious', Cinergie il cinema e le altre arti 4, 166–82.
Botting, Fred (2014), *Gothic* (London: Routledge).
Byron, Glennis (2013), 'Introduction', in Glennis Byron (ed.), *Globalgothic* (Manchester: Manchester University Press), 1–10.
Carroll, Noël (1990), *The Philosophy of Horror or Paradoxes of the Heart* (London: Routledge).

Davis, Blair (2012), *The Battle for the Bs: 1950s Hollywood and the Re-birth of Low-budget Cinema* (New Brunswick, NJ: Rutgers University Press).
DeVos, Andrew (2010), 'The More You Rape Their Senses, the Happier They Are: A History of Cannibal Holocaust', in Robert G. Weiner and John Cline (eds), *Cinema Inferno: Celluloid Explosions from the Cultural Margins* (Lanham: The Scarecrow Press), 76–100.
Hantke, Steffen (ed.) (2004), *Horror Film: Creating and Marketing Fear* (Jackson: University Press of Mississippi).
Kavka, Misha (2002), 'The Gothic on Screen', in Jerrold E. Hogle (ed.), *The Cambridge Companion to Gothic Fiction* (Cambridge: Cambridge University Press), 209–28.
Kawin, Bruce (2012), *Horror and the Horror Film* (London: Anthem Press).
Kaye, Heidi (2015), 'Gothic Film', in David Punter (ed.), *A New Companion to The Gothic* (Oxford: Blackwell), 239–51.
Koven, Mikel J. (2006), *La Dolce Morte: Vernacular Cinema and the Italian Giallo Film* (Lanham: The Scarecrow Press).
Lovecraft, H. P. (1927), *Supernatural Horror in Literature* (Abergele: Wermod & Wermod).
Pierse, Alison and James Byrne (2013), 'Creepy Liver-Eating Fox Ladies: *The Thousand Year Old Fox* and Korea's *Gumiho*', in Alison Pierse and Daniel Martin (eds), *Korean Horror Cinema* (Edinburgh: Edinburgh University Press), 35–47.
Prawer, S. S. (1980), *Caligari's Children: The Film as Tale of Terror* (Oxford: Oxford University Press).
Reyes, Xavier Aldana (2014), 'Gothic Horror Film, 1960 – Present', in Glennis Byron and Dale Townshend (ed.), *The Gothic World* (London: Routledge), 388–98.
Schneider, Steven Jay (2003), *Fear Without Frontiers: Horror Cinema Across the Globe* (Godalming: FAB Press).
Schneider Steven Jay and Tony William (2005), 'Introduction', in Steven Jay Schneider and Tony William (ed.), *Horror International* (Detroit: Wayne State University Press), 1–12.
Taves, Brian (1993), 'The B Film: Hollywood's Other Half', in Tino Balio (ed.), *Grand Design: Hollywood as a Modern Business Enterprise, 1930–1939* (New York: Charles Scribner's Sons), 313–50.

PART I

AMERICA

1. ITS, BLOBS AND THINGS: GOTHIC BEINGS OUT OF TIME

Justin D. Edwards

It walked in the woods.
   It was never born. It existed. Under the pine needles the fires burn, deep and smokeless in the mold. In heat and in darkness and decay there is growth. There is life and there is growth. It grew, but it was not alive. It walked unbreathing through the woods, and thought and saw and was hideous and strong, and it was not born and it did not live. It grew and moved about without living. (Sturgeon 1993 [1940], 303)

This passage from Theodore Sturgeon's story 'It' (1940) anticipates the Gothic phenomena of 1950s b-movie schlock: those Its, Blobs and Things that come from some other place – the void of outer space or the mysterious black lagoon – and threaten to disrupt the everyday life of middle America. As in the unabashedly camp movie *Swamp Thing* (1982), the 'It' of Sturgeon's story is a massive creature of organic matter. It is a colossal, powerful and destructive veggie-monster-Thing comprising the moss and mould that has accumulated over decades on the soil of a boreal forest. It gives off the fetid odour of rotting plants and drops 'little particles of muck behind it' as it lumbers through the growth, leaving behind a trail of mulch (318). This 'thing of the mold' does not eat (318). It does not breathe. It does not sleep. It cannot be shot or stabbed. It does not distinguish between tree life, canine life and human life. It kills out of curiosity. It is unnameable because it defies classification: it is decay alongside growth, movement without life, strength without solidity, maturity without birth. It is a Thing that confounds ontological and phenomenological conceptions of being or sentience. It is outside human-centred relationships or anthropocentric conceptions of the biosphere. It is a non-human object that threatens life and cannot be enframed by the subject through an ordering for human use or even categorised within language.

Most important, though, is that Sturgeon's veggie-monster is outside of what we often conceptualise as a coupling of being and time. This Thing cannot distinguish between day and night; it must learn that perception is altered with the passing of the sun. The time-cycles of sleeping and waking, hunger and sustenance, do not apply. And temporal units of time – seconds, minutes, hours – or the marking of events in reference to time occurrences have no currency. This Thing exists but was never born, a situation that negates any sense of beginning, a temporal origin, and thus confounds the conception of time as experience within the being. But it also challenges the notion that time is the condition of possibility of experience in what Heidegger (1962) identifies as the vital link between being and time for human subjectivity (39).

In Sturgeon's text, time is not the horizon of being. And because the Thing's beginning-in-birth cannot be established, it is outside of being-in-the-world (being there) in any historical, temporal sense of being. This radically alters any human conception of time wherein subjectivity underlays temporality. But it also challenges claims that temporality is the prerequisite for experience. This is because Sturgeon challenges formations of time that are tied to subjectivity by imagining a temporal world outside the subject. This leads us into a wilderness of thought where Things that once lay in the background of subjectivity come to the foreground and reveal a weird aura. It is here that we find a site for the critical revaluation of existing norms where temporal subjectivity loses its privileged place and we move into the realm of speculation.

In this chapter, I examine American B-movies from the 1950s alongside the fiction of early twentieth-century US Gothic texts that frame Gothic monsters within the fundamental paradox of the unnameable Thing, an unknown life form that comes from a non-human temporal realm. The Thing thus gestures to a world outside of the subject wherein the 'weird' challenges us to revaluate existing norms and where the gaze from a particular human subject position loses its privileged place. The Thing replaces the subject with an object; or, better yet, subjectivity is superseded by the degraded 'thingness' of an object that has lost its use-value. To call the Gothic creature a Thing is to foreground a sense of disunity and incoherence when compared with the human experience, not just identifying it as a foreign entity, but also placing it in a nonhuman realm where it cannot speak for itself. Perhaps a better way to express this positioning is not in the word 'nonhuman' but in the word 'unhuman', which links it to the uncanny and the possibilities of something that will come back to haunt the human without it being fully integrated into humanity. In this respect, the unhuman is closely tied up with notions of alienation and anonymity and opens up the possibility of an alien subjectivity as a spectre that haunts any coherent sense of cohesion in the human self.

In the Gothic creature called the Thing, I suggest, the subject becomes an alien materiality, not only in terms of becoming other, but also in its unknowability. While the unhuman may be a force of opposition, a threat, it does not necessarily negate humanity. In fact, it is the inclusion of the human in the unhuman that might, in the end, allow the Thing to speak. For although the Thing, in some instances, extends beyond the human body and crawls into another body, it retains some semblance of a human body. The movement from subject to object to Thing underscores the limits of alterity, and the fear of becoming unhuman arises out of a consciousness about the potential effacement of subjectivity. In the experience of the unhuman, the reality of materiality (thingness) persists despite the apparent extinction of subjectivity, for it is precisely because the Thing returns that its reality is accented outside the subject, a subject that becomes alien to itself.

TIME FOR THE B-MOVIE THING

An important B-movie corollary to Sturgeon's 'It' is *The Thing from Another World* (1951) directed by Howard Hawks and Christian Nyby. Here, the Thing is a plant-based creature which is discovered frozen in ice near an American North Pole research camp. A scientist, Dr Carrington, and an Air Force Captain, Patrick Hendry, accidently destroy the UFO that brought the Thing to earth. They extract the block of ice holding the alien and transport it back to base camp. The monster accidently thaws and begins to wreak havoc: it kills sled dogs, attacks Dr Stern, breaks into the greenhouse and consumes two members of the research team, stringing up their bodies and draining them of blood. When the Thing's arm is severed by one of the dogs, the microscopic examination shows it to be vegetable rather than animal matter, revealing the Thing to be a highly evolved form of plant life. As the veggie-monster's arm warms to ambient temperature, the body part ingests some of the dog's blood and the hand begins to move. The alien arm becomes a thing of its own and, as the palm of the hand opens, the researchers discover seed pods that have the power to reproduce the monstrous Thing.

The movie repeats the Gothic trope of the monstrous creature – the dangerous Other – sucking human blood, but at the centre of the film is a homage to Mary Shelley's *Frankenstein* (1818). The Arctic setting that is prominent in both texts combines with the 'mad' scientist and foreboding about unchecked scientific enquiry. Like Victor Frankenstein, Dr Carrington seeks 'the secrets that would give us a new science' and 'the keys to the stars'. He secretly uses the creature's pods to grow new life (using fertiliser and blood plasma); he

Figure 1.1 Carrington grows alien pods in *The Thing from Another World* (1951)

considers the porous unconnected cellular growth of the alien to be intellectually superior (mastering interplanetary travel) and unimpeded by the emotions and desires of the animal-human. But his attempts to create new life only lead to destruction – the death of those around him – and he is threatened and nearly killed by the Thing he tries to reproduce.

Dr Carrington's and Victor's attempts to envision the inner workings of life on Earth are resisted on both a conceptual and experimental level. The experiments lead to destruction, not creation, thus refuting all interrogations that might assuage the desire for knowledge and lead to a comforting and homely relationship to the world. Rather, the stitching together of a new creature and attempts to grow alien pods only thwart the human desire for homeliness on Earth. If the place they inhabit, the planet, is knowable, then it is only because it draws a limit against what cannot be known. The earth shifts beneath the scientists' feet. Within the sublime landscape of the extreme north, the irreducible element persists blindly, revealing itself in moments that generate disorientation, anxiety and fear. This unhomely paradigm is heightened in *The Thing* when the technological instruments of the crew go awry; as they get closer to the Thing, the navigational devices and Geiger counter cease to function, thus making the ominous terrain increasingly disorienting. It is here that the crew find the contact zone for a foreign place, an alien civilisation.

Yet this contact zone is more than just a site where two different cultures meet: it is an encounter that disrupts the homeliness of the planet. The crew are forced to grapple with a potential asymmetrical power relation where the superior intelligence and technology of the Thing cannot be contained or controlled by the inferior technology of human weaponry. This sparks an extreme form of the uncanny that does not just disturb the individual's sense of identity but also the subject's fundamental state of existence. This is the moment when anxiety transforms into fear and marks the point of losing touch with the primary moment of being. Indeed, when Captain Hendry's crew find the Thing frozen in the ice, the moment of vision becomes the moment of anxiety and fear as they must confront a spatial lack (where does this Thing come from?) and a temporal lack (when did this creature arrive? And when did its civilisation evolve?).

The Thing haunts the base from within the ice. The guards express their unease – a creepiness – when they are alone in the room with it. One guard believes the Thing can see him; he puts a blanket over the ice block, resulting in the ice melting and the release of the creature. It then physically haunts the base. Like Frankenstein's creature, it can live exposed to the harsh conditions of the Arctic; it is elusive and nobody knows when it will reappear. This haunting is translated into the movie's aesthetics, for the dark black-and-white corridors on the base throw off shadows in the dim light, and the lack of windows transforms the base into what look like underground passages. This *mise-en-scène* repeats the visual imagery of James Whale's 1931 version of *Frankenstein*, so it is not surprising that, when the Thing appears, it bears a striking resemblance to Whale's slow-moving and hulking image of Frankenstein's creature. The use of electricity is also crucial to both films, but with an important twist: the electrical machines spark Frankenstein's creature into life whereas the Thing is lured into a wired-up corridor and electrocuted to death.

The Thing from Another World is based on the novella *Who Goes There?* (2011 [1938]) by John W. Campbell, which includes the discovery of an alien life form frozen in ice. The creature, though apparently dead, is hideous and has telepathic powers and shape-shifting abilities. This monster moves away from a two-legged humanoid creature and towards a mysterious Thing that does not conform to a recognisable bodily form. In a genealogy of Gothic it is important to contextualise Campbell's novella in relation to Lovecraft's Gothic text 'The Unnamable' (1925), which begins with the narrator's reflection on how a giant willow tree in an old cemetery uses its tentacle-like roots to extract 'spectral and unmentionable nourishment' from the buried corpses (Lovecraft 2014, 274). This image of an organic Thing consuming human flesh sparks a nocturnal discussion in the graveyard between the narrator, Carter, and his highly rational friend, Joel Manton. This leads to a philosophical dialogue that pits phenomenology against a kind of ontological supernaturalism: Carter takes the position that there are mysterious things beyond the laws of matter that cannot be understood or named; Manton, on the other hand, asserts that all things can be known by the 'five senses' and nothing can be really unnameable because all things have 'fixed dimensions, properties, causes and effects' (275).

By adopting this position, Manton gives voice to a science of phenomena, a phenomenological position that relies on an understanding of consciousness in relation to the objects (or things) of direct experience. That is, phenomena and the appearance of things are understood through the perception of the first-person point of view and, as a result, the meanings of things are based on how they appear to us or the ways we experience things. Thus, the significance of objects, events, the flow of time, the self and others can only be determined in the 'life world', a position that reduces the world of things to an anthropomorphised world, enclosed at all times with an unbreakable alliance between subject and world, best exemplified in Heidegger's notion of *being-in-the-world*.

But what if we cannot find a meaning for a thing? What if it cannot be explained in our life world? Indeed, Lovecraft's narrator speaks of a Thing of such 'grotesque distortions' that no 'coherent representation' can 'express or portray so gibbous and infamous a nebulosity as a spectre of malign, chaotic perversion', a 'vaporous terror' that is the 'shriekingly *unnamable*' (278). This passage begins with a horror that is imaginable because it can be articulated in the language of the oak tree that consumes human corpses. But Carter and Manton are then confronted with a form of monstrosity that is unspeakable. This Thing signals a nameless and unknown terror that resists the articulation and categorisation that would place it in the order of things. Consequently, the unnameable figure of monstrosity is the harbinger of category crisis precisely because its liminality refuses easy compartmentalisation and demands a radical rethinking of boundary and normality. The Thing challenges stable borders in a way that is all too fearsome and horrific; it cannot be managed in the rational processes of logical classification within Western European phenomenology. The terrifying Thing cannot be put into words. It haunts the darkest corners of human subjectivity and language.

Under such circumstances, we can glimpse the horizon of speculation that calls into question phenomenology as a beacon of integrity because it forces us to think outside of the subject. And in moving outside phenomenology, we also move beyond linguistic idealism, for what appears to Manton and Carter, as well as what they experience, and what they are aware of, is not a function of the language they use. Their cognitive states cannot be registered in language, nor can language here make up the objects of the experience. By the end of the story, linguistic idealism and phenomenology are untenable. Manton is attacked by a mysterious Thing and, when he regains consciousness, he cannot find words to describe the phenomenon that attacked him: 'No – it wasn't that way at all. It was everywhere – a gelatin – a slime – yet it had shapes, a thousand shapes of horror beyond all memory. There were eyes – and a blemish. It was the pit – the maelstrom – the ultimate abomination. Carter, *it was unnamable!*' (280).

Lovecraft's story suggests that human beings are not, and perhaps never were, at the centre of things. For it challenges the human-centric persistence on thinking through its own centrality, its ontological superiority. If we replace the premise 'I think' with 'It lives', what endures is the Thing, a Thing that, according to our thinking, should not exist, for it is an anonymous mass of materiality with unknown origins. This mysterious beginning of the Thing gestures to an alien time: something that is outside of human time and human history and breaks down the classification of life forms: life as plant, life as animal, life as subject. Yet the Gothic narrative of the story centres on the struggle between the body as possessor of the subject and the body as possessed by the subject. The temporality that arises out of this alien life form presents us with a body that is discombobulated, a body out of joint. A body that we cannot conceptualise in time, for it has no beginning and end that we can understand, so it does not conform to the temporal conditions of a human-centric time-history.

Lovecraft's story anticipates the cheapo scary B-movies that have flourished in the USA, particularly during the 1950s. These It and Thing movies are perhaps best exemplified by, among others, *The Thing from Another World* (1951), *It Came from Outer Space* (1953) and *It Came from Beneath the Sea* (1955). In *It Came from Beneath the Sea*, for instance, a giant tentacle-Thing emerges in the Pacific Ocean and, after running amuck in the sea, attacks the Golden Gate Bridge. The city is in peril. The National Guard is mobilised. And as the trailer warns, 'The H-Bomb blasted it loose from the depths of the Pacific, but not even the H-Bomb can kill it!'. As in many other 'It' movies, the 'Thingified' body is a shape-shifter: its tentacles grow and increase and change form. This Thing is the 'It' machine; it ruptures the symbolic realm, for the threat is not just the eradication of the human, but also something the human cannot name or describe. It resists linguistic transparency and is, by extension, unresolvable.

A particularly interesting example is *It! The Terror from Beyond Space* (1958), which is more than just a monster-running-amuck picture. This is, in part, because it gestures towards the haunted house movie sub-genre through images of 'The Dark Old Spaceship' shot in a shadowy Gothic manner. The plot revolves around a spaceship sent to Mars to pick up Carruthers, who is stranded on the planet with a dead crew. Carruthers is suspected of killing his men, but he knows the real cause of his crew's death. After leaving Mars, the captain of the rescue ship uncovers several deaths among his fellow astronauts.

A mutated Martian (the last of its kind?) is concealed as a stowaway in the spaceship's ventilation shafts. Its Nosferatu-esque shadow skulks through corridors and stairwells as it murders the crew (often in eerie silhouette) and spreads a bacterial infection through its claws. The creature is unstoppable. The crew tries rigging the grates with grenades. They try flooding the lower levels with poison gas. They electrify a staircase. The creature will not die. One of the crew muses on the origin of the beast: a great civilisation once existed on Mars, but suffered a catastrophe of some kind. Their people returned to barbarism... and only this creature remains.

This speculation about an otherworldly civilisation gestures to a realm where the concept of life is not held by a subject whose history is tied to life as it is understood from a human perspective. This speculative narrative poses a significant question: can thinking move outside the limitations of its own history to conceptualise the alterity of the Thing? In answering this question, I suggest that a film like *It! The Terror from Beyond Space* represents a history – a conception of historical time – that is outside the birth of the human. Beyond human time, another origin exists, which the subject can only articulate in the most vague and abstract terms: It, Thing, Them. Without any personal relation with this timescale, the subject is faced with a silent void. The terror here arises out of a spatial and temporal realm that confounds human-centricity – the very basis of phenomenological thought – when the subject discovers that something beyond the human conception of time has a sense of belonging in the universe. This forces a recognition of another (non-human) time that ruptures the unity of the (human) self in the present, without being fully integrated into the subject through language. This other origin marks a point of dissonance for the subject, an unknowable mass of materiality that becomes the site of a parallel history.

If, as the title suggests, the terror is *beyond* space, then it is also beyond time. Or, to put this another way, it is outside of any human-centric conception of time that merges the spatial and the temporal to forge a sense of subjectivity. Being beyond space and time means entering a void where there is only silence and where the finitude of the human's voice remains unanswered. On the one hand, terror arises when It attacks humans (so it can be justifiably killed in self-defence); on the other hand, terror arises beyond space because there is no possibility for dialogue; we can never know It's narrative of origin or history as these relate to time and space. The other does not speak back. Without the possibility of communication, the cosmic void is an oppressive site, breaking the human's need to be heard and thus offering us a mirror from which we must see the limits of narcissism. Beyond space, where there is silence without witness, there is nothing. Nothing, that is, to hear your voice.

Yet in the film the terror that is generated from the great beyond is conveyed, in classic Gothic form, through the dark figure that stalks its prey, attempting to consume human life by sucking all liquid from the bodies of its victims. The black-and-white film stock emphasises the shadows that are projected on the walls of the gloomy and labyrinthine corridors, representing a cinematic and advanced-technological version of the subterranean passages of the eighteenth-century Gothic novel. The space ship is also a place of absolute isolation – shades of the remote Gothic castle – where the confinement of the pressurised environment is heightened in the claustrophobic and disorienting air ducts (where some of the action takes place), anticipating scenes from Ridley Scott's *Alien* (1979) and echoing earlier Gothic texts. Gothic aesthetics from the past are incorporated into an imagined future (the film is made in 1958 and set in 1973).

The advancements of interplanetary travel in the near future imply a teleological sense of human time as related to technological progress and scientific evolution. Alien time, though, points to the opposite, a devolution or reversal of a former 'civilisation' on Mars that has deteriorated into its base and primal origins. The It from beyond space is not beyond the B-movie clichés of an uncontrollable atavistic physicality that disrupts the teleology of a civilised, 'mature', future. The alien Thing is a devolved form of Martian civilisation that also threatens human civilisation and cannot be stopped by human weapons. This invokes contradictory ideas of temporal development that underpin the Gothic narrative: the human pushes forward by scientific and technological advances, but is then confronted with a reversal of this temporal axis by It, a Thing that embodies decay, mutation, deterioration and devolution. Being witness to devolution is also being conscious of one's own effacement: the end of time. For once It is finally killed (deprived of oxygen), It's species is extinct, displaced in the density of the void beyond space and relegated to the horror of darkness as It becomes nothing. There is no-Thing.

But what happens when the Thing cannot be forced into extinction? On this terrain, we are required to take seriously an origin that is other to our experience so that human-centricity is reconsidered and the phenomenological validity of the Earth as ground loses its solid legitimacy. Another agency then emerges out of a Thing from beyond time and outside of taxonomy that resists descriptive experience and resists knowledge, thus marking a fissure within the subject. Because the Thing cannot be integrated into human subjectivity on either a spatial or a temporal plane, it ruptures a sense of unity for the self in the present by gesturing towards the site of a parallel history, a past where the subject cannot locate a sense of belonging or orient himself in relation to the other site. The emergence of another timescale reveals a history that coexists alongside the human subject in the present and leads to a doubling – a temporal doppelgänger – that both mirrors and distorts human life and experience. The temporal doppelgänger is the history of the subject's alterity, offering an alternative time that might or might not include the moment of separation that establishes categories of life: plant, animal, human. And this conformation with another alterity also forces a recognition that we – human beings – are in fact nothing less than an alien life form.

Suddenly, the Thing is in our presence, our present. If it was there all along, it was invisible. But the abrupt appearance of It forces us to confront the visibility of the invisible. It embodies another agency, but not with a body that is understood or, in some cases, even recognisable as a bodily form. It does not relate to the lived dimensions of the human body or correspond to our experiences of being a bodily subject. This new body – the Thing's body – confronts us now, in our time and place, but it also embodies a dimension beyond immediate spatio-temporality. For if our human bodies anchor us in the immediacy of the moment and tie together the present, past and future, then the appearance of this new body bears witness to a foreign time and place that has been hitherto inaccessible to – or perhaps untouched by – human bodies, the lived experience of the human.

In narrative terms, the vision of a buried past coming into the present is a recurring motif in the Gothic mode. When the Gothic combines with sci-fi, the past that disrupts the present is often an alien past that was not repressed, but was not known. Yet this sudden disruption of the past-in-the-present is no less threatening, for while the temporality of the invading alien-monster belongs to the present, it also incorporates the futurity of death (the possible death of humanity) and the pre-history of an unknown alien birth and civilisation.

The Blob's Body

This is the case in *The Blob* (1958), which depicts a formless Thing that is alien to our sense of bodily form and experience. In the original 1958 version of the film, the blob emerges when a meteorite falls in the country outside of a small town in Pennsylvania, bringing with it an alien creature. The grounded comet is discovered by a farmer and some teenagers, and a strange primordial goo attaches itself to the farmer's hand. The teenagers take him to the local doctor, but the physician and his patient are no match for this alien Thing; they are consumed by it. The citizens of the small town refuse to listen to the teenagers who have witnessed the blob's destructive power. In the meantime, the alien life form ingests everything in its path: it grows and grows. It threatens people at the grocery store and the movie theatre before it engulfs the diner, oozing in through the windows. Weapons cannot stop it. But eventually the townspeople realise it can be frozen. They use fire extinguishers to freeze the blob and an Air Force jet transports it to the North Pole. Here, it is not killed, but contained, frozen in time and place. The film ends with the words 'The End' . . . which then morphs into a question mark.

In *The Blob*, we see the stirrings of an embryonic life form emerge from the expanse of an infinite void. The comet that hits the earth ignites a Thing that is reanimated from the depths of an abyssal time. The blob's origin is not revealed but its amorphous bodily mass forces us to think outside an anthropomorphised spatio-temporal cosmos, reminding us of our tenuous relationality wherein we are tied to our perception of the world. The materialisation of the blob with its Jell-O-like, unstructured body reveals a temporal plane (a mysterious history) that is at odds with our understanding of both Earth and the body. In its earthly form, the blob is a fluid and unbound shape that cannot be classified in relation to other forms we call life and, as a result, this blob – this alien materiality – ruptures the earth/body relation in terms of its unknown origin *and* its unknowability. This suggests that human life is only one figuration of the body, which is at all times surrounded by foreign bodies that are beyond our embodied experience and at the limit of description: we cannot know how a non-human life form experiences the world through its body. This reverses the human drive to colonise the cosmos, for in this narrative the cosmos colonises humans (Trigg 2013, 34–6).

Early in the film, when the blob first attaches itself to the arm of an elderly labourer, the human subject can be seen as sharing its bodily experience with the alien subject. As the blob grows, the Gothic narrative develops by focusing on the struggle between the body as possessor of the subject and the body as possessed by the subject. Such ambiguity means that the 'sharing' of the body becomes an intrusion, so the farmer becomes physically of the self and *other* than the self at the same time. As in other body horror films like David Cronenberg's *The Fly* (1986) or Stuart Gordon's *From Beyond* (1986), *The Blob* plays out the battle over the ownership of the human body, thus signalling an uncanny dualism wherein the singularity of the human self is disordered and a coherent personal identity is thrown into doubt. The two beings become, if only for a moment, a symbiotic organism, with each spatio-temporal realm inhabiting the same body.

Of course, the battle over the body is a losing cause: the lived dimension of the human is eventually absorbed by an alien body. But it is significant that this alien invasion is played out on a temporal plane: the alien enters the human's body in a moment that is irreversible; this leads to a phase of symbiosis, which is one period in a drawn-out process wherein the human body becomes incorporated into non-human corporeality. This invokes a Gothic narrative that, in the context of *The Blob*, suggests that the human body is shadowed by an alien subjectivity, thus forcing the characters to wonder if they have possession of their bodies. A question then arises that is implied, though never articulated, in the film: if I lose possession of my body, then who – or perhaps more significantly *what* – am I?

It would be too simple to answer this question in relation to the context of the 'birth of the teenager' in post-Second World War America. Yes, it is a teen B-movie that buys into and constructs this birth. But the film cannot

Figure 1.2   The blob outside the movie theatre in *The Blob* (1958)

be reduced to a symbolic register wherein the teenager's transitional body suddenly becomes alien to the subject. For in *The Blob*, the body that becomes alien moves into a dimension beyond its immediate spatio-temporality as a human condition solely located in an Earthly history. Becoming blob means becoming integrated into another body connected to another time and another place.

The blob intrudes on a teleological version of time that conflates progress with new technology. Viewed in De Luxe color, the film stages the relationship between a black-and-white past and a technologically advanced present brought to us in Technicolor. As the film builds to its climax, there is a film-within-the-film: the teenagers go to a 'spook' B-movie, which happens to be John Parker's B-movie *Daughter of Horror*, a black-and-white low-budget production made with a high camp value, a film which was first released in 1955 and then rereleased to theatres by EPI in 1957 (Davis 2012, 96).

At the start of this scene, the audience laughs heartily at the dated aesthetics of this self-styled scary movie. The arrival of a being from another place and time occurs as Parker's film gestures back to a black-and-white B-movie age just as the colour film we are watching highlights the future of B-movies (in terms of aesthetics, production values and its star, Steve McQueen). As audiences of *The Blob*, we are invited to contribute our own laughter, placing us figuratively in the same position as those watching *Daughter of Horror*. But if the first part of this scene imagines a present and future that distances itself from a less advanced technological past, the second part reverses this temporal axis. For as the blob enters the theatre and mounts its attack, the temporal plane is disrupted by the presence of another time, threatening the audience with difference *and* sameness: the alien body, with its mysterious origins, cannot be incorporated into the symbolic order *and* threatens to incorporate human bodies into its mass of materiality. The audience moves from laughing at the past from the superior position of the present to the primal screams of prey being hunted.

As laughter becomes scream, we hear how the Thing sparks a response that is outside of language, a form of communication that does not allow for dialogue, resulting in a breakdown in relationality. Even when the response to the Thing is not a scream, it is beyond language; as the policeman says, 'it's the most horrible *thing* I've ever seen in my life'. We can only speculate about what this thing might be and recognise that becoming-blob is too terrible to describe. As the blob engulfs the place of human consumption (the diner), it has the potential to consume and continue to grow until it has incorporated all life on the planet. The loss of human life on earth is also the end of human time. Time is up, eaten by a foreign entity with an unknown origin, incorporated into a foreign temporal plane.

With the appearance of the blob, the singularity of the sovereign self is thrown into question and there is a discrepancy between the experience of the body as one's own and the reality of the body as belonging to the other. This is because, in the assemblage of material zones, the unity of the human body is lost in its integration into the blob's foreign body so the human body moves into a different space and time – even while the blob remains grounded on earth – whose origins began elsewhere. From this perspective, the body is a point of convergence wherein two temporalities merge, but when the human body is consumed by the blob it is no longer anchored in the immediacy of the present, personal perception or experience. Nor does the human body continue to be tied to the past or the future. Instead, it is integrated into a mass of lived materiality that is a foreign expression of corporeal dynamism. This subsequently limits human time and imposes another temporality, for the rupture of lived time is encroached on by a time that is outside human consciousness.

Beyond the sphere of personal existence, another subject intervenes and imposes a past that has never been part of a human present and a future that cannot be imagined or articulated. The threat to selfhood is not just the process of being consumed; it is also the glimpsing of a foreign self – an alien subjectivity – that is inaccessible in thought, communication or language. This knowledge, along with the potential loss of the human body, signals an anxiety about being disembodied and ontologically displaced. This paves the way for an agency from another time and place, but it also raises an ambiguity about the human body – the sense of it as possessor and possessed – as we must reconsider what is living and non-living, alien and non-alien, human and unhuman.

For we are forced to ask a significant question: what happens when the human body becomes blob? Perhaps this break of the body from an experience of selfhood is not absolute. Perhaps it enables a reconfiguration of the body as both self and other. If the body contributes to its growth as alien, then the consumption is not a departure from the lived body but a continuation of it.

End Thing

The body of the It, Thing or Blob is not just anterior to humanity but is, in some sense, opposed to human existence. In its unhuman form, its body becomes the site of a deadly and threatening force, a figuration that is uncanny and thus gestures to spectrality. In fact, the Thing is unhuman precisely because the reality of the material body continues to exist even after subjectivity has been eradicated. Even as the subject becomes one with nothingness, the physical presence persists, and there is an inversion that arises out of the distortion of interiority and exteriority. Nothing remains except materiality, so much so that even spectrality is condensed within its material form. The spectral – that which outlives the death of the corporeal – remains located in the undead, uncanny and unhuman figure. The body becomes spectre and spectrality becomes corporeal: the confounding Thing returns from the void of perception and language.

What I have sought to put forward in this chapter is that the temporality of Its, Things and Blobs marks an aspect of the human that is outside both conceptions of the body *and* human time. As materialised abjection, the Thing is a figure of primal terror because it is a site wherein the revenant of the unhuman is housed in a nameless body. At the visible level of the corporeal, this foreign body is a construction of the threat from an alien time and place. On the level of the real, this becomes the unnamed Thing. At the level of the spectral, the residual trace that is left over from the eradication of subjectivity returns and intrudes on the Real. The question is not just what space this Thing has come from, but also what time-place (origin) the It inhabits. The Thing's origins are at the limits of description and anterior to subjectivity. The response of fear and anxiety that arises here is not contained within the human body's lived experience. Instead, Gothic in this context breaks our bond with experience or any conception of something that can be associated with human time. Fears and anxieties arise out of an unutterable and altogether confoundingly unreal reality that cannot be contained with any historically based human conception of life. From the expanse of an infinite void, the stirrings of an embryonic life emerge. From nowhere, life unfolds. A miracle of being in the yawning abyss of non-existence. The void is spatial but it is also linguistic and temporal: Its, Things and Blobs come from a space–time continuum that is as unnameable as the body that emerges from it.

BIBLIOGRAPHY

Cahn, Edward L. (1958), Director. *It! The Terror from Beyond Space*. United Artists.
Campbell, John W. (2011), *Who Goes There?* (London: Gollancz).
Davis, Blair (2012), *The Battle for the Bs: 1950s Hollywood and the Rebirth of Low-Budget Cinema* (New Brunswick, NJ: Rutgers University Press).
Hawks, Howard and Christian Nyby (1951), Directors. *The Thing from Another World*. RKO.
Heidegger, Martin. (1962), *Being and Time*, trans. John Macquarie and Edward Robinson (Oxford: Blackwell).
Lovecraft, H. P. (2014 [1925]), 'The Unnamable'. *The Complete Fiction of H. P. Lovecraft* (New York: Race Point), 274–80.
Sturgeon, Theodore. 'It' (1993 [1940]), *The Ultimate Egoist: The Complete Stories of Theodore Sturgeon*. Vol. 1, ed. Paul Williams (Berkeley: North Atlantic Books), 303–27.
Trigg, Dylan (2013), *The Thing: A Phenomenology of Horror* (Winchester: Zero Books).

2. RE-SCRIPTING BLAXPLOITATION HORROR: *GANJA AND HESS* AND THE GOTHIC MODE

Maisha Wester

During the 1970s, a plethora of low-budget, kitschy Horror films aimed at Black audiences flooded American cinemas. These films were often filled with excessive intra-racial violence, gratuitous nudity, and sympathetic monsters who were invariably products of systemic racism. However, Bill Gunn's *Ganja and Hess* (1973) eschews the violence and monsters typical of such movies. A Blaxploitation-aimed project, the film is Gothic in its portrayal of racial turmoil as characters struggle with questions of assimilation, desire and racial community. The Gothic is invaluable to expressing the film's concerns while also evading the stereotypes and trappings that plagued Black Horror films of the era.

The fate of Gunn's film, however, reflects back upon the expectations and limitations imposed upon Black B-films of the era. The production company pulled the film from theatres, edited it and rereleased it with additional violence and sex scenes. However, Gunn's example proves significant for later Black filmmakers. Movies like *Def By Temptation* (1990) and *Tales from the Hood* (1995), while returning to the kitsch of the Blaxploitation films, resist readings as simple Horror movies. Like Gunn's film, these later movies turn to Gothic tropes to emphasise the psychological terror of negotiating modern Black identity.

Blaxploitation films were, by their very definition, B-films. Quickly produced on low budgets, the films appealed to Black audiences by exploiting their fantasies of resistance against systems of White dominance. The films were 'aimed directly at young Black males who imagined themselves machine-gunning all the balls on the pool table, then doing likewise to "absolutely, positively every last (white) motherfucker in the room"' (Patterson 2002, 5). Blaxploitation movies often contained gratuitous Black female nudity, consequently reproducing ideologies about Black female sexual accessibility and hypersexuality. The Black Horror films produced during the era followed this formula. Populated with sympathetic Black monsters, disempowered Black anti-heroes, vicious white antagonists and Black heroines, they were unsparing in their depiction of violence, mayhem and revenge.

In Blaxploitation Horror, Black actors occupied lead roles as monsters fighting against an unjust and virulently racist system; they stood as figures of Black strength, protest and militancy. For instance, Blacula was presented as an unwilling product of racist violation; his violence was therefore a mixture of righteous rage and vengeance. Likewise, Diana, a.k.a. Sugar, turns to voodoo in order to fight the exploitative system of white economic power embodied by white mobsters in *Sugar Hill* (1974). Audiences took pleasure in watching the 'monsters' violently topple figures that metaphorised oppressive social institutions; such identification was 'a potentially empowering act for many filmgoers' (Benshoff 2000, 32).

The problem with such films was that they were 'Horror' films, and therefore unambiguous in their moral articulations. Their horror assumed physical terms, leaving explorations of psychological torment and oppression under-explored. Though the monsters were sympathetic, there was no question about their monstrosity; the brutality and extensiveness of their violence only reinforced their coding as destructive, aberrant force, even if they were the creation of a heinous social system. This is most apparent in the make-up used to depict the monsters as visibly excessive: 'Black monsters tend to be more animalistic than white monsters: when Blacula gets his blood lust up, for example, he becomes almost lupine, with a hairy face and brow, a trope usually not used for more debonair White vampires. The possessed woman in Abby also has facial hair and a deep voice (drawing on gender-bending queer fears as well as bestial/racial ones)' (Benshoff 2000, 42). Additionally, a common element of the female monsters in these films was their wanton sexuality, as exemplified by Abby, who is barely human in her demonic possession (41). Such representation reinforced problematic racial and sexual ideologies, deeply embedding Black sexuality and identity as monstrous (31) even as they appealed to the fantasies of Black audiences. Furthermore, though the monsters fought against antagonists who metaphorised racist oppression, their fight was invariably restricted to individuals; the larger systems of oppression remained unchallenged and unaffected. Lastly, the monster's struggle expired with him/her, suggesting that change was ultimately limited and fleeting.

Bill Gunn's film was commissioned to be another Blaxploitation Horror film by a studio hoping to replicate the success of *Blacula*. Gunn, however, refused to pander to the studio's exploitative desire, and instead created what Toni Cade Bambara defines as 'conscious cinema' (quoted in David 2011, 28). Briefly, Ganja and Hess centres on the cultural tribulations, emotional intimacy and psychological trauma of Ganja Meda and Dr Hess Green, a vampire couple. Hess is a wealthy anthropologist who is transformed into a vampire when his assistant, George Meda, stabs him with an ancient African dagger three times, 'Once for the Father, once for the Son, and once for the Holy Ghost'. Arising a vampire, Hess feeds on the Black inner-city population. Shortly after the attack, Meda's wife Ganja arrives in search of her husband; finding Hess instead, she begins a relationship with him, enjoying the luxuries of his sprawling suburban home but also disdaining his Black servant Archie. Eventually, Hess makes Ganja a vampire, and the two rejoice in their new life together. However, Hess suffers a crisis of spirit and eventually seeks redemption, first through a Black church and then through suicide. He invites Ganja to join him, but she refuses; rather, she inherits his massive home, kills Archie, and selects a new partner to join her.

The film 'subverts genre and, as a result, asks audiences to imagine an alternative to the Black insatiable Other that is punished narratively with trauma, injury, social ostracism, or death' (David 2011, 28). Notably, Gunn's blood-drinking protagonists are called 'addicts' whose thirst metaphorises 'capitalism and cultural imperialism, dramatizing ... how some human beings live off the blood, sweat, and toil of others – what one latter-day commentator called a "symbolic portrayal of a completely Europeanized Black man"' (Benshoff 2000, 43). Gothic tropes allow Gunn to do what Horror tropes could not for other Blaxploitation films: avoid replicating ideologies of Black monstrosity and of aberrant Black sexuality.

Gunn's Gothic Addicts

Ganja and Hess is marked by a number of Gothic elements. The isolation exemplified by Hess's home alternates with scenes of an equally silent landscape populated by 'degenerate' people like pimps and prostitutes. *Ganja and Hess* refuses to rely on inhuman violence to emphasise the terror of historical oppression and the chaos it causes in modern Black life. While there is bloodshed in the film, it is not the centre of the struggle. Rather, Gunn uses claustrophobic framing techniques to dehumanise individuals and suggest conflict before it ever occurs. Likewise, the eerie score – atonal chanting and high-pitched cries – proves jarring as the film seems to scream in pain during moments of intra-racial violence. The film's tension is consequently achieved via mood and sound, rather than carnage. Further, the film frames bodies to

GANJA AND HESS AND THE GOTHIC MODE

Figure 2.1 Meda and Hess discuss suicide, betrayal, racial isolation and racial violence in a scene evoking Jim Crow violence

render them grotesque at times. In the scene in which Meda first contemplates suicide, the shot fragments his body and Hess's, revealing only his legs hanging from the tree and Hess's upper body; the noose hangs between them as Meda's seemingly disembodied voice accounts for the threatened violence. The scene recalls the history of horrific racist violence in the USA, specifically the dehumanising objectification Blacks suffered throughout the process of lynching. Read as less than human by dominant society and therefore assailable, Black bodies were literally subject to dismemberment in the midst of lynching, as texts such as Dora Apel's *Imagery of Lynching* and James Allen's *Without Sanctuary* reveal in their analysis of the horrific 'keepsakes' from previous eras.

The psychological nature of the film's tension and the intense isolation of the characters embody the solitary nature of their struggle to grapple with the collision between two contending forces: Western (White) modern culture and Black ancestry. As a colonising discourse, the former privileges itself as the location of the normative and demonises the latter as 'primitive' and monstrous. Manthia Diawara and Phyllis Klotman explain that the opening song should not be read as a way of evaluating the Black protagonists; rather, the opening song narrates the course of world history from a destructive Western Christian perspective (Diawara and Klotman 1991, 304). This problematic standpoint deems the dagger, and thus the culture it originates within, 'diseased'. The song occurs alongside shots of Western art – sculptured alabaster marble statues. The tight framing of the statues disorients the viewer, suggesting that, although this is the dominating discourse under which the characters live, it is alienating in its vision. The statues are cold and utterly disconnected from living people and context, an aspect emphasised by the scene which immediately follows the introduction – a wide shot of a Black congregation mid-song. The complete decontextualisation of the art deprives it of its philosophical and emotional functions, an issue which recurs in Ganja's and Hess's discussion of his home and its artistic decorations. Art in the opening scene and in Hess's home serves as a sign of taste, and therefore a consumptive practice in capitalist economy. There is nothing to connect to in it. In contrast, the first scene of the Black church emphasises community and a counter to alienating and objectifying capitalist consumption.

Ganja and Hess illustrates the radical anti-racist possibilities of Gothic texts, reclaiming its protagonists from cultural discourses which mask them as monstrous, demonising their bodies and desires as deviant. There are no normalising figures decrying vampirism in the film; even Reverend Luther, a figure whose Christianity associates him with hegemonic discourses overly committed to defining 'deviance', refuses to marginalise Hess as 'monstrous'. Luther's first lines of the film firmly humanises Hess, deeming him an 'addict'. Hess is more of a Gothic Byronic anti-hero than outright Horror monster; his psychological and social conflicts doom him to disastrous behaviour even as he desires community and love.

Hess is a victim, turned into a vampire through assault, rather than an inherent villain. To become a vampire he had to be stabbed three times with a Myrthinian dagger – 'once for the Father, once for the Son, and once for the Holy Ghost' – emphasising his 'addiction' as the creation and product of Christianity. Further, the film emphasises Christianity as a violating Western system that co-opts the cultural artefacts of the African cultures it demonises and eradicates. Hess, as a Black scholar of ancient African cultures, struggles between these two positions – one which demonises and the other which is demonised. The Byronic anti-hero's damning conflict here is the challenge to resolve the tension. Likewise, the *mise-en-scène* of the film's beginning re-emphasises that he is a product of history. After leaving the museum of hyper-white artefacts, Hess and Meda travel to Hess's home: 'The camera travels with them, giving the impression that a great deal of space has been covered. The viewer feels s/he has embarked on a journey beyond land and sea. The song in the foreground makes references to a pre-Christian era, to slavery, and to Christendom. They arrive at Green's house. The song stops' (Diawara and Klotman 1991, 305). The timing of the song's end suggests that history has brought them, and us, to the conflict played out in Hess's house and life.

Hess's isolation and alienation is emblematised by his house, a sprawling dark Gothic manse. At one point, Ganja comments upon the home's constant chilliness:

Ganja: Why am I always cold . . . Are you always cold?
Hess: Um hmm.
Ganja: What have you done about it?
Hess: Grown used to it.

Populated by artefacts instead of family, 'the mansion has all the trappings of the most successful haute bourgeoisie, yet also seems in a state of sumptuous decay' (Diawara and Klotman 1991, 301). The house is made to manifest Hess's struggle and psychological state; outwardly successful and thriving, he suffers inwardly, his suicide ultimately revealing his degenerated state as a (result of) hyper-consumer(ism). Indeed, in the previous excerpt, Hess's reply and solution reveal that he is as 'cold' as the house itself, alluding to both his physical and his emotional state.

One of the sources of Hess's alienation is his assimilation into dominant White capitalist society. He has impeccable tastes and manifests his success in White bourgeois materialist terms, with an estate, cars, servants and clothes. His son receives the best private school education, speaking French as easily as English. The child's proficiency in French proves significant given that his father is a professor of African cultures. Instead of providing his son with an education that would introduce him to the language and cultures of Hess's research and ancestry, Hess's decision – to enrol the child in a predominantly white private school where he learns a language of colonisers – places the boy

Figure 2.2 Crumbling black statue at elite private school reflects Hess's cultural and spiritual state

at a further remove from Blacks. His son's education reveals Hess's research in ancient African artefacts as superficial rather than a source or desire for ancestral connection. An eerie shot of a statue on the school grounds embodies the reality of Hess's position and the threat of the Western culture he privileges. The statue is of a black-skinned figure, isolated and crumbling, the black paint flaking off to reveal a grainy rotted whiteness beneath.

While the homes in Hess's neighbourhood represent social status, Hess's racial isolation proves problematic and, in fact, rewrites the threat manifested by vampires in early Gothic literature. Historically, vampires such as Dracula have 'figured as . . . dangers from without. The vampire is the monster that threatens the White middle-class male protagonists' (Jones 1997, 152). The threat Dracula posed was his ability to 'pass', infiltrating an unwitting, homogenised society; an unnoticed interloper, the vampire could destroy and contaminate the population from within. However, Hess's encounter with Meda in the tree reveals that exactly the reverse is true. Meda argues that Hess should not worry over his suicide; Hess counters that the tree and rope are his property, and he is the only Black person on the block. Meda's death, while recalling historical White violence against Black bodies, threatens Hess with a repetition of that violence. Further, Meda's statements of his neurosis and paranoia may be generalised to a comment upon Black men under (White) social surveillance and manipulation. Hess's isolation in the neighbourhood makes him hyper-visible, a vulnerability he seems aware of on the basis of his comments about the rope and tree. Thus, Hess is the one in danger in this neighbourhood as 'interloper', not his White middle-class neighbours. There is no chance of Hess 'passing', and as the only Black in the neighbourhood, he is utterly susceptible to violation at the hands of the Whites who outnumber him.

Ganja and Hess equates and worries over various kinds of intra-racial violence, suggesting that such violence is part of Hess's monstrous inheritance. Here again, the film's use of Gothic tropes rather than Horror proves important. Horror would produce and dismiss Hess as wholly monstrous, thus reproducing the very violence the film decries; as previously mentioned, Blaxploitation Horror films often fell into this trap by rendering their protagonists inhuman monsters. *Ganja and Hess*, however, rejects this trend through its subversive use of the Gothic tropes. As a supernatural being that never appears other than human – unlike the wolfish, hairy Blacula – the film erases visual signs of Hess's monstrosity. We are left instead to ponder the complex problem of his behaviour.

Meda is the first to articulate the film's concerns about intra-racial violence as he sits in the tree with the noose. Remarking that he feels that he is both a victim and a murderer, Meda expresses the condition of Black artists in the USA. He is invariably the victim of racism, and his art must therefore reflect his victimisation at the hands of White America, 'but he also cannot create without involving Black America' (Diawara and Klotman 1991, 308). Meda indicts himself and all artists as contributing to the problem of cultural (mis) representation and the production of Blackness. Likewise, Hess, as a Black professor of ancient African culture, doubly participates in this construction, embodying a kind of Blackness while also interpreting and defining other Black cultures as 'primitive'. Hess's lifestyle and profession consequently argue in support of specific types of Blackness – white capitalist assimilated and self-isolating – as civilised while implicitly colluding in the definition of alternative forms as degenerate. Through the scene's extended dialogue between Meda and Hess on this topic, the film emphasises cultural representation and engagement as a location in which grievous intra-racial violence occurs. Black-on-Black assault is first psychological before it is ever physical. Hess's Black house staff illustrate that he already participates in this level of violence, feeding on their labour to sustain his existence.

The scenes leading to Hess's first 'hunting' expedition explicitly links vampirism to intra-racial violence on a psychological, economic and physical level. The camera lingers on Hess drinking blood before cutting to a long shot of him driving past a cemetery; this immediately cuts to a scene featuring a conversation between a Black pimp and his hooker, both of whom Hess will soon feed upon. The juxtaposition of the scenes links Hess's habits and existence to death, despite his material splendour, and also links the pimp and prostitute to consumption and fatality. The economic and emotional relationship between pimp and hooker can easily be read in vampiric terms, as the pimp thrives upon the body (work) of his prostitute. Yet both also feed upon the body of the prostitute's clients, who are also Black, given that the prostitute works out of a Black nightclub.

Although the physical confrontation between Hess, the pimp and the prostitute is certainly graphic, it does not depend upon goriness for its shudder. Rather, the eeriness of the soundtrack signals the disquiet we feel at witnessing this moment of intra-racial violence. Throughout the fight, tribal chanting plays in the background; at the climax of the fight, as Hess drags the prostitute down the hall, the song reaches its peak in a screaming pitch. The film therefore signals this assault as an ancestral betrayal, literally screaming at the moment in which one Black person murders another. That this vampiric violence should be understood as a kind of violating internalised racism is apparent in the connections between Black corpses and European artistic production. In contrast to the screaming tribal music, European Baroque music plays in the background during the scene in which Ganja and Hess dispose of their Black victims' bodies. Thus the film links the Black corpse to White artistic production, figuring the corpse as the 'art' produced by White culture.

If Hess is both anti-hero and monster, Ganja should be understood as both seductress and violated heroine. Ganja seems to consume men in the way as

Hess consumes blood. Although she confronts Hess about her husband's body, she neither reports Hess nor seeks personal justice; instead, she continues her relationship with him. However, although she seems cold and calculating she is revealed as another victim well before Hess makes her a vampire – notably without her consent.

Ganja's initial appearance and articulation of her own monstrosity prove misleading. As she calls to announce her arrival, the camera reveals only her red lips speaking into the mouthpiece of the phone and her manicured hand, associating her early on with tools she later uses to seduce Hess while also refusing her the ability to look back at the camera. She explains that Hess's driver 'can't miss me 'cause I'm that evil'. The fragmentation of her face and observation, however, point to her as disempowered: she cannot look at us but he/we can easily see her. Like the film's revision of the vampire's isolated position in homogenised community, her difference, which seems to signify power, in truth renders her vulnerable.

Ganja is initially positioned as a femme fatale through her powerful gaze, which she uses to assess situations, judge social standing and seduce men. Upon first arriving at Hess's home, for instance, Ganja does not immediately approach Hess but instead stands back to look at the house and Hess. As her eyes rove over the house and man before her, there is no sign that she distinguishes man from material, much less acknowledges the dominance he claims as male and home owner. Throughout the rest of the film, Ganja wields her gaze to both articulate her desire and render herself desirable. As Marlo David explains, the breakfast scene in which Ganja questions Hess about Meda illustrates how Ganja uses her gaze to seduce, gather information and claim authority. Ganja seductively pulls the pit from Hess's black cherry; savouring the juice it leaves on her fingers, 'she twists it around her tongue, lets it linger just a moment while she sucks the juice from it. The dark juice from the cherry simultaneously evokes blood, blackness, and sex . . . Hess watches her in this act, and Ganja returns his gaze directly – watching him watch her – and she experiences pleasure from it' (David 2011, 34). David explicitly connects pleasure to Ganja's gaze, and that pleasure seems to repeat the typical depiction and threat of the femme fatale figure. However, what Ganja really seems to savour is the play of seduction with an equal; the seductive power of her enjoyment at being looked at and looking stems from Hess's thrill at her returned gaze. While David reads Ganja's use of the erotic as illustrating how she is 'the boss' in such moments, it also emphasises a female desire for male appreciation of, not domination over, such authority. Traditional Horror and Gothic texts would position her as a villainous female because these moments illustrate that she invites neither saving nor conquest. But the moment of 'romantic' conquest positions her more clearly as Gothic heroine; Hess 'claims' her by making her his victim. The anti-hero ultimately creates his own distressed heroine.

Unsurprisingly, Ganja has been victimised before meeting Hess. Her narrative of her childhood explains her siren-like behaviour, consequently disrupting easy readings of her as a femme fatale by repositioning her as an innocent, undefended victim. As Ganja explains it, her coldness stems from a lack of affection from her mother, the one person who should protect and empathise with her. However, her mother defines Ganja as a disease and calls her a 'slut'. While Ganja longs for her mother to say 'I love you', her mother can only say that Ganja is beautiful. From these exchanges, Ganja concludes that she would always take care of herself, no matter what.

While Ganja's conclusion proves accurate, the exchanges with her mother produce Ganja's self-definition as 'evil'; the pleasure she finds in the seduction and consumption of men also illustrates a fulfilment of her mother's articulation of Ganja as a beautiful 'slut'. Ganja's determination to embody her mother's ideas of her as 'evil' and 'slut' proves an attempt to appropriate the definitions that were hurtful to her as a child, thereby rendering them a source of power and invulnerability. Consequently, Ganja's sexually desiring gaze conveys not only power but another unspoken desire – to hear 'I love you'. It also hides Ganja's vulnerability and history of suffering, and therefore the ways in which her seductress persona is a projection and consequence of her distressed damsel-hood. The psychological violence Ganja suffers as a child further comments on the intra-racial violence witnessed throughout the film. Ganja reveals the lasting ramifications of psychological torment and how it produces indifference between members within an oppressed community.

The solution to Ganja's trauma is the experience of love and the ability to express emotional desire in various ways, including but not limited to sex. Indeed, after Ganja concludes her narrative of her mother's neglect, the film cuts to a scene of horseplay between Ganja and Hess. The moment of emotional intimacy followed by playfulness suggests healing and connectivity in a relationship that was already sexual, and articulates another one of the film's concerns, the reclamation of Black sexuality from stereotypes of deviancy. In both Horror and the Gothic, Black characters have often been totalised as 'monsters'. This totalising replicates dominant culture's very real gothicisation of Blacks as less than human and their corporeal difference as sign of non-heteronormativity. Much of lynching history is explicitly connected to the dehumanising of Black sexuality and reduction of Blacks to sexual predators. Consequently, representation of Black sexuality is a particularly fraught terrain. Audiences have been taught to 'expect horrific, monstrous, and nihilistic stereotypes of black sexuality'; there is little 'space for black bodies and movies engaged in eroticism and sensuality without attaching violence to them' (Stallings 2011, 146). Unfortunately, Blaxploitation films often reproduced this kind of exploitation, featuring empowered Black female leads that 'showed she meant business by taking her top off in the first scene – then blowing a man's head off with a shotgun' (Patterson 2002, 5). Notably, the recut and rereleased versions of Gunn's film feature just this kind of sexually exploited Black bodies.

Ganja and Hess repeatedly and explicitly articulates various forms of Black intimacy and eroticism. In doing so, the film reclaims Black men and women from definitions of deviant hypersexuality, redefining sexual females as other than villainous sirens and sexual males as other than miscegenating rapists. Further, the film's cinematography explicitly acknowledges how sexual aberration is racially coded as 'darkness' and dismisses this coding. James E. Hinton, Gunn's cinematographer for the film, recalls how a lighting technician interrupted shooting the first scene, explaining they needed to change the light to make the dark-skinned lead actor Duane Jones seem fairer-skinned. Hinton refused, with Gunn's support, to lighten anyone's skin in the film, 'since we have many different skin hues and tones' (quoted in David 2011, 31). His decision particularly resonates in the film's sex scenes, which are shot in dark spaces against which the actors' bodies are also dark. Commenting upon Hinton's decision, David concludes that in these moments, the film produces a radical redefinition of Blackness and Black eroticism beyond the normative constructs. Sexual representation instead is marked as 'critical to the aims of collective survival and individual self-actualization' (29). Gunn thus reclaims Black sexuality and erotic subjectivity from the locale of the fetish/the deviant/the monstrous.

Significantly, 'vampire' literally occupies the place of the unspeakable in this film, as a term which is never once uttered despite the protagonists' blood-drinking habits. In rendering the term literally unspoken, Gunn acknowledges the trauma done to Blacks who have been socially coded as monstrous, parts of their bodies, culture and psychology erased under different names for deviancy. In American cultural myth both vampires and Blacks 'threaten' deviant sexuality and miscegenation upon an unwitting, innocent, White (female) population. Even 'defanged' vampires serve this function, because no matter how 'human' they attempt to be by '[struggling] to suppress or sublimate the very qualities that make them into vampires – their bloodlust, their immortality, their prowess ... vampires by their very nature cannot be good' (Derakshani 2007). Although the primary complaint in the previous excerpt is about the transformation of the vampire into a figure of denial, the critic's concluding point proves particularly important for understanding Gunn's refusal to name his protagonists 'vampires': the monster, though 'pervasive and culturally specific' (Goddu 1997, 129), carries with it a historical function as locus of negative ideology and signification. Vampires are doomed to be 'bodies of excess, monsters [which] provide profitable sites to explore the localized collisions and collusions between the boundaries of different identities' (128). The vampire in fiction consequently functions much like Blacks in dominant American culture;

the construction of 'deviance' and 'excess' in each provides a foil against which the national identity can define itself, its notions of normativity, and onto which it can abject its anxieties.

Furthermore, in refusing the term 'vampire', Gunn also acknowledges the subversive potential of Gothic monsters once freed from the cage of pre-established signification. Jeffrey Cohen, for instance, notes that naming the monster illustrates the culture's need 'to apprehend and to domesticate (and therefore disempower) that which threatens' (quoted in Goddu 1997, 127). The absence of stabilising figures such as vampire-hunters reiterates Gunn's rejection of traumatising metaphors which re-trap Blacks within social discourses of deviancy. Consequently Gunn's Black couple can become the complex multi-faceted centres of their own stories. Unnamed, they are offered the possibility of escaping domestication and destruction.

Blood-drinking proves more fluid in the film than traditional depictions of vampirism, and figures for a number of socially sanctioned destructive relations, particularly Western capitalist relations. That Hess's vampirism is particularly of a Western kind is evident in the film's opening and the order of events. The narrator explains Hess's addiction at the start of the film; however, this explanation arrives before Meda stabs Hess with the dagger, turning him into a vampire. The opening statement therefore suggests that Hess is a monstrous consumer before he becomes a supernatural being; his addiction rather signifies Hess's capitalist consumption before it is made a referent for his blood-thirst. Shortly after this explanatory opening, we glimpse the materials that bedeck Hess's life. Significantly, Ganja draws our attention to Hess's excessive consumption, asking why he chooses to live in such a large house given that he has no family there. Consequently, Hess's consumption of people merely realises the extreme end of his tastes for 'finer things' which are invariably the cultural products and labour of other people.

However, the film also associates vampirism with an African ancestry. The dagger is, after all, African in origin. The scenes of an ornately dressed Black woman walking through the African grasslands provide visual connection between a lost heritage and the contemporary Black, vampiric figures. Likewise, Hess's vampiric baptismal speech to Ganja also contains comments emphasising rebellion against dominant Western social norms: 'the only perversions that can be comfortably condemned are the perversions of others. I will persist and survive without God's or society's sanctions. I will not be tortured, I will not be punished, I will not be guilty.' Hess's observations about the practice of condemnation prove poignant in articulating the construction and naming of monstrosity; the first sentence explicitly describes the construction of otherness as part of a process of denial. As such, social and religious sanctions prove useless. Most importantly, Hess's conclusion emphasises the retributive treatment social and religious Others suffer, naming the internalisation of guilt as part of this castigation. Refusal of such treatment proves a way of refusing to be defined and treated as Other. Importantly, this speech initiates Ganja fully into vampirism; Hess stabs her a second time, leading to a second vampiric rebirth. The speech alongside the creation of the vampire in the film therefore suggests that embracing vampirism can also prove revolutionary and self-empowering.

Gunn's film consequently posits two futures for his Black vampires. One future follows the arc of typical Horror narratives, concluding with the 'monster's' defeat and death. Yet the return to normalcy promised by this arc is undone by the second future, embracing the Gothic un-ending for radical meaning: the 'monster' wins and lives to reproduce disruptive (readings of) Blackness. More importantly, in juxtaposing these two fates, the film illustrates how return to 'normalcy' is death for those deemed always and already beyond the centre.

The 'monster' loses by embracing and assimilating to Western normative values. Hess, despairing of his existence, seeks redemption through embracing Christianity in Reverend Luther's church. The scene initially seems one of uncritical embrace by Black community – Hess approaches the pulpit where Luther baptises him as the congregation sings 'Just as I am (I come)'. Likewise, Hess essentially resigns the dominance associated with his class position; Luther, who occupies a servile position as Hess's chauffeur, now commands as Reverend and symbolic patriarch who welcomes Hess into his community. However, the redemption of community offered in the scene is undercut by the premise of their collectivity – Christianity. Consequently, Hess submits to the welcoming arms of a Black community and to the punitive, normalising ideologies of Western culture. Notably, Hess clarifies the problem of religion as it colours individuals earlier in the film, explaining to Ganja that they can only die in the shadow of the cross, because 'nothing can live in the shadows'.

The film indicts Christianity early on as a warping and colonising tradition. The opening song, in telling the history of the world, remarks: 'I came to be addicted to the truth/until the Christians came.' The lyrics indict Christianity of displacing African experience and history with a fictitious narrative, one which claims the authority of 'history' and which demonises alternative cultures and narratives. Further, the film implicitly remarks upon the hypocrisy in Christian narratives through this opening song and the refusal to use the term 'vampire' to define the characters' blood-drinking. Given that the consumption of blood is invoked in Christian religious practice in the sacrament, Christianity merely replaces one form of blood-drinking with another. Notably, Hess's meeting with a White administrator at the film's beginning – shortly after the numerous shots of hyper-White European art – is accompanied by a voiceover which narrates the ritual of Christian sacrament. The conjunction between the scene of the Western art objects, Hess's meeting with a White administrator

– presumably in the same museum as that housing the Western art – and the voice over suggests that Christianity is but another dehumanised, lifeless, alienating and alienated White consumptive practice. But most importantly, the manner of Hess's suicide critiques the function of Christian religion in the West. Hess's explanation that 'nothing can live in the shadows' implicitly acknowledges the ways Christianity casts such shadows and denotes it as destructive. Taken together, the film's various references to Christianity mark it as a colonising enterprise that withers and destroys the lives of the colonised who fall under its shadow, displacing their culture with empty materials and alienating ideologies. Consequently, Hess's baptism signifies his submission to problematic Western culture; in so submitting himself, he dies.

Ganja, however, refuses Hess's invitation to join him in suicide; her survival illustrates a moment when the 'monster' wins. Although Hess creates her without her consent, her determination to survive illustrates a refusal to lose herself in victimisation as well as a refusal to internalise definitions which would stamp her as aberration. In other words, she manages to seize control of her situation and, in doing so, seizes power and authority over her life. In part, Ganja's survival illustrates her ability to negotiate a complex existence – to straddle the boundaries between the normalising West and radical Afrocentricism. Ganja's initial arrival from Amsterdam suggests that she is inherently positioned to negotiate the two positions. Her elegant dress suggests that she is highly cultured and participates in Western consumerism; however, her speech uses Black idiom, suggesting she remains connected to her racial culture. Perhaps these pre-existing qualities make it unnecessary for her to 'resolve her vampirism', which 'does not provide guilt or conflict, only occasional discomfort'; perhaps Ganja's 'life as a vampire Other is not distinct from her status as a black woman Other . . . In other words, Ganja maintains her fierce determination to be an independent individual, an erotic subject, and her vampire identity actually enhances these qualities' (David 2011, 36). David's observations imply that it is the absoluteness of Ganja's pre-existing Otherness, socially pre-determined as inherently deviant because she is a Black woman, which enables her to survive. Ganja's decision to live therefore constitutes a radical refusal to assimilate to oppressive norms which will never allocate her any position of authority, power or normalcy. She becomes the hero of her own story.

The concluding scene depicting Ganja's survival particularly manifest the radical nature of her decision. As a Black man rises out of the pool and runs towards her, naked and dripping water from his Afro, Ganja watches in pleasure from a balcony above, an approving smile on her face. She thus assumes the position of authority and claims Hess's wealth. More importantly, as the man runs, he jumps over Archie's prone corpse. Although the scene suggests Ganja's violence, in truth Archie's death, the man's leap over his body and

Ganja's smile define the kind of Blackness Ganja privileges in her survival. In the breakfast scene, Ganja invites Archie to articulate his overworked and abused state as he serves the meal. When Archie does not respond, she orders him to bring more food, as if determined to aggravate his labour through repeating the excessive consumption to which his employer, Hess, is already subjecting him. In another scene, Ganja requires Archie to carry in all of the grocery bags and insists he help her out of the car, though she is empty-handed, before finally slamming the door to the house in his face. Although such moments seem to indicate Ganja's cruelty, they must be understood as her response to his refusal to claim any power for himself, which is particularly evident in Archie's explanation of the origins of his employment with Hess: Archie simply notes that he 'came with the house'. Archie consequently represents an utterly subservient form of Blackness, one which repeats previous eras of Black dehumanisation and oppression. His death and vaulted body emphasise Ganja's determination to reject Black subservience. Instead she privileges a man whose hairstyle suggests cultural pride and whose nudity suggests a rejection of the physical shaming connected to Black sexuality and physicality.

Cruel Cuts of Capitalism

The critical reception of Gunn's film marked it as ground-breaking, with it winning the Critics' Choice award at the 1973 Cannes Festival. Yet this reception did not save it; the film was pulled from theatres a week after it opened, and sold to a distributor who re-cut it as a sexploitation film now called *Blood Couple* a.k.a. *Double Possession*. The new posters advertising the rereleased film highlighted its new conjunction between hypersexuality and deviancy, proclaiming 'The Devil wanted their souls – she wanted their bodies . . . and more!'. While Gunn's original poster emphasises the tension between a Black man and a Black woman – their sombre faces looking in opposite directions but seeming to grow out of the same central space – the poster for the rereleased film centres around Ganja's monstrosity. Her face appears contorted in two shots – her mouth gaping in a scream as blood drips from her chin in the largest image, while the smaller one reproduces a scene from *Nosferatu* as she ascends a staircase, a black figure with clawed hands. Further, this second image is juxtaposed against headshots of the men in the film, stressing they are her unwitting victims. Thus the film was re-imprisoned in the cage fashioned for Blaxploitation films as sites where the B-movie and adult film industry collide (Stallings 2011, 147). Black female sexuality became the site of horrific deviance, given the poster suggests that Ganja is more gluttonous and evil than the Devil. The fate of Gunn's film illustrates the unfortunate truth of the battle waged behind the scenes in the Blaxploitation film industry: 'even if directed by a black filmmaker with the best intentions, white studios and distributors could enact artistic violence on products by projecting their own distorted gazes on black bodies and sexuality' (146).

In the decades following the initial release, re-cutting and rerelease of *Ganja and Hess*, Black directors have built upon the ideologies about Black Gothic and Black Horror film while also struggling to retain full artistic licence of their work. Most recently, Spike Lee released an updated version of the film titled *Da Sweet Blood of Jesus* (2014); the modern film, like the original, refuses to emphasise the horror as supernatural monstrosity. *Def by Temptation* (1990) is another independent film which confronted financial troubles and sought alternative methods of financing rather than witness the corruption of its narrative. The film uses typical Gothic tropes to convey the degeneracy and threat of New York after dark, featuring numerous scenes in dark smoky rooms populated by people who are emotionally disconnected from each other. Although the scenes of the succubus's attack are graphic, the atmosphere of the film borrows heavily from the Gothic tradition outside of these scenes. Further, the film's focus on sexual objectification and social disconnection recalls the ideas of communal alienation and violence in *Ganja and Hess*.

Tales from the Hood (1995) similarly revised the formula for the popular television Horror series *Tales from the Crypt* to centre the stories around individual Black heroes without reinforcing pervasive stereotypes. Although the bulk of the film clearly fits within the Horror genre, its piece 'Boys Do Get Bruised' deploys Gothic tropes to depict the child's helplessness, the hero's defeat and the reality of the 'monster'. The vignette is about a young Black boy named Walter who regularly suffers the wrath of his mother's abusive boyfriend Carl. The story plays upon Horror expectations of explicitly grotesque 'monsters', displacing these ideas with a very human but all-too-real monster: a cruel, dominating, physically abusive man. The horror stems from the silence around Carl's violent control of the family and the mother's role in the attacks on her child through this silence. Further, while the child's teacher expresses his concern, visiting his home to confront the parents and battles with the abuser, it is the child that ultimately defeats the story's 'monster'. Intra-racial violence at the familial level thus displaces physical monstrosity as the source of terror in the segment.

Perhaps the clearest ancestor of *Ganja and Hess* is Kasi Lemmon's *Eve's Bayou* (1997). Although it doesn't qualify as a B-film, given its $4 million budget and star-lined cast, the film reproduces many of the qualities and concerns of Gunn's film. The plot of the film centres on Eve Batiste, the young fiery daughter in a family of five. Eve, witnessing her father's affair with a neighbour, attempts to understand and stop her father's misdeeds after she thinks she sees him kiss and then hit the family's eldest daughter. Ultimately, the film and Eve conclude that it is impossible to know what really happened that summer, only that the family is forever changed as a result. The film's location in the Louisiana Bayou, its uncertain anti-hero and his distressed wife, its mysteriously widowed woman – who loses several husbands – and its emphasis on the illegibility of life-changing events prove Gothic. The movie also recalls many of *Ganja and Hess*'s ideological concerns over representing the complex lives of the Black middle class, its representation and rejection of stereotypes of Black hypersexuality, and its determination to represent the complexity of Black desire.

The reception of *Eve's Bayou* illustrates a shift for Black Gothic films. Unlike Gunn's film, which was pulled and distorted to better fit the Blaxploitation genre, *Eve's Bayou* received critical acclaim. Some critics went so far as to suggest that 'To hail *Eve's Bayou* as the best African American film ever would be to understate its universal accessibility to anyone on this planet' (quoted in Mask 1998, 27). Mia Mask explains how 'This statement of unwavering support is also contradictory, implying that ethnic art – in this case African-American cinema – cannot evoke the pathos or poignancy ascribed to mainstream (read: white) cultural products' (37). Thus the problematic ideology latent within the assault on Gunn's film and the reception of Lemmon's is that, for the film to be a 'Black' film, it cannot be artfully Gothic, but should be B-Horror and speak only to Blacks in stereotypical ways. If, like Lemmon's film, it depicts a rural, affluent Black family instead of the stereotypical youth in the urban ghetto, then it is a 'universal film' at best. Or as Gunn's film showed, it is doomed to disfigurement. Producing a Black Gothic film, B or otherwise, thus proves a struggle fraught with numerous threats. Yet as *Ganja and Hess* stresses in its discussion of Black complicity in violent stereotypes, to do otherwise is to allow others to define Blackness. As Audre Lorde notes, this is ultimately more dangerous than the violation which threatens Black alternative film, because 'If I didn't define myself for myself, I would be crunched into other people's fantasies for me and eaten alive' (Lorde 2007, 137).

Bibliography

Benshoff, Harry M. (2000), 'Blaxploitation Horror Films: Generic Reappropriation or Reinscription?', *Cinema Journal* 39/2, 31–50.

David, Marlo D. (2011), '"Let It Go Black": Desire and the Erotic Subject in the Films of Bill Gunn', *Black Camera* 2/2, 26–46.

Derakshani, Tirdad (2007), 'Vampires Defanged; What Happened to Those Vintage Bloodsuckers of Pure Evil? Modern Versions Seem Like Victims Destined to Do Good', *The Philadelphia Inquirer*, E01.

Diawara, Manthia and Phyllis R. Klotman (1991), 'Ganja and Hess: Vampires, Sex, and Addictions', *Black American Literature Forum* 25/2, 299–314.

Ganja and Hess, film. Directed by Bill Gunn. USA: Kelly/Jordan Enterprises, 1973.

Goddu, Teresa (1997), 'Vampire Gothic', *American Literary History* 11/1, 125–41.

Jones, Miriam (1997), 'The Gilda Stories: Revealing the Monsters at the Margins', in Joan Gordon and Veronica Hollinger (eds), *Blood Read: The Vampire as Metaphor in Contemporary Culture* (Philadelphia: University of Philadelphia Press), 151–67.

Lorde, Audre (2007), 'Learning from the 60s', in *Sister Outsider: Essays & Speeches* (Berkeley: Crossing Press), 134–44.
Mask, Mia L (1998), 'Eve's Bayou: Too Good to Be a "Black" Film?', *Cinéaste* 23/4, 26.
Patterson, John (2002), 'The Exploitation Game: The life, death and rebirth of black film-making', *The Guardian*, 8 February, 5.
Stallings, L. H. (2011), 'Poster Gallery: Coming Attractions', *Black Camera* 2/2, 146–8.

3. ALUCARDAS AND ALUCARDOS: VAMPIRIC OBSESSIONS, GOTHIC AND MEXICAN CULT HORROR CINEMA

Enrique Ajuria Ibarra

There is a pivotal scene in the Mexican film *Alucardos, retrato de un vampiro* [*Alucardos, Portrait of a Vampire*] (2010), directed by Ulises Guzmán, where the main themes of this narrative of dark obsessions with a cult horror film converge. Manuel and Eduardo, the protagonists, are fans of Juan López Moctezuma's film *Alucarda, la hija de las tinieblas* [*Alucarda, Daughter of Darkness*] (1977), where a young girl is possessed by a demon and terrorises a convent with her vampiric cravings. The young men study medicine and are granted access to the mental institution where the famous director is being treated. They are convinced by López Moctezuma to help him escape from his room, and they hide him in their home for a while. López Moctezuma suffers from depression and from Alzheimer's, and eventually becomes confused and scared in Manuel's and Eduardo's place. The protagonists decide to help the old man recover his memory and drive him to one of the filming locations of his vampire film: a real forest and park in the outskirts of Mexico City called Desierto de los Leones. Eduardo leads López Moctezuma along several footpaths in the forest. The montage sequence shows a series of images about the filming of the original *Alucarda* interspersed with the final, completed scenes of this same film. A cross-cutting in Guzmán's film also displays a medium close-up shot of Manuel putting on make-up and dressing up as Alucarda inside the car. Once he is ready, Manuel approaches López Moctezuma and Eduardo. The two young men are convinced that López Moctezuma has come back to reality: stepping into one of the filming locations and seeing his vampiric creation represented by Manuel have allowed López Moctezuma to remember his identity and to recover his personality traits from the past.

This sequence confirms the aim of Guzmán's film. The obsession the two protagonists harbour towards the vampire Alucarda rules their lives up to the point when Manuel obtains full gratification in using his body as a vessel to re-create López Moctezuma's character. When Manuel dresses up as Alucarda and faces the old director, his fantasy of becoming Alucarda is finally realised. This scene not only contains themes of fanaticism, idealisation and representation; it also demonstrates that *Alucardos* rescues other motifs explored in López Moctezuma's film. Indeed, the transmutation and re-presentation of Alucarda by Manuel possesses a phantasmatic and spectral function: a projected image of the desire of two avid fans, a representation of a figure that rules their identities, a fictional character that haunts the fractured memory of its creator.

Alucardos prompts us to review the cinema of López Moctezuma and allows us to consider his contribution to Gothic horror in Mexico. His works demonstrate that Gothic motifs are appropriately blended into a cinematic aesthetic that privileges the fantastic, the surreal and the baroque. Gothic in López Moctezuma's films demonstrates that hyperbole and negativity also feature prominently in more regional cult and independent film productions, such as in Mexico. When *Alucardos* cites *Alucarda*, we can consider the former to be a vampire film because it works through a textual invocation that helps revive a corporeal and spiritual obsession framed in the mythical desire of two fanatics. The citational relationship between these two films evidences a Gothic body creeping under the mask of horror. The recovery of the past, although idealised and imagined by the two fans, is manifestly Gothic: an undertone that prompts us to reconsider the link between B-movie, horror and cult. The imaginary features of the film once it has been watched induce a revisiting which impels it to cult status. Gothic in *Alucarda* is not just formal or intertextual, but, as *Alucardos* helps demonstrate, it suggests that the value of the B-movie in terms of cult should be glanced at through Gothic as well. If they are truly considered B-movies, *Alucarda* and *Alucardos* also help us question the validity of lowbrow, independent filmmaking, as its marginal othering provides the basis for a highly effective and critical view of the dark, and often overlooked, anxieties of modernity. This is further determined by the B-movie status, which, once again, works as the negative, low-brow side of the recognised film industry. Instead of supporting veracity, work with Gothic, as well as abject horror, rescues the past and reconfigures it in a nostalgic fantasy image that grows stronger with its validation and legitimation by avid fans.

Gothic Citations

Reception of *Alucarda* was not positive in Mexico upon its limited release in theatres. Emilio García Riera notices that López Moctezuma filmed it during 1975, but it was not released until 1978, and it ran in cinemas for two weeks only (García Riera 1995, 186). García Riera also claims that criticism of the film's production values, aesthetics and themes was harsh, and that reviewers considered it one of the ten worst films ever made (1995, 186). With a plot very different from previous Mexican horror films',[1] *Alucarda* was considered too risky and shocking. Justine arrives at a convent to receive a strict religious education. Here, she meets Alucarda, a young girl with whom she quickly establishes a close friendship. Alucarda is mysterious and attractive, and both girls develop an intimate relationship that eventually leads them to be tempted by the devil. They become possessed, and they soon wreak havoc in the convent: they claim that Satan is their master and Alucarda acquires supernatural powers, such as telekinesis and the ability to trigger spontaneous combustion in objects and people. The main priest in the convent decides to conduct an exorcism on the girls. With the help of monks and nuns, they torture the young women with the purpose of liberating their souls. But the exorcism gets out of control: Justine dies in the torture rack and becomes a violent vampire with an unquenchable thirst for blood. Finally, Alucarda uses her powers to burn the convent down and kills the people that tortured them.

López Moctezuma's film is characterised by a grotesque and baroque aesthetic. The *mise-en-scène* presents settings that allude to a long-forgotten past. The convent already lies almost in ruins, and its interior looks similar to a cavern: the walls are not taken care of, they are not painted, and the chapel houses religious figures that seem to have been formed naturally on the rocks. The constant use of hard and low-key lighting in the climactic scenes of the exorcism and the burning of the convent create a strong contrast between light and darkness that intensifies these violent and supernatural acts. The nuns' robes are made of gauze similar to those used for Egyptian mummies, and these are constantly stained with blood. Alucarda stands out from the rest of the characters with her ominous long, black dress and abundant thick black hair. Additionally, a few characters in the film also feature deformities and a shabby appearance. The world of *Alucarda* is mostly dreamlike and surreal, although more akin to a nightmare. The film features a black mass and a satanic orgy, and the exorcism scene contains copious amounts of physical and psychological violence. To purify the souls of the two young protagonists, the monks and nuns flagellate themselves in an act of contrition first. During the exorcism, Justine and Alucarda are constantly abused: Justine is crucified naked at the altar, and the executioner inflicts several wounds on her body to let the demon out (Figure 3.1).

MEXICAN CULT HORROR CINEMA

Figure 3.1 Justine is tortured by the executioner in *Alucarda*

The theme of the narrative and its critical view of an abusive and hypocritical Catholic Church also lines up with very clear and identifiable Gothic motifs. *Alucarda* is well informed by a negative aesthetic, a feature Fred Botting has emphasised in his most recent look at Gothic. Alucarda shares the same characteristics Botting ascribes to traditional Gothic romances, that is, it is 'overtly but ambiguously, not rational, depicting disturbances of sanity and security, from superstitious belief in ghosts and demons, displays of uncontrolled passion, violent emotion or flights of fancy to portrayals of perversion and obsession' (Botting 2014, 2). In the film, demonic manifestations, exaggerated expressions of feelings and sentiments and perverse practices frame the characterisation of Alucarda and the monks and nuns of the convent. This ambiguous representation questions the discursive parameters that define monstrosity: is Alucarda a monster because she is transgressive and other? Or is the real monster the religious institution that violates the integrity of the body and the mind when it forces its authority upon the young protagonists?

Additionally, the close and intimate relationship between Alucarda and Justine haunts heteronormative idealisations of sexuality. As a demonic and vampiric figure, Alucarda represents an otherness that threatens the religious structure of the convent. By means of her overt sexuality and evil practices, she becomes this monstrous figure that Botting suggests features in the Gothic text. Thus, 'monsters combine negative features that oppose (and define) norms, conventions and values; they suggest an excess or absence beyond those structures and bear the weight of projections and emotions (revulsion, horror, disgust) that result' (2014, 10). In *Alucarda*, monstrosity is manifested through non-normative sexualities and the desire to know what should not be known – destined futures, black masses, the pleasure of the body and blood – which challenge social norms and values represented in the film by a religious institution. Alucarda's actions allow for a projection of horror and disgust that results in abjection. This abjection becomes a serious issue when the attitude and behaviour of nuns and monks become horrific in themselves: their flagellations and the exorcism ceremony are represented very graphically and violently. Julia Kristeva acknowledges that abjection is a bodily experience, which questions the corporeal sense of inside and outside as a physical mark of subjectivity (Kristeva 1982, 3, 5). Catholic acts of contrition seek to expel a monstrous negative residing inside the body by breaking the corporeal barrier that may keep any spiritual hideousness within. The execution of hegemonic powers awakens a horror towards the norms and conventions that rule us socially and culturally. An abjection of feminine monstrosity faces the rationality of a legitimised institution: the monster is monstrously punished and destroyed by the religion that once nurtured it. The confrontation also elicits the inevitable destruction of the convent by a fire ignited by Alucarda's supernatural powers.

Alucarda's most prominent features are its fantasy horror narrative. The themes explored in the film are elaborated through a series of intertextual references to the Gothic tradition. In fact, *Alucarda* is a loose adaptation of *Carmilla* (1871–2), by Sheridan Le Fanu, and the film associates this vampire narrative with references to *Justine* (1791), by the Marquis de Sade, and the films *The Devils* (1971), directed by Ken Russell,[2] and *The Exorcist* (1973), directed by William Friedkin. These texts share notions of sexuality, lost innocence, and the crisis patriarchal and religious institutions experience when they encounter the other and the unknown. López Moctezuma re-assesses these obsessions in a film that stands out because of its fantastic, dark and disturbing narrative, and because it distances itself from the religious and moral instincts of Mexican culture. Its representation of otherness is thus also reinforced when the film is classified as a B-movie, or an underground cult horror film. Nonetheless, this category validates its cultural signification when it faces a public that becomes fascinated with the film's look at other horrors and pleasures.

Similarly, Ulises Guzmán's film recovers a passion for alternative cinema and finds in Alucarda and her creator the motive to develop a story of obsessions, madness and vampirism. *Alucardos* is a documentary that tells the encounter between Manuel, Eduardo and Juan López Moctezuma. In his review of the film, Vicente Gutiérrez interviews Guzmán, who claims to have been approached by Manuel and Eduardo and told him of their encounter with the mythical director (2011). The two protagonists are two young men whose lives have been affected by Alucarda. Guzmán's film establishes a believable authenticity of the events presented on screen with interviews and testimonials from people who have actually met López Moctezuma, such as celebrated cultural analyst Mexican Carlos Monsiváis and Tina Romero. The film narrates a reality that helps frame the myth of López Moctezuma as a peculiar, bohemian and eccentric man. Manuel and Eduardo's fantasies help establish an idealisation of the director and his films. When they meet, their close relationship partially imitates the relationship between Alucarda and Justine in López Moctezuma's film.

Intertextual and referential features in both films generate a ghosting that is moulded out of a factual situation, but is reworked through the documentary into an imagined reproduction of real encounters that have nevertheless been processed by two fanatics. Trangressions of heteronormativity are disturbingly evidenced in Le Fanu's *Carmilla*, as well as Sade's *Justine*; these become spectral and empty remnants that are then refilled with the supernatural anxieties that plague *Alucarda*'s view on sexuality, to then be re-imagined and resignified under the light of Manuel and Eduardo's fanaticism. This ghosting process is reminiscent of Jerrold E. Hogle's view that the ghost of the counterfeit in Gothic fiction is a process that pulls 'discourses back toward disintegrating and hollowed-out antecedents and simultaneously [allows] those past forms to be transferred into a newer and ideological structure of relationships, including newer modes of symbolic exchange, through which the middle class works to define itself' (Hogle 2012, 504). In this sense, Gothic in *Alucarda* and *Alucardos* permits us to unravel regional cultural anxieties through visual explorations that are emptied out of previous signifying determinants in order to address current concerns over modernity through ghosted replications and imitations.

Alucardos is plagued by these very spectres and obsessive ghosts. Manuel and Eduardo get to meet Moctezuma after the enigmatic Francisca makes a phone call. Francisca is an unknown being that disturbs the development of the plot in the film: she prompts new twists, and her presence distorts the image on screen. Her irruption into the narrative works like a ghosted counterfeit: a spectral presence that fuels the fanaticism of the young men and torments Moctezuma. Guzman's film reveals that Francisca was an actress who burned and died in the set of *Alucarda*, and her spirit has come back for revenge.[3] She shows herself before Moctezuma dies and incites the revival of the filming of *Alucarda*. The ghost of Francisca collapses time and space, and manages to revive Moctezuma's dreams, fantasies and terrifying obsessions. She also revives a passion for Alucarda, the character, that moves beyond the mere image on screen. Yet, she cannot become a factual spectre because of the nature of the film form – a documentary – that questions the limits between reality and fiction. On the other hand, this counterfeiting also demonstrates how elaborations of cultural imagining are always worked through the realm of the idealised image of the past. Alucarda becomes embodied through Manuel, who at the same time revives and brings back the young vampire from cultural oblivion. Alucarda lives as a cinematic and textual image, and she is only legitimised as a veritable and popular figure through Guzmán's film: the image source that originated her through citational and referential processes that allude to other Gothic literary figures.

Thus, as a vampiric figure, Alucarda exercises cultural memory, a phenomenon that Simon Bacon and Katarzyna Bronk claim is an essential part of the vampire; that is, it works as

> a memory from the distant past that is buried under the surface of everyday experience and, while not being overt, shapes and informs the structure of how we see and comprehend the present and even envision the future. As such, the figure of the vampire becomes a way in which communities not only record the time they are living in, but also how the present is joined to and contains memories of the past. (Bacon and Bronk 2014, 1–2)

This constitution of cultural memory is achieved with the citational vampire because, according to Ken Gelder, vampire cinema is 'a mode of citation or excitation: a way of setting something in motion, of summoning something (or of being summoned by something), and of being taken out of one's self' (Gelder 2012, 51). The collapse of space and time, past and present, liberate a dark and vampiric trait: Alucarda is a vampire and a demon, and is defined by her citations as a transgressive, metaphorical figure in social, cultural and sexual terms. *Alucarda* fashions the vampire through clear intertextual references to Gothic fiction. Additionally, the two films evidence their vampirism since they work as a referential and self-referential structural hinge. Jeffrey Weinstock argues that 'vampire movies ... endlessly and in so many ways talk about vampires and vampire movies' (Weinstock 2012, 1). On this occasion, the vampire figure flows and moves across two spatial and temporal instances in Mexican cinema, and retrieves and mystifies a dark character that is also transgressive and alternative. *Alucardos* is also noted for being a vampire film where the vampires themselves and the spectres start to invade the constitutive space of the film itself, both physically and narratively. Manuel's and Eduardo's obsession for Alucarda feeds the vampiric spirit of the film, and simultaneously makes the protagonists enjoy their fantasies and obsessions. Their passion for Alucarda transforms their personality, as if this cinematic vampire had turned them into vampires too. Guzmán's film accomplishes this citation through performativity too: Manuel reclaims Alucarda when he dresses like her. This performative citation is an action which Gelder considers 'visible' and which 'invokes' precedent vampire figures 'living under their shadows, returning to them over and over' (2012, vi–vii). *Alucardos* brings back this particular vampire film – a Mexican independent cult horror feature – from cultural oblivion and revives it through its spectral narrative and its idealised mystification of both Moctezuma and Alucarda in the imaginary of two fanatics.

Alucardos is spectrally obsessed with Moctezuma's cinema. Its references to *Alucarda* are not the only ones that refer to the Mexican director's work. Through his impersonation as a madman, the film also cites his film adaptation of Edgar Allan Poe's 'The System of Prof. Tarr and Dr. Fether', in *La mansion de la locura* [*The Mansion of Madness*] (1973). The spectral apparitions of spirits from Moctezuma's personal past and film production, the obsessions of two *Alucarda* fanatics, the motifs of entrapment, madness, death and vampirism, make *Alucarda* a citation in vampire cinema. Thus, this underground, cult Mexican horror film keeps the notion and cultural value of the vampire alive. At the same time, its intertextualities work phantasmatically, as they persistently and hauntingly bring to attention a fascination for vampires and exorcisms rarely seen in Mexican horror cinema. These citations link Gothic and horror motifs that mystify Moctezuma and his film productions.

B-Movie and Otherness

Doyle Greene claims that López Moctezuma was unable to become a major name in the Mexican film industry, and that he turned to more experimental, avant-garde artistic ventures, where he became friends with midnight-movie director Alejandro Jodorowsky (Greene 2007, 46). With films such as *El topo* (1971) and *The Holy Mountain* (1973), Jodorowsky cemented his status as a filmmaker who broke conventions in the Latin American film industry, not just in terms of form and technique; also, his narratives seem to lack any structure, and his plot developments mostly resemble those of dreams and hallucinations, with a variety of characters and situations that are clearly surrealist. While Jodorowsky indulges in metaphorical and metaphysical ruminations, López Moctezuma's films go beyond the shock of surreal imagery and also present a shock that is more deeply ingrained in the realm of body horror. If Paul Wells defines this genre as 'the explicit display of the decay, dissolution or destruction of the body, foregrounding bodily processes and functions under threat, allied to new physiological configurations and re-definitions of anatomical forms' (Wells 2000, 114), then López Moctezuma's focus on corporeality does push boundaries with explicit use and abuse of the body and blood. Although clear relationships can be noticed between the work of these two directors in the use of lavish scenarios, weird characters and extreme bodily performances, López Moctezuma departs from surrealism to enter into more physical confrontations that question normative discourses of modernity, religion, subjectivity and gender.

López Moctezuma's films are very different from studio-produced Mexican horror films, which evidence a strong influence from Universal Studio horror films of the 1930s and 1940s, as well as from the Hammer horror films of the 1950s and 1960s. He finds inspiration from more obscure and less popular international directors, mostly associated with B-movies, and with cult and exploitation cinema. Greene notices that López Moctezuma's films, mainly *The Mansion of Madness* and *Alucarda*, evidence an influence from the 'drive-in era of Roger Corman and American International Pictures . . . in tandem with silent German horror and the Universal horror classics' (2007, 47). Kirsten Strayer expands this list of influence to other directors such as Federico Fellini, Luis Buñuel, Mario Bava and Jess Franco, thus embracing 'avant-garde cinematic expressions and splatter gore' (Strayer 2014, 115). These comparisons situate López Moctezuma's film work outside the mainstream film industry, and even outside narrative and genre conventions.

Although not as fragmented as Jodorowsky's films, *The Mansion of Madness* and *Alucarda* reveal through bodily excess, gore and violence the failure of reason and of religious or clinical institutions. For Hogle, this has been a staple feature in Gothic fiction since the eighteenth century: the anxiety and confrontation of 'threats to life, safety, and sanity kept largely out of sight or in shadows or suggestions from a hidden past' (Hogle 2002, 3), most particularly in Western culture. As Strayer states, López Moctezuma 'embraces the European élan of modernity as madness' and 'adapts radical politics and aesthetic strategies employed by art and independent cinema', which emphasise strategies of spectacle, shock and sensation in their criticism of modern discourse and modern institutions (2014, 116). As mentioned previously, reviews for *Alucarda* rejected the cinematic style of López Moctezuma for these very reasons: the excessive and shocking visuals of the film depart from idealised – and even romanticised – aesthetics of horror. With evident citations of vampires, satanism and sexuality, the film shows perhaps too much, makes manifest that which has been rejected by modern Mexican decorum influenced mostly by Roman Catholicism. The film flaunts that which has been abjected, or in Kristeva's words, that which is 'opposed to I' (1982, 1). *Alucarda* breaks subjectivity and social decorum with excessive blood, corporal punishment and animated vampire corpses. Alucarda's power springs from within her mind and body to destroy everything sacred, as it evidences a cruel and hypocritical religious institution represented by the nuns and priests. Considered poor, cheap and bad, *Alucarda* is thus judged not suitable to be art cinema, or an A-list movie. The film that is produced in the margins stays there, slowly being considered another B-movie – a small production with low-quality value – but with a growing appreciation of it as cult horror.

Nevertheless, a problem arises if we wish to consider López Moctezuma as a B-movie director because of American-oriented connotations regarding the film industry. B-movie is a concept that has been applied to American low-budget and independent films, typically employing a hardly-known cast, engaging with non-mainstream genres (such as horror), and directed by non-commercial directors. As such, B-movies may also be associated with cult and exploitation cinemas, with many of these films also gathering such a following as to be considered classics by their fans.

To speak of B-movies is to address also non-commercial or non-Hollywood productions. They are films that are usually considered to be at the bottom end of movie theatre programmes, quietly gaining their audiences at the margins of A-film distribution and screenings. It is this low-key and constant othering, often differenced from big-budget productions, that creates a niche for everything non-American, non-glamour, non-Hollywood, including foreign films that do not enjoy a massive distribution strategy and are usually relegated to smaller screenings in alternative theatres and festivals. Such is the case with several Latin American films, whose lower production budget and non-massive distribution in the USA provide enough reason to call them B-movies.

In his study of mexploitation cinema, Greene considers that the American viewer is at odds with the Mexican horror film, because 'mexploitation's unorthodox formal strategies force the (American) viewer to alternate between accustomed, comfortable, traditional Hollywood codes and unfamiliar, "disruptive, counter viewing codes" – codes specifically suited to a Mexican audience' (2005, 16). In this sense, Greene argues, the American viewer is inevitably distanced from the Mexican film production code, as well as the local cultural discourse that frames these movies, but Dolores Tierney claims that Greene has fallen into the trap of othering. She notices 'some postcolonial awareness' (Tierney 2014, 132) in Greene's view: the emphasis on recognising an 'other' cinema that can only work as counter-cinema because of its status of difference from the Hollywood norm (2005, 17–18). The cult following of Mexican films by American audiences poses a problem regarding the status of these productions. Thus, Tierney argues that criticism focusing on Latin American cult cinema mostly addresses this issue of 'US metropolitan audiences' who display a 'viewing protocol' from 'a potentially dominant group that thrills in seeing the cultures of the peripheries failing to copy the culture of the center' (2014, 131). Tierney notices that cult cinema (like other associated terms, such as B-movies) is an outside concept that seeks to frame the idea of cult in Latin American film cultures, and that it is necessary to acknowledge this issue in order to understand 'how cult cinema fits in with new ways of conceiving the region's cinema' (2014, 130). As such, Guzmán's film *Alucardos* provides

Figure 3.2 Manuel and Eduardo pose next to an altar made of merchandise from the film *Alucarda* in *Alucardos*

insight into the notion of cult and B-movie Gothic within Mexican cultural parameters: it is not an outsider audience facing Moctezuma's film, but rather two avid Mexican fans who help determine the cult status of both director and film as part of Mexican popular culture (Figure 3.2).

In *Alucardos*, Manuel and Eduardo are devoted fans of *Alucarda*, both the film and the character, mostly because it provides them with a fictional representation of that which is different, that which does not conform to the norm: darkness, the macabre, the rejection of social institutions, the rejection of heteronormative conventions of sexuality as portrayed by Alucarda's and Justine's intimate relationship. Both characters confess during the course of Guzmán's film that they have always felt themselves to be different from the norm, both in the way they approach reality and in their own constitutions of subjectivity. When Manuel confesses he is intersex, he reveals that his difference could be mediated with López Moctezuma's film. He recognises in Alucarda (the character) a vessel for the alternative, a representation with which he can feel himself aligned: Alucarda does not conform to the norms of decorous heteronormativity, and she is also repudiated and ostracised by the society that once nurtured her. Also, her supernatural powers turn her into a monstrous freak, and Manuel sees in her the confidence to recognise his own body as transgressive or alternative. David Church argues that cult fans see in their films a 'sense of "uniqueness"' and 'perceived difference from "mainstream", non-cult movies', and that this allows for representations of other bodies, disabled bodies, 'freakish' bodies to be featured in films that are considered to be cult (Church 2011, 3).[4] Even though Church concludes that the representation of disability in these films does not resolve perceptions of inequality aimed at disabled bodies (2011, 3), he claims cultists find a sense of inclusivity within their own social experience, instead of accepting 'easy condemnation' (2011, 16). Thus, the relationship between other bodies and other forms of subjectivity finds a receptacle for difference, even though this otherness is still considered transgressive by the mainstream norm. Manuel is able to claim his own subjectivity thanks to this: he is able to take his intersexuality as his defining feature, thus cementing his identity and recognising his alterity through his very own cult fanaticism.

Manuel and Eduardo love Alucarda and López Moctezuma's film. It is their obsession that moves them to kidnap the director. It is their fanaticism that allows them to get in touch with Tina Romero (the actress who portrayed Alucarda) as the closest physical rapport they can have with their beloved vampire girl. This fictional character comes to life spectrally: she is a manifested persona that does not materialise corporeally, but exists through Manuel's and Eduardo's collection of items related to *Alucarda*, as well as their contact with the people involved in creating, impersonating and making Alucarda. As such, this cult devotion – which has also determined their own subjectivities in the alternative world of cult fandom – provides the opportunity to understand how lesser-known Mexican film productions may develop an audience that recognises the film as an alternative, transgressive, yet valuable visual cultural product in Mexico. Even if its underground production, limited release and lack of mainstream recognition has not allowed López Moctezuma's film to be considered a prominent example of Mexican cinema (an A-movie), it nevertheless works its way through film history through the alternative B-route. Whether B-movie or cult film, the relationship between *Alucardos* and *Alucarda* must be recognised by the way *Alucarda* is imagined in Guzmán's film, as much as *Alucarda* imagines the Gothic fictions to which it alludes.

Notes

1. Although Mexico had previously experimented with the horror genre in the 1930s, 1940s and 1950s, during the late 1950s and 1960s horror productions became more formulaic and relied on standardised features that starred the Mexican wrestler El Santo. Doyle Greene notices that most horror films in Mexico turned to more exploitation standards, and that, even though they were 'consigned to camp or cheese status', they 'may in fact represent a form of alternative and even experimental cinema through their very disregard of conventional form, coherent narratives, and cinematic realism' (Greene 2005, 13). *Alucarda* detaches itself from this standardisation of Mexican horror wrestler films. Even though the latter should also

be critically evaluated to determine their contribution to film, as Greene argues, it is also important to understand what makes López Moctezuma's works stand out from the mexploitation horror films that preceded them.
2. There is an exceptional similarity between Russell's and López Moctezuma's films. Doyle Greene acknowledges that both films share a thematic line that criticises Roman Catholicism and sexual repression, but that '*Alucarda* liberally incorporates supernatural overtones and implications in its violence and eroticism: occultism, demonic possession, and vampirism' (Greene 2007, 71). It should also be noted that, while *The Devils* also criticises the political corruption of Roman Catholicism, with Cardinal Richelieu's scheme to get rid of Urbain Grandier, *Alucarda* focuses more on criticising the Catholic Church's modernism and its implication in the legitimation of abusive practices under the guise of faith and divine reasoning.
3. In his review of *Alucardos*, Todd Brown claims that this tragedy actually did happen: in 'a last minute decision' López Moctezuma burned 'the set of Alucarda for real while filming', and this 'led to the death of an extra while others were severely injured' (2011).
4. Church cites films such as Tod Browning's *Freaks* (1932), and Jodorowsky's *El topo* and *The Holy Mountain*, as clear examples of cult films that feature prominently disabled bodies considered to be part of this transgressive, freakish spectacle.

Bibliography

Bacon, Simon and Katarzyna Bronk (2014), 'Introduction', in Simon Bacon and Katarzyna Bronk (eds), *Undead Memory: Vampires and Human Memory in Popular Culture* (Bern: Peter Lang), 1–17.
Botting, Fred (2014), *Gothic*, 2nd edn (London: Routledge).
Brown, Todd (2011), 'Morbido 2011: Alucardos, Retrato de Un Vampiro, Review', *ScreenAnarchy*, 28 October, <http://screenanarchy.com/2011/10/morbido-2011-alucardos-retrato-de-un-vampirto-review.html> (last accessed 3 November 2017).
Church, David (2011), 'Freakery, Cult Films, and the Problem of Ambivalence', *Journal of Film and Video* 63/1, 3–17.
García Riera, Emilio (1995), *Historia Documental del Cine Mexicano*, Vol. 17 (Guadalajara: Universidad de Guadalajara).
Gelder, Ken (2012), *New Vampire Cinema* (London: BFI/Palgrave Macmillan).
Greene, Doyle (2005), *Mexploitation Cinema: A Critical History of Mexican Vampire, Wrestler, Ape-Man and Similar Films, 1957–1977* (Jefferson, NC: McFarland).
Greene, Doyle (2007), *The Mexican Cinema of Darkness: A Critical Study of Six Landmark Horror and Exploitation Films, 1969–1988* (Jefferson, NC: McFarland).
Gutiérrez, Vicente (2011), 'López Moctezuma: La historia de un genio maldito', *El economista*, 28 February, <http://eleconomista.com.mx/entretenimiento/2011/02/28/lopez-moctezuma-historia-genio-maldito> (last accessed 3 November 2017).
Hogle, Jerrold, E (2002), 'Introduction: The Gothic in Western Culture', in Jerrold E. Hogle (ed.), *The Cambridge Companion to Gothic Fiction* (Cambridge: Cambridge University Press), 1–20.
Hogle, Jerrold E. (2012), 'The Gothic Ghost of the Counterfeit and the Progress of Abjection', in David Punter (ed.), *A New Companion to the Gothic* (Oxford: Wiley-Blackwell), 496–509.
Kristeva, Julia (1982), *Powers of Horror: An Essay on Abjection* (New York: Columbia University Press).
Strayer, Kirsten (2014), 'Art, Horror, and International Identity in 1970s Exploitation Films', in Dana Och and Kirsten Strayer (eds), *Transnational Horror Across Visual Media: Fragmented Bodies* (London: Routledge), 109–25.

Tierney, Dolores (2014), 'Mapping Cult Cinema in Latin American Film Cultures', *Cinema Journal* 54/1, 129–35.
Weinstock, Jeffrey (2012), *The Vampire Film: Undead Cinema* (New York: Wallflower Press).
Wells, Paul (2000), *The Horror Genre: From Beelzebub to Blair Witch* (London: Wallflower Press).

Filmography

Alucarda, la hija de las tinieblas (Alucarda, Daughter of Darkness, Juan López Moctezuma 1977)
Alucardos, retrato de un vampiro (Alucardos, Portrait of a Vampire, Ulises Guzmán 2010)
The Devils (Ken Russell 1971)
The Exorcist (William Friedkin 1973)
Freaks (Tod Browning 1932)
La mansion de la locura (The Mansion of Madness, Juan López Moctezuma 1973)

4. GOTHIC FORESTS AND MANGROVES: ENVIRONMENTAL DISASTERS IN *ZOMBIO* AND *MANGUE NEGRO*

Daniel Serravalle de Sá

The zombie holds a special place within Gothic culture, for it is not rooted in the literary tradition that includes Horace Walpole's *The Castle of Otranto* (1764), Mary Shelley's *Frankenstein* (1818) and Bram Stoker's *Dracula* (1897). The origins of zombies lie in religious practices that originated in Africa and found a syncretic expression in Haiti and Cuba, but also in places like New Orleans, Salvador-Bahia and Rio de Janeiro. These cultural manifestations are united by their common characteristics of incorporation, magic and sacrifice in the form of offerings made to the saints or *orixás*.

The zombie has moved slowly from Afro-Caribbean and Black American religious practices into cinema screens. Yet the cinematic representations of the zombie embody monstrous and spectral dimensions that tie them to a European literary Gothic tradition. The first zombie films produced in the 1930s and 1940s depict voodoo ceremonies, and zombies as bodies without minds, as well as figures who exist on the threshold between life and death. This early cinematic zombie is associated with voodoo and does not depict the graphic violence of the late twentieth- and twenty-first-century flesh-eating zombie. Victor Halperin's *White Zombie* (1932), Jean Yarbrough's *King of the Zombies* (1941) and Jacques Tourneur's *I Walked with a Zombie* (1943) are iconic examples from this early cinematic tradition, depicting zombies who shuffle across the set, often in somnambulistic trances. The decaying corpse hungry for human flesh is largely an innovation of George Romero's low-budget, black-and-white film *Night of the Living Dead* (1968) and, a decade later, films such as Lucio Fulci's *Zombi 2* (1979) and Marino Girolami's *Zombie Holocaust* (1980), which consolidated the zombie in cinema by depicting gory scenes of cannibalism.

The late twentieth and early twenty-first centuries included the emergence of the zombie in new manifestations and forms: the zomromcom, the comic zombie, the zombie parody, the fast-moving zombie and the zombie virus. For instance, in Dan O'Bannon's *The Return of the Living Dead* (1985) a gas leak reanimates corpses into zombies who can talk and consume human brains; Danny Boyle's *28 Days Later* (2002) and Paul W. S. Anderson's *Resident Evil* (2002) introduce fast-moving zombies (the latter based on the 1996 third-person shooter video game *Biohazard/Resident Evil*). Zombies have taken on many different forms, and with that many different historical meanings in a variety of contexts, so they reflect a wide range of socio-political issues: critiques of consumer culture (George Romero's *Dawn of the Dead*, 1978), the first Iraq war and US presidential elections (Joe Dante's *Homecoming*, 2004), xenophobia and Nazi history (Tommy Wirkola's *Dead Snow*, 2009), terrorism (*The Terror Experiment*, 2010 and *Ozombie*, 2012) (Edwards 2015, 1–14). These examples of zombification, whether they arise through contamination, sorcery or brainwashing, are frequently linked to the loss of rational and emotional responses that constitute humanity: the ability to think, feel empathy, express sympathy.

In this chapter I discuss two Gothic zombie B-movies – zombBie-movies – made in Brazil: Petter Baiestorf's *Zombio* (1999) and Rodrigo Aragão's *Mangue Negro* (2009). These films represent a small fraction of a genre that is currently thriving in Brazil, and one of the primary reasons for such popularity of zombie movies in Brazil is that they are cheap films to produce. My reading of *Zombio* and *Mangue Negro* will move from contextualisation to analysis, and I seek to provide insights into the Gothic dimensions of these Brazilian zombie films.

These films include those Gothic images of decay, degeneration and destruction which are related to contemporary anxieties about environmental devastation. Considering that Brazil's widespread image is that of an optimistic tropical country, these films, I suggest, expose the underbelly of national history and identity. Moreover, the zombie's insatiable appetite for human bodies is, I argue, particularly meaningful in the Brazilian context where the recent history of the exploitation of labour, political unrest, alienation and, more specifically, environmental disaster underscore both of these films.

Zombio and *Mangue Negro* take place in ecological settings that highlight the natural location. The visual focus on the high-arched forest canopies and aerial mangrove roots is reminiscent of the visual forms and features found in Gothic architecture and consistent with Robert A. Scott's observation that the Gothic style 'originated in forests' (2003, 119) and – although this is contentious among art historians – Scott maintains that the idea has 'persisted with incredible tenacity, and one hears it occasionally even today' (2003, 119).

My ideas about environment, nature and ecology are informed by Timothy Morton's *Ecology without Nature* (2010), *Hyperobjects* (2013) and *Dark Ecology* (2016), in which he develops a theory of environmental art and explores different ways of taking a critical and reflexive artistic stand on environmentalist issues. Morton argues that humans are embedded in nature, which is the surrounding medium and the materiality that sustains life. The key question, however, is how the human being, as a social and political animal, determines its insertion within nature. According to Morton, 'Ecological awareness is a detailed and increasing sense, in science and outside of it, of the innumerable interrelationships among lifeforms and between life and non-life' (2013, 128). In this sense, what makes humanity ecological is its interconnection and coexistence with nature and, in *Zombio* and *Mangue Negro*, this concept is powerfully associated with the depiction of survival.

ZOMBIO: SUNSCREEN, POLLUTED RIVERS AND GOTHIC FORESTS

Independent Brazilian filmmaker Petter Baiestorf is based in Palmitos, a small town in the state of Santa Catarina, from where he has made over thirty short, medium-length and feature films. In collaboration with his business partner César 'Coffin' Souza, he has developed a cinematic aesthetic called Kanibaru Sinema, a comic 'Japanisation' of the words 'cannibal cinema', with the purpose of producing films in any format with micro-budgets. The basis of their conception of cinema is articulated in their book *Manifesto Canibal* (2002), in which Baiestorf and Coffin Souza attack those filmmakers who 'have everything and do nothing', thus voicing their dissatisfaction with mainstream cinema. As an alternative, they propose an approach to cinema that is 'anthropophagic, primitive, savage, nihilist, atheist and chaotic, but with such a damn pureness that [it] is capable of frightening the colonised and colonisers' (37).

This nonconformist approach is reminiscent of a previous generation of filmmakers who emerged in the 1960s in Brazil and produced low-budget films of gut-wrenching intensity, though they rarely made horror films. Known as Cinema Marginal or *udigrudi* (a comic spin on the English expression 'underground'), these films from the 1960s depict underworld characters in a 'degraded sub-world, [which is] traversed by grotesque processions, condemned to the absurd, mutilated by crime, sex, and exploitation, hopeless and fallacious [but which], is, however, animated and redeemed by its inarticulate wrath' (Gomes 1995, 248). Further connections between these two generations of filmmakers can be observed in their use of random locations, untrained actors and improvised dialogues, all of which combine to produce a fragmented and often incoherent fictional world.

Produced by Canibal-Mabuse, the medium-length film *Zombio* (1999) was originally released on VHS, and the producers claim to have spent only 78 US dollars making it. It is the first zombBie movie made in Brazil, initiating a massive list of productions that continues to grow. After the DVD release in 2009, pirated copies were uploaded onto YouTube and, in 2013, Baiestorf posted links on his Facebook profile for free downloads of his films. In this 45-minute film, Euclides (César Souza) and Tânia (Denise V.), two eco-tourists, think they have found a small paradise on a remote island on the Uruguai River, which is on the border between Argentina, Brazil and Uruguay. However, when exploring the island, they find a sinister old lady (Petter Baiestorf), who is a serial killer, as well as a band of zombies commanded by a diabolic priestess (Rose de Andrade). There is much blood splattering, gratuitous nudity and amateurish special effects, all of which would appeal to fans of movies by Lucio Fulci (to whom Baiestorf dedicates the movie), John Waters, Brad F. Grinter, George Kuchar and José Mojica Marins.

In the opening scene, the couple spread sunscreen lotion on each other and discuss the risk of skin cancer in the tropics. This dialogue introduces an ecological leitmotif which is developed throughout the movie, and which links their desire for a meaningful relationship with nature to its presence as a potentially destructive force. The couple acknowledge that the interconnectedness that permeates all dimensions of life is an entangling web apart from which no being, object or construct can independently exist, the interconnectedness that Morton refers to as ecological thought. As the couple cross the river to the remote island, a more ominous space emerges: they glimpse a dark underside to the tropical vegetation.

The mysteries of the Brazilian forest offer a Gothic setting, and this combines with the threat of environmental disaster that is often found in ecoGothic texts. According to Hughes and Smith (2013):

> debates about climate change and environmental damage have been key issues on most industrialized countries' political agendas for some time. These issues have helped shape the direction and application of ecocritical languages. The Gothic seems to be the form which is well placed to capture these anxieties and provides a culturally significant point of contact between literary criticism, ecological issues and political process. While the origins of ecoGothic can be traced back to Romanticism the growth in environmental awareness has become a significant development. (5)

The political urgency of ecological issues is often self-consciously elaborated in many contemporary Gothic novels, films and television series, from Cormac McCarthy's *The Road* (2006) to Sánchez and Myrick's *Blair Witch Project* (1999) to AMC's *The Walking Dead* (2010–).

EcoGothic and 'dark ecology' are central in Baiestorf's *Zombio*. The island on Uruguai River unleashes an uncontrollable environmental force on the couple, which will ultimately lead to their destruction. As Euclides and Tânia embrace on the banks of the river, the first zombie emerges from the water; as it staggers towards them, Euclides says: 'this guy is rotten; it must be the pollution in the river'. Contaminated water here is an explanation for the existence of the zombies, a consequence of human environmental destruction. As a backlash to industrialisation, this is a concern that can be traced back to the period when the Industrial Revolution began to take effect. In this sense, *Zombio* updates eighteenth-century Gothic themes such as the environmental disaster as a consequence of industrialisation and its impact on nature. Environmental anxieties, as an aspect of contemporary Gothic, surface here and speak to a threat that looms on the horizon and that derives from the far bigger problem of pollution, which is causing global warming and the contamination of the world's freshwater rivers and lakes.

The zombie attacks the couple, but they manage to kill it. In the struggle, Tânia is covered in putrid fluids and Euclides is bitten. Contaminated with something that will gradually turn him into a zombie, Euclides is overcome by uncontrollable rage. Meanwhile, on another location on the island, a blonde girl is held captive by a weird (and bearded) old lady. The lady is in fact a sexual predator wearing a shawl (a ridiculously bad disguise) and she tortures the girl with a knife. As the sinister lady fetches firewood, the injured girl manages to flee. At sundown, the couple move quickly through the forest and seek shelter. Their journey is impeded by slimy green zombies, which they slay with a machete. Tânia perceives that Euclides is losing control; he is increasingly violent and he brutalises the bodies of the zombies they kill. Tânia initially refuses to brutally attack the zombies but, in due course, she relents and relishes the act of killing. It becomes clear that there is something botanical about the zombies; they are in part decomposing vegetable matter. The couple then discover the blonde girl and, believing she was a zombie, Tânia strikes her with the machete. But her blood is red. In this long sequence, the zombies stumble through the forest (Figure 4.1) and become easy prey for the couple, who violently attack the undead (Figure 4.2).

We soon learn that the diabolical priestess controls the zombies by making them drink a green sap from her veins. Elsewhere in the forest, Euclides begins drooling green liquid and, without his support, Tânia is soon overwhelmed; she is ruthlessly disembowelled and consumed by zombies. The sinister old lady, who was searching for the fugitive girl, runs into a group of zombies. She tries to resist them but she is captured, eviscerated and eaten alive. The film reaches a climax when the zombies take Euclides to the priestess, who has morphed into a monster (Figure 4.3). One of her hands has becomes a phallic green finger; the other hand is a piranha-like snakehead. Surrounded

Figure 4.1   Night shot of zombies walking in the forest

by zombies, as in a black mass, and her monstrous hand bites Euclides on the shoulder, completing his zombification. Here, the high-arched forest becomes the priestess's Gothic cathedral, where she transforms herself into a monstrous shape-shifter. She is a kind of guardian to the remote island and the zombies are her territorial army, resisting the presence of intruders and the devastation that humans may bring. In the end, Euclides places his hand over her penis-like hand and they walk into the fog, a newly-wed couple.

The zombies overwhelming the intruders on the island is symbolic of the revenge of a natural world that has been ravaged by environmental destruction.

Figure 4.2 Evisceration special effects

Nature reasserts its balance by consuming the remnants of the peculiar death spectacle that occurs in the forest. Despite the doom and destruction, the Gothic tropes of environmental anxiety and ruination point to a form of salvation, for the ending is not apocalyptic. Rather, the couple who disappear into the haze suggest that there is a future for new beings, and new life to come. Toxic substances and environmental destruction have been exploited and harnessed to produce new life forms.

An explanation of this film is offered in the short film *Revisitando Zombio*

Figure 4.3 Priestess morphs into a bestial monster

(*Revisiting Zombio*, 2009), a documentary in which Baiestorf and Coffin Souza return to the island on the Uruguai River where *Zombio* was filmed. Drinking cans of beer and without the support of a crew, the filmmakers talk about the stories behind the film production, ten years after its release. When they arrive at the location by the river, the presence of pollution and debris resurfaces and they discuss the environmental destruction of the river and comment on how they had to clean up the spot at the time and how they will do it once more. Although Baiestorf and Souza do not claim to be environmental activists,

Zombio contains a Gothic discourse of decay and destruction that is related to environmental anxieties, pollution and natural disasters.

Mangue Negro: Global Warming, Ethnicity and Gothic Mangroves

In *Mangue Negro* (*Mud Zombies* 2009), although there is no precise explanation of what has given rise to a plague of zombies, the mangrove's environmental deterioration is mentioned several times in the film as a consequence of global warming and similar human-induced activities. Produced by Fábulas Negras, with a budget of 16,000 dollars, *Mangue Negro* was filmed in the coastal town of Guarapari in the state of Espírito Santo, and is Rodrigo Aragão's first feature-length film. The location of the film is significant, for in November 2016, the coastal state of Espírito Santo suffered irreparable environmental damage due to a flood of contaminated water moving downstream from the site of a mining dam breach in the state of Minas Gerais. The mudslide of mining waste and chemicals left a path of devastation that impacted on the livelihood of many communities and caused long-term damage to the local ecosystem. The dam rupture at the Samarco iron ore mine, owned by BHP Billiton and Vale, is the worst environmental disaster in Brazil's history.

Mangue Negro received an award at the Buenos Aires Rojo Sangre festival, the oldest event of its kind in Latin America. It also received honourable mentions at the London International Festival of Science Fiction and Fantastic Film and at the Yubari International Fantastic Film Festival for its make-up techniques. The director is a self-taught make-up artist, who claims to have learned his skills by emulating other movies' special effects. Unlike Baiestorf with his 'savage' cinema, Aragão aspires to make low-budget films that do not shy away from mainstream studio productions. Recently, Aragão directed two other B-movies which, alongside *Mangue Negro*, form a terror trilogy: *A Noite do Chupacabras* (*The Night of the Chupacabras*, 2011), which draws upon a family feud and the popular legend of a blood-sucking alien creature, and *Mar Negro* (*Dark Sea*, 2013), which tells the story of a strange fish that spreads a disease and turns people and sea animals into predatory killers.

Mangue Negro is set in an isolated region of the Brazilian coastline, where a deprived community ekes out an existence fishing and catching crustaceans from a mangrove. Thriving where land and water meet, tropical mangroves are complex ecosystems that protect the coastline, managing the daily rise and fall of tides and forming a barrier against storms and hurricanes. Mangroves are a relatively common ecosystem in Brazil and they have a major ecological and cultural significance for many communities which rely on the crabs, mussels and fish that live among the roots. In the film, the existence of a mangrove population is threatened by the gradual disappearance of aquatic life. When dead bodies emerge from the muddy waters, attacking the inhabitants of the community and transforming them into zombies, a frightened and reticent local, Luís (Walderrama dos Santos), fights the monsters and saves the life of Raquel (Kika de Oliveira). Luís is hopelessly timid and can hardly speak to Raquel, but he is skilled with an axe that can help them through the cannibal-zombie infestation, and the splatter scenes satisfy the most gore-ravenous viewer.

Despite the conventional aspects of the plot, there is technical accomplishment in the film's use of make-up artistry and editing, for the story is narrated by a series of jump-cuts that seek to convey a sense of a fast-paced simultaneity to the events in the storyline. Another insightful moment in the film takes place when the opening credits roll and the names of the actors and crew move from side to side on the screen, mimicking the sideways movement of a crab. Moreover, Aragão employs different types of POV shots, including first-person reverse shots and what is known as the 'shaky cam', the film resembling Peter Jackson's early works (scenes shot from many angles) and Sam Raimi's *Evil Dead* (1981) in the way it manages to submerge the spectator in the action (Figure 4.4).

Mangue Negro is also remarkable in the way it uses a Gothic discourse of disintegration and death to represent environmental disasters. In the first scene, which functions as a prologue to the narrative, two men row down a river estuary surrounded by the distinctive mangrove vegetation. Local inhabitant Agenor (Markus Konká – the only professional actor in the film) recalls a bygone era when he could fish and pick enough mud crabs to feed his family and even sell part of his catch. The character's speech turns this once benevolent and idyllic ecosystem into a dark space of ruination and decay, foreshadowing the grim events that are about to come. As the camera cuts from the actor's face to the shrubs and different tree species that rise out of the tangle of roots in the mud, the vegetation gains an eerie aura. The aerial root system of the vegetation appears to be standing on stilts above the water, resembling the flying buttresses of Gothic cathedrals but also a labyrinthine space of entrapment and disorientation (Figure 4.5).

Gothic forms are presented here as multi-faceted phenomena, both aesthetic and discursive, demonstrating an inclination to spawn a variety of settings across various topographies and geographies. The tropical mangrove becomes infused with recognisable Gothic motifs (displacement, isolation, sublime wilderness) which are based upon Brazilian cultural circumstances and associated with environment disaster. In terms of ecological coexistence, the depletion of the mangrove's resources and wildlife occurs because 'we coexist in an infinite web of mutual interdependence where there is no boundary or center' (Morton 2007, 23). The desertification of the mangrove ecosystem is thus the consequence of anthropocentric violence against other life forms on earth, a side effect of an agrarian society that gradually progresses to intensive farming,

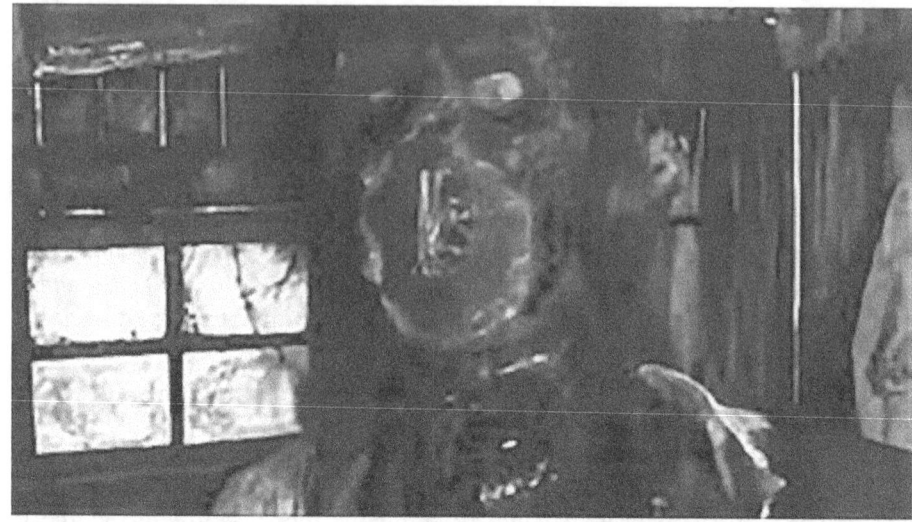

Figure 4.4 A POV shot of Luís shooting a zombie in the back of the head

overfishing, speciesism, excessive consumption. The Gothic's dark ecology that emerges here reveals how we are haunted not only by our past, but also by our future, since all things are connected in this hermetic spider web.

Due to the extinctions of crabs and fish, a herd of zombies arises from the dead and reflects the ever-changing ecological niches. The emergence of the zombies' plague functions in *Mangue Negro* as an ecological self-correction mechanism, arguably a natural force that emerges to drive out humans from the mangrove in an attempt to restore environmental balance. The first zombie

ENVIRONMENTAL DISASTERS IN *ZOMBIO* AND *MANGUE NEGRO*

Figure 4.5   A flooded tropical mangrove and a tide-out mangrove with its aerial roots

appears when fisherman Batista (Reginaldo Secundo) stumbles upon a rotting body while catching crabs; he is shocked by the ghastly scene and he falls on sharp barnacles, injuring himself and eventually becoming a zombie. Although the process of zombification is not explained, the film suggests it is related to primal and destructive forces connected to global warming and other man-made ecological destruction. In the film, the ecosystem is not presented merely as a backdrop, but functions as a central character, which conceptually establishes a point of contact with the environment.

Moreover, *Mangue Negro* is associated with the Gothic by means of the recent Brazilian history of the exploitation of labour and alienation: it articulates critiques of the underbelly of Brazil's stereotypically cheerful surface. While Batista turns into a zombie, Luís gathers courage to ask Raquel out, but, when he arrives at her family's shack, the scoundrel, Júlio (Júlio Tigre), is groping Raquel, who manages to push him away. Júlio goes into the shack to speak to Raquel's father, Seu Antônio (Antônio Lâmego), whom he controls financially by purchasing the crabs he manages to catch. The connections with the Gothic here are twofold: Júlio's sexual advances represent coercive forms of sexuality exercised by older men on younger women – Schedoni in Ann Radcliffe's *The Italian* (1797) is an iconic example of such male harassment. The second aspect is the method of bonded labour by means of which Júlio keeps Seu Antônio trapped in a helpless cycle of debt reinforced by an economic disparity that echoes the enslavement and exploitation found in William Godwin's *Caleb Williams* (1794).

As Luís and Raquel flee through the mangrove at night and try to reach the highlands to escape the zombies, they stop at the house of Dona Benedita, an elderly *mãe de santo* (priestess), who is able to cure Raquel of the zombie disease. The presence of the priestess alongside the drumming rhythms of the soundtrack creates an atmospheric scene that establishes a connection with African-Brazilian *candomblé* religion. As she sends the couple on their way, Dona Benedita refuses to leave her shack in the mangrove, either because she knows how to avoid the zombies or because she knows the end of her lifestyle has been realised. *Mangue Negro* is a socially significant film in the sense that it presents characters who symbolise Brazilian people and culture, representing types such as the local fishermen and the artisanal crab pickers to the *mães de santo*, who use natural products to cure illnesses, and the con-men who exploit the already deprived locals (Figure 4.6).

Brazilian mangrove communities are usually populated by people of indigenous African descent, many of whom found refuge in this remote environment during slavery. In this sense, the film gestures back to the Brazilian history of subjugation, genocide and colonisation. The threats to the mangrove ecosystem establish a new order for the dark-skinned people in the film, and they must confront the ecological violence of flesh-eating zombies. Although *Mangue Negro* is not a call for political action, it addresses historical Brazilian experiences of violence and anxiety that can be traced back to the early days of colonisation and are now being projected onto the dark future of environmental disaster.

ENVIRONMENTAL DISASTERS IN *ZOMBIO* AND *MANGUE NEGRO*

Figure 4.6 Old *candomblé* priestess and night shot of a zombie in the mangrove

NATURAL DISASTERS AND THE STATE OF THE NATION

Eighteenth-century Gothic elements enter into the Brazilian B-movies *Zombio* and *Mangue Negro* by means of similarities in the treatment of discourses, settings and themes, highlighting the centrality of the natural environment and the zombie as a trope of devastation and disaster. The zombies here stand in for the ghosts of classical Gothic, whose transnational discourse is capable of capturing local histories of violence and anxieties and fostering debates about exploitation, unrest and alienation, which often inhere in the representation of the landscape.

Issues concerning environmentalism are also nationally modulated and this connection has been an enduring element in the Gothic literary tradition. However, in the early Gothic novels, there is little or no sense that environmental damage could threaten the entire planet. It was only in the Gothic films of the 1960s and 1970s that such apocalyptic scenarios became more prevalent, questioning the effectiveness of governments and the breakdown of social institutions. This has been particularly evident in the so-called 'revenge of nature' films where biomes threaten to destroy mankind, including, among many others, Alfred Hitchcock's *The Birds* (1963), George McCowan's eco-horror *Frogs* (1972) and Peter Weir's *The Last Wave* (1977). The already-mentioned zombie films *Night of the Living Dead* (1968) and *Dawn of the Dead* (1978) artfully articulate the overthrow of humanity by means of infection and plague, presenting zombiedom as an incurable disease that gradually takes over the world.

In the Brazilian films, the Gothic discourse helps to draw out a dystopian ecological world-view, acknowledging paradigms that help to reinvigorate debates about violence and anxiety, race and class, economic speculation and exploitation, and national identities, as well as environmental disasters that threaten ecological coexistence. In the wake of this, the depiction of a backlash from nature destabilises a culture of globalisation that ignores mutual interdependence in the web of life and often disguises the unyielding pursuit of economic growth behind the governmental and market-driven rhetoric of sustainable development. Haunted by the future, these Brazilian films anticipate the imminent threats represented by our failure to prevent an all too predictable environmental disaster.

The dispersal of the Gothic over diverse temporal contexts and geographical spaces does not negate historical or national specificities. In *Zombio* and *Mangue Negro* the merger of Gothic, environmentalism and nationhood relies upon many of the same tropes and characters that engender other state-of-the-nation narratives. In discussing historical allegory in film, Ismail Xavier explains why it has been a privileged mode of interpretation during particular historical moments. He notes that recognising such dimensions requires the ability to perceive a correspondence between specific circumstances of the text and the historical context, for national allegories often serve as a means of offering a 'disguised comment on the present' (1997, 354). Moreover, he argues that the identification of 'national allegories require[s] the understanding of private lives as representative of public destinies' (1997, 335). This relates directly to *Zombio* and *Mangue Negro*, for the Gothic emerges as the prominent mode for dealing with the environmental disasters that threaten the nationhood of Brazil, a country that is defined in the national imaginary as linked to the sublime landscapes of the Amazon as well as a tropical paradise of vast beaches, sun and clean water. As a cultural metaphor, the zombies in these films arise out of the consciousness about environmental destruction that is slowly developing in Brazil. As agents of nature the zombies seek revenge for the damage done to forests and mangrove ecosystems, unleashing pestilence and death with overwhelming power and violence on the species responsible for ecological imbalance and the devastation of the natural world.

BIBLIOGRAPHY

Baiestorf, Petter and César Souza (2002), *Manifesto Canibal* (Rio de Janeiro: Achiamé).
Edwards, Justin D. (2015), 'Zombie Terrorism in an Age of Global Gothic', *Gothic Studies* 17.2, Nov., 1–14.
Gomes, Paulo Emílio Salles (1995), 'Cinema: A Trajectory within Underdevelopment', in Johnson Randal and Robert Stam (eds), *Brazilian Cinema* (New York: Columbia University Press), 224–55.
Hughes, William and Andrew Smith (2013), Introduction. *Ecogothic*. Manchester: Manchester University Press. 1–14.
Mangue Negro (Mud Zombies, Rodrigo Aragão 2009).
Morton, Timothy (2007), *Ecology without Nature: Rethinking Environmental Aesthetics* (Cambridge, MA: Harvard University Press).
Morton, Timothy (2010), *The Ecological Thought* (Cambridge, MA: Harvard University Press).
Morton, Timothy (2013), *Hyperobjects: Philosophy and Ecology after the End of the World* (Minneapolis, MN: University of Minnesota Press).
Morton, Timothy (2016), *Dark Ecology: for a Logic of Future Coexistence* (New York: Columbia University Press).
Scott, Robert A. (2003), *The Gothic Enterprise: A Guide to Understanding the Medieval Cathedral* (Berkeley and Los Angeles: University of California Press).
Xavier, Ismail (1997), *Allegories of Underdevelopment: Aesthetics and Politics in Modern Brazilian Cinema* (Minneapolis: Minnesota University Press).
Zombio (Petter Baiestorf, 1999).

PART II

EUROPE

5. MUMMIES, VAMPIRES AND DOPPELGÄNGERS: HAMMER'S B-MOVIES AND CLASSIC GOTHIC FICTION

John Edgar Browning

The Gothic literary movement came to haunting, bloody life in the British Isles in the 1790s. Like some dead, repressed thing it clawed its way out of the English, Irish and Scottish subconscious and took hold of the popular imagination of the nineteenth century. In 1930s and 1940s Britain, however, the cinema was to have none of it. Horror was at this time all but completely censored into oblivion, or it was refused a certificate entirely. And even if a picture did receive an 'H' certificate (for 'Horror'), children were forbidden to see it, which meant that English studios would often avoid releasing horror pictures altogether, whether because of the censors or the special effects (both affecting cost and revenue). The outcome was to result in Hollywood's iron grip on the monster market. Even still, it was to be a market in touch with its roots across the Atlantic. The Gothic horror that kept American film studios afloat during the Great Depression of the 1930s was, after all, at its heart *British* Gothic horror, through such classics as *Dracula* (alongside the Spanish-language version filmed and released concurrently), *Frankenstein* (1931), *Dr Jekyll and Mr Hyde* (1931), *The Mummy* (1932), *Bride of Frankenstein* (1935), *Werewolf of London* (1935), *Dracula's Daughter* (1936) and *Son of Frankenstein* (1939). Gothic horror never lost its British accent either, even in America. For, indeed, many of the films that helped to found the horror genre in Hollywood not only had their roots in English Gothic literature, but were performed by British expatriates who, unlike many American silent film stars, already had ready-made stage acting and, in particular, *speaking* experience, actors like Boris Karloff (*Frankenstein*), Charles Laughton (*Island of Lost Souls*), Elsa Lanchester (*Bride of Frankenstein*), Herbert Bunston (*Dracula*), Ernest Thesiger (*Bride of Frankenstein*), Claude Rains (*The Invisible Man*), Bramwell Fletcher (*The Mummy*), Lionel Atwill (*Mark of the Vampire, Son of Frankenstein*), Elizabeth Allan (*Mark of the Vampire*), Lester Matthews (*Werewolf of London*) and others. The result was to give early Gothic horror films a certain authenticity and quality that, arguably, elevated them from 'B products', in the process enabling them to resonate, in profound ways, with American audiences. Unfortunately, even this could do little to keep American horror pictures fresh and new. Times were changing, and technology booming. By the 1950s, the genre, now tired and musty, had all but given way in America to gimmicky, formulaic science fiction thrillers. What Gothic horror needed, it's obvious to us now, was a facelift, and who better to give it than the British, the Gothic's original masters?

By the decade's end, Gothic horror would re-emerge across the Atlantic, finding in England's Hammer Film Productions a grand new home with the release of *The Curse of Frankenstein* (1957) and *Horror of Dracula* (1958). Shocking violence, unabashed sensuality and lavish set designs in all-new, magnificent Technicolor would come to be hallmarks of Hammer's new virile strain of Gothic cinema, one that was distinctly British and Grand Guignol in flavour, with red – the studio's trademark shade – coming to symbolise both a break from black-and-white celluloid and censorship's loosening grip on motion pictures in general, and horror in particular. The result was to breathe new life into the Gothic, but the tricky part was doing it without getting sued for copyright infringement by American powerhouse Universal Studios. This chapter will show, through a predominantly socio-economic lens, how extraordinary leaps were made at the hands of Hammer in not simply retelling familiar Gothic classics but re-envisaging them for audiences thirsting for gore. In the process, the studio would '[r]evitalize, redefine, and revolutionize horror movies around the world', to borrow Jonathan Rigby's careful phrasing (Rigby 2004, 57). Hammer – at what would be the confluence of de-censorship and technological advancement in film processing – effectively birthed Gothic horror cinema's second golden age through reinventing the genre as a whole.

Gothic Horror Comes Home

During its heyday, Hammer came to dominate the Gothic horror market, in part through worldwide distribution partnerships with major American studios, and it enjoyed in the process considerable financial success and freedom. But at the start of the 1950s, this could not have been further from the truth. The studio needed an edge, and it would come in the most unlikely of ways – a near-derelict studio space and a film workers union strike.

In 1951, Hammer leased a mid-eighteenth-century country estate house on the banks of the River Thames called Down Place and made, exclusively at that time, low-budget, high-yield B-movies. The interior of Down Place was in substantial need of repairs. Even so, the site's lenient restrictions on construction work encouraged Hammer to remodel and refit Down Place into a custom studio, often room by room (and picture by picture, as needed), maintaining in the process the structure's Gothic, antiquated charm. This, combined with the beautifully diverse countryside that made up the estate's grounds, would later add to Hammer's unique look and flavour. By year's end, Hammer's one-year lease at Down Place was nearly up, and the studio's marked success led it to begin looking to more conventional production spaces. Perhaps fortuitously, a union strike prevented Hammer's relocation, so the studio elected to purchase Down Place, which it renamed Bray Studios after the nearby village of Bray. Within a few years, the studio would turn its sights on low-budget science fiction infused with the Gothic, a decision that would have a lasting effect on horror history. Afterwards, the studio would never be the same again.

Hammer's first essay into Gothic horror was a comparatively gentle one. In 1955, the studio adapted Nigel Kneale's popular BBC Television science fiction serial, retitling it *The Quatermass Xperiment* (from the original 'Experiment') in order to play up the new 'X' certificate (which replaced the 'H' certificate in 1951).

This time, after years of gradual decline in censorship, the film studio aimed to cash in on the adult market, and the gamble paid off, very, very well. The distinct look and feel Bray Studios brought to life in the centuries-old rooms and halls of Down Place, coupled with Hammer's systematic, cost-conscious approach to production, imbued even a low-budget picture like *The Quatermass Xperiment* with a sense of style and quality. This new-found success immediately led the studio to produce *X the Unknown* (1956) and *Quatermass 2* (1957) using the same formula as the first picture. The fusion of science fiction and Gothic horror in these quality, albeit low-budget, black-and-white films – Gothic science fiction, or 'Martian Gothic', we might call them today (Figure 5.1) – proved to be an economic boom for the studio (Gatiss 2010, episode 2). More importantly, it left behind in the mouths of English audiences a distinct taste for Gothic horror. Hammer was quick to recognise that the time might finally have arrived for a full-on horror show, but one wonders if the studio actually realised just how perfect the timing was. And thus was born Gothic horror's second golden age, once more behind the macabre visage of the same two monsters who had earlier inaugurated America's golden age in the 1930s.

Figure 5.1 A rocket crashes into England's countryside in *The Quatermass Xperiment* (1955)

Hammer's Gothic Revival

Out of Bray Studios came two consecutive masterful productions: *The Curse of Frankenstein* (1957) and *Horror of Dracula* ([US title] 1958; *Dracula* [UK]). Both starred Peter Cushing and Christopher Lee, and both were to set the standard for a new approach to Gothic horror that at the time was nothing short of revolutionary. *The Curse of Frankenstein*, 'reportedly earning 70 times its production cost', Mark Gatiss aptly points out, and continuing with the theme of the X certificate, embraced Gothic horror more fully than did its predecessors at Hammer (2010, episode 2). However, as would be the case with *Dracula* (1958), *The Curse of Frankenstein* was not merely a remake of the Universal picture; in fact, legally it could not be, not even the make-up (Figure 5.2). Instead, both films were to be re-imaginings of the original novels. (Indeed, if either one of the new Hammer versions contained material original to any of the Universal adaptations or sequels – that is to say, anything in the film that did not come from Mary Shelley's or Bram Stoker's novel – litigation could be threatened.) This meant that Hammer was forced to produce two very different stories from Universal's copyrighted pictures, yet the studio did

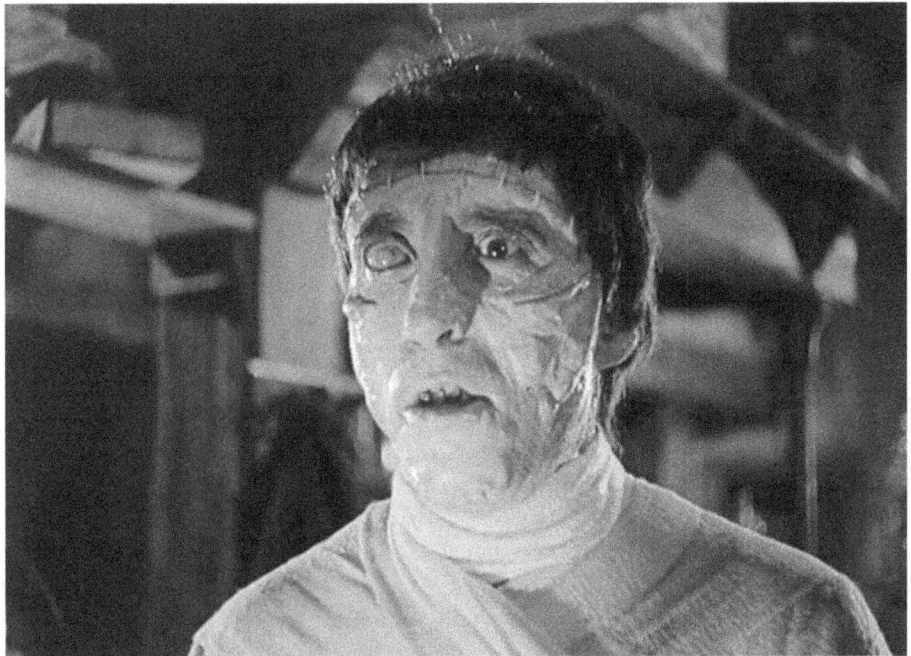

Figure 5.2 Christopher Lee dons his macabre make-up as the Monster in *Curse of Frankenstein* (1957)

not stop there. Hammer imbued its films with qualities that, for the British Board of Film Censors (BBFC), went above and beyond even an X certificate, a dangerous gamble that proved crucial both to Hammer's financial success and the revival of the entire horror genre.

Hammer shot both *The Curse of Frankenstein* and *Horror of Dracula* in Eastmancolor, an innovation that was less than a decade old. Even before production began, however, color's projected use gave worry to the BBFC, whose own Audrey Field warned, 'We are concerned about the flavour of this script, which, in its preoccupation with horror and gruesome detail, goes far beyond what we are accustomed to allow even for the "X" certificate' (Norman 2010). But Hammer did not budge, going so far as to include shots of blood (in vivid colour) and even allowing the camera to linger on the red gore. Cushing's performance as Baron Frankenstein and Lee's portrayal as the Monster, together with Bray Studio's atmospherically Gothic *mise-en-scène* at Down Place, helped to turn a modestly budgeted film into an instantly lucrative sensation throughout England and America. Audiences on both sides of the Atlantic, including (with improved dubbing techniques and facilities) a host of non-English markets, were already anticipating a sequel when Hammer commenced preparations for *The Revenge of Frankenstein* (1958), scheduled for release the following year. Yet, there was something in *The Curse of Frankenstein* audiences had not anticipated. The film's more sexually suggestive undertones, as compared to the Universal version, were more fully developed, a feat that would have proven nearly impossible under the more rigid censorship of the 1930s, especially in horror pictures (Browning 2014, 225–36). Even still, this was to be merely a trial run at macabre cinema for the studio. Arguably Hammer's real, proverbial 'first taste' of sex and blood was to come next.

Cushing and Lee returned to the screen as Dr Van Helsing and Count Dracula in *Horror of Dracula*, the second of Hammer's *pièces de résistance*, although, unlike *Frankenstein*, *Dracula*'s screen copyright belonged to Universal for another four years until the novel became public domain in 1962. But Hammer did not want to wait that long, so after a deal was struck with Universal, Hammer released in 1958 its filmic version of *Dracula*, and like *The Curse of Frankenstein* Hammer's vampire picture was fundamentally a reimagining of the original novel. Yet, in other ways, *Horror of Dracula* (Figure 5.3) merely brought to the surface much of what was already present in Stoker's novel, albeit at times merely sub-textually.

The BBFC's Audrey Field once again took notice, remarking on an early draft of the script:

Figure 5.3   Count Dracula (Christopher Lee) embraces Mina (Melissa Stribling), his not-unwilling victim, in *Horror of Dracula* (1958)

> The uncouth, uneducated, disgusting and vulgar style of Mr Jimmy Sangster cannot quite obscure the remnants of a good horror story, though they do give one the gravest misgivings about treatment ... The curse of this thing is the Technicolor blood: why need vampires be messier eaters than anyone else? (quoted in Kinsey 2011, 80)

Simply put, the 'eating' was messy because 'sex' is messy. In this, Hammer was leagues ahead of other studios at creating subtext, for indeed not only did the studio shoot its vampire picture in glorious Eastmancolor, but it showed the audience actual vampire fangs (American cinema did not per the censors, forced instead to keep the phallic iconography tucked neatly away), on-screen penetration (American cinema either obscured this action behind a vampire cape or performed it off-screen, again per the censors) and copious amounts of blood. The result was a rather suggestive combination the likes of which had never before been seen in mainstream vampire cinema. This, together with *Horror of Dracula*'s Gothic atmospherics, music and dark mood, and the film's reliance upon gore and shock, absolutely riveted British and American audiences. The film proved immensely successful, breaking box-office records on both sides of the Atlantic. Lee's portrayal eclipsed, practically overnight, the symbolically castrated and penectomised Dracula of 1930s and '40s American cinema, a feat by anyone's standard.

The Face(s) of Horror

David Pirie notes that with the success of *Horror of Dracula*, Hammer's American distributor, Universal International, gave the English studio the full run of its horror film library without any further copyright problems (2008, 34). So it was that Lee returned in what was to be the first of such pictures, Hammer's *The Mummy* (1959), which broke even *Dracula*'s box-office receipts, both in the USA and the UK (Kinsey 2002, 166). Lee would also return a year later in Hammer's *The Two Faces of Dr. Jekyll* (1960), though he would not play the role of the maniacal doctor. Even still, the latter film was just the start of what was to come in the 1960s. Hammer's three-film cycle with *The Curse of Frankenstein*, *Horror of Dracula* and *The Mummy* ignited a horror boom in the 1960s, one that would mirror Hammer's example through the use of gore and violence, stretching as far away from the Home Counties as Italy with *Black Sunday* (1960). Of Hammer's initial Gothic horror run, Peter Hutchings observes:

> Hammer film-makers were in the business of producing not just marketable films but also 'good' films, with this 'goodness' or quality ultimately forming part of the films' distinctiveness in the market. The Hammer

approach promoted an attention to detail in production and costume design, camerawork and lighting, performance, editing and music, among other things, and an accompanying concern to push low budget to its limits, to make a film appear more expensive than it actually was. (Hutchings 2003, 35)

Hammer's success would even encourage American studios to revisit Gothic horror. Mostly notably, Roger Corman began producing a slew of (out of copyright) Edgar Allan Poe pictures that proved to be highly successful.

Times were changing still in other ways. Observe Britain's teenage youth, for example, who themselves comprised an ever-growing (albeit largely untapped) market that found itself increasingly at odds with the establishment. Sensing this, Hammer reciprocated by playing to those feelings with great effect through its prolific horror output from 1960 through to the mid-1970s. In the 1960s, Hammer horrors were fast becoming the fashion of the day, though inevitably a couple of monsters were more indelible than the others. Indeed, 'none of the Universal house themes', writes Pirie, would prove to be 'as remunerative a source of material for Hammer as Bram Stoker or Mary Shelley' (2008, 34). Fans of Frankenstein and Dracula did not have to wait long either.

Hammer's *Frankenstein* sequels commenced in 1958 with *The Revenge of Frankenstein*, followed by *The Evil of Frankenstein* (1964), *Frankenstein Created Woman* (1967), *Frankenstein Must Be Destroyed* (1969), *The Horror of Frankenstein* (1970) and *Frankenstein and the Monster from Hell* (1974), in each case (with the exception of *The Horror of Frankenstein*) returning Peter Cushing to the lead role of Baron Frankenstein. The studio's *Dracula* sequels commenced in 1960, if only in name, with *The Brides of Dracula*, which introduced audiences to 'Baron Meinster' (David Peel), a vampire disciple of Dracula's playing opposite Peter Cushing, who reprised his role as Van Helsing. To satisfy adoring audiences (and, most especially, Hammer's American distributor), the British studio eventually convinced Christopher Lee to don the cape again in *Dracula: Prince of Darkness* (1966). The film was met with great success. What's more, with *Dracula*'s entrance into the public domain in 1962, there was nothing to stop Hammer – with or without Universal's permission – from returning Lee to the role a further five times with *Dracula Has Risen from the Grave* (1968), *Taste the Blood of Dracula* (1970), *Scars of Dracula* (1970), *Dracula A.D. 1972* (1972) and *The Satanic Rites of Dracula* (1973). Cushing returned as Dracula's adversary in the latter two films, as well as in Hammer's final *Dracula* picture the next year with *The Legend of the 7 Golden Vampires* (1974), a horror/kung fu hybrid starring John Forbes-Robertson as Dracula.

The studio's 'rags' to riches story does not end with the Dracula and Frankenstein archetypes alone. Hammer owes a small debt to the studio's ragged Egyptian monster as well. The 1960s and early 1970s also saw three mummy pictures (albeit narratologically unrelated to Lee's 1959 picture), beginning with *The Curse of the Mummy's Tomb* (1964) and followed by *The Mummy's Shroud* (1967) and *Blood from the Mummy's Tomb* (1971). All three films were cost-conscious productions. Indeed, despite Hammer's success, the studio never forsook its economical approach to production, shooting back to back a number of horror films during the 1960s that used the same costumes and sets, which the studio disguised by featuring them on separate double bills. Hammer's efforts were rewarded in 1968 with the Queen's Award to Industry, an honour conferred, appropriately enough, on the steps of Castle Dracula during the filming of *Dracula Has Risen from the Grave* (Rigby 2004, 179).

Industry accolades and fan adoration aside, invariably Hammer was inundated by criticism for its unabated use of gore, violence and sexual innuendo, as Ian Cooper aptly discusses at length in *Frightmares: A History of British Horror Cinema* (2016, 51–2). But the more the studio did so, the more audiences loved them for it, a symbiosis that proved key to evolving the genre into what it would become in the 1970s. This relationship, however, was to be a temporary one, as would be Hammer's jubilation. The market was poised to shift once again, signalling an end to Hammer's horror dynasty in but half a decade.

America, 'New' Horror and Hammer's Decline

Due to ever-declining box-office revenues, Motion Picture Association of America (MPAA) president Jack Valenti issued, on 7 October 1968, a press release outlining 'a radically new motion picture production code', notes Jon Lewis in *Hollywood v. Hard Core: How the Struggle Over Censorship Created the Modern Film Industry* (NYU Press, 2002, 135). This new movie rating system, Lewis rightly adds, 'was adopted at a crucial moment in Hollywood history' (135). Cultural and political turmoil in America had crescendoed by the late 1960s, forcing the cinema to evolve alongside a disquieted public. As for Valenti, he 'understood . . . that content regulation had less to do with specific scenes in specific movies than with a complex set of industrial and political relationships' (136). Lewis continues:

> 'When I became president of the [MPAA] in May 1966,' [Valenti] wrote, 'the slippage of Hollywood studio authority over the content of films collided with an avalanching revision of American mores and customs.' Late sixties culture, Valenti reminds us, was characterized by 'insurrection on the campus, riots in the streets, rise in women's liberation, protest of the young, doubts about the institution of marriage, abandonment of old guiding slogans, and the crumbling of social traditions.' (136–7)

The new production code's effect was an immediate one, notes Lewis, encouraging 'the production of a more diverse range' of motion pictures (141).

With the release of films like Roman Polanski's *Rosemary's Baby* (1968), Hammer found itself in the precarious position of trying to keep pace with the new horror market booming around it, the very market it had helped to develop. People had been going to Hammer films for their sex and violence since the late 1950s, but Hammer's competitors, especially those in America, began saturating the horror film market by the late 1960s and early 1970s with even bloodier exploitation movies, as with dark independent horror such as *Night of the Living Dead* (1968), films that were gorier and often more explicitly sexualised. This, coupled with the loss of Hammer's American funding from Universal International around the same time, prompted the studio to adapt. Some of Hammer's first attempts at appealing to the new horror market and its younger audiences came in accentuating the violence in *Scars of Dracula*, a film in which, writes Kim Newman, 'vampirism [is] grafted on to an ultra–violent "meat" movie' (2011, 33). The attempt would ultimately fail, and in doing so it prompted Hammer to abandon period films nearly altogether in favour of more contemporary-set productions. *Dracula A.D. 1972* and *The Satanic Rights of Dracula*, both set in swinging 1970s London, as well as *Blood from the Mummy's Tomb*, a contemporised version of Bram Stoker's *The Jewel of Seven Stars* (1903), were three of Hammer's such attempts. Both Lee and Cushing reprised their roles (Cushing as a descendant of Van Helsing), but this did little to help the success of the films. Hammer was in trouble, but it still had one trick left.

Audiences had all but outgrown Hammer's (now dated) level of gore, so they began turning in increasing numbers to American horror cinema, whose more lax censors allowed for more gore and more violence. Realising this, Hammer opted to elevate its films' sexual content, an area it *could* compete in as per the British censors at the time. This new initiative was not lost on Michael Style (Figure 5.4), producer of Hammer's *Lust for a Vampire* (1971) (the second instalment in Hammer's lesbian-themed *Karnstein Trilogy*, which was based loosely on Sheridan Le Fanu's 1872 vampire novella *Carmilla*), who said of Hammer horror films at that time: 'You need a lot of murders, a lot of blood – I ordered five gallons of blood for [*Lust for a Vampire*] – you need a good, strong villain – a really villainous-looking villain, a good hero, a certain amount of sex, lots of action, and lots of pretty girls' (Gatiss 2010, episode 2). However, Jimmy Sangster, long-time Hammer screenwriter and sometime director, believed that the studio's increased reliance upon nudity and sex was, in part, what led to its downfall, in particular because it 'became more important than the horror' itself (ibid.). And fall Hammer did. After the mid-1970s, Hammer produced a few more horror pictures before abandoning them altogether in favour of television productions.

HAMMER'S B-MOVIES AND CLASSIC GOTHIC FICTION

Figure 5.4 Mircalla/Carmilla Karnstein (Yutte Stensgaard) takes Amanda (Judy Matheson) in a lesbian embrace in *Lust for a Vampire* (1971)

The death knell of Hammer came ostensibly with the release of such American pictures as *The Exorcist* (1973) and *The Texas Chain Saw Massacre* (1974), followed by *The Omen* (1976), *Jaws* (1977) and *Halloween* (1978). Recalling eerily Dracula's plight from Transylvania to England (then back to Transylvania) in Bram Stoker's novel, Gothic horror – after briefly immigrating to America – returned to England, where it died on its native soil. The historic value of this horror's transmigration is measureless, but its singularly greatest utility lies in reviving British horror and helping to birth modern horror, a mode which has far outlasted the 1970s.

BIBLIOGRAPHY

Browning, John Edgar (2014), 'Classical Hollywood Horror', in Harry M. Benshoff (ed.), *A Companion to the Horror Film* (Malden, MA: Wiley Blackwell), 225–36.

Cooper, Ian (2016), *Frightmares: A History of British Horror Cinema* (Leighton Buzzard: Auteur).

Gatiss, Mark (2010), *A History of Horror with Mark Gatiss*, Episode 2, 'Home Counties Horror' (BBC Productions).

Hutchings, Peter (2003), *Dracula: The British Film Guide 7* (London: I. B. Tauris).

Kinsey, Wayne (2002), *Hammer Films: The Bray Studio Years* (Richmond: Reynolds & Hearn).

Kinsey, Wayne (2011), '"Don't Dare See It Alone!": The Fifties Hammer Invasion', in Darryl Jones, Elizabeth McCarthy and Bernice M. Murphy (eds), *It Came From the 1950s!: Popular Culture, Popular Anxieties* (Basingstoke: Palgrave Macmillan).

Lewis, Jon (2002), *Hollywood v. Hard Core: How the Struggle Over Censorship Created the Modern Film Industry* (New York: New York University Press).

Newman, Kim (2011), *Nightmare Movies: Horror on Screen since the 1960s* (London: Bloomsbury).
Norman, Barry (2010), 'Vampires, Vamps and How I Cut My Teeth on Hammer Horror', *Dailymail.com*, 29 November, <http://www.dailymail.co.uk/tvshowbiz/article-1333970/BARRY-NORMAN-Vampires-vamps-I-cut-teeth-Hammer-horror.html> (last accessed 3 November 2017).
Pirie, David (2008), *A New Heritage of Horror: The English Gothic Cinema* (London: I. B. Tauris).
Rigby, Jonathan (2004), *English Gothic: A Century of Horror Cinema*, 3rd edn (London: Reynolds & Hearn).

6. FANTATERROR: GOTHIC MONSTERS IN THE GOLDEN AGE OF SPANISH B-MOVIE HORROR, 1968–80

Xavier Aldana Reyes

The portmanteau 'fantaterror' amalgamates the terms 'fantástico' (literally 'fantastic', although in Spanish the word conveys a meaning closer to that of 'supernatural' in Anglophone cultures) and 'terror' (indistinguishable from 'horror', but more ubiquitous). Popularised by director, scriptwriter and actor Jacinto Molina, famous under his artistic name Paul Naschy, fantaterror was coined to refer to the Spanish answer to the type of violent and titillating films that have come to be known as 'exploitation cinema' within the European and American contexts (Mathijs and Mendik 2004; Shipka 2011). Since 'exploitation cinema' may also cover genres such as the Western or softcore films, other terms have cropped up to refer to the horrific side of the transgressive and provocative B-movie cinema that flooded Spanish screens in the 1960s and 1970s. 'Euro-horror' is a popular label in the Anglo-American world, but Spanish cinema critics and writers, in an attempt to emphasise the uniqueness of the various occult, dark, sensual and weird elements of films such as *La residencia / The House That Screamed* (Narciso Ibáñez Serrador, 1968) or *Mil gritos tiene la noche / Pieces* (Juan Piquer Simón, 1982), have come up with other less catchy ones like 'cine bizarro' (bizarre cinema) (Diego 2014) or else simply called them 'cine negro' (film noir) (Luque Carreras 2015). Seldom does one find 'cine de terror' (horror cinema) explored as such in Spanish scholarship; it is normally discussed in broader surveys of supernatural cinema (cine fantástico), which sometimes mingle horror, science fiction and fantasy. The word 'Gothic' has been used even more rarely by those who have most rigorously studied the country's horrific output. The term has only gained currency, unsurprisingly, in Anglo-American academia, where scholarly interest in the Gothic has been systematically developing since the 1980s and, especially, since the 1990s.

Given Spain's reluctance to acknowledge the Gothic as a national mode, a stance born out of many decades of the sustained critical championing of social realism as the quintessential artistic form of expression for the country's writers, fantaterror now stands as the most productive term with which to refer to genre filmmaking between 1968 and 1980, the golden age of Spanish horror. Since Spain's historical situation, under Franco's dictatorship from 1939 to 1975, had a significant effect on cinematic censorship (although it relaxed gradually from 1962, and was finally lifted in 1977), the focus has inevitably remained industrial: how did horror manage to flourish in an era of repression? Is the work of filmmakers like Jesús Franco and Jorge Grau political in its emphasis on power-hungry tyrants, creatures from the id and evil religious figures? In this chapter, I want to approach fantaterror's vast textual body thematically; I want to offer a brief analysis of the type of Gothic figures that populated the mode in Spanish cinema of the period. While I do not remain oblivious to the financial underpinnings of the films covered, I am more interested in the type of figures that blossomed in Spanish B-movie Gothic – why were they popular? How well did they travel to and from Spain? – than in their possible economic origins. At stake is the nature of the Gothic as a transnational and transmedia mode, the result of various levels of adaptation (from literature to film, but also from one culture to another). Although the global aspects of the Gothic have only begun to be probed in the twenty-first century (Jacobs 2000; Byron 2013; Elbert and Marshall 2013), it is important to highlight the mode's glocal qualities, its capacity to remain inherently local yet eminently exportable.

Although a number of isolated precedents may be located in the early twentieth century, Gothic horror cinema in Spain largely coalesced into a cultural force to be reckoned with as a result of two B-movie successes: Enrique López Eguiluz's *La marca del hombre lobo / Frankenstein's Bloody Terror* (1968), a colourful and well-executed update of recognisable Gothic formulas by then used and abused by Universal Studios and Hammer Horror, and Narciso Ibáñez Serrador's aforementioned *The House That Screamed*, a sadistic Gothic boarding school psychosexual nightmare that attempted to look like an international production. Together they constituted the foundation for the horror that was to follow suit: an eminently transnational, low-budget, exploitational form of national cinema which riffed off widely recognised Gothic myths and settings, but which could not help but adapt to a specific national context. Sold largely to the American market and made with a mixture of local and international talents and funding, the resulting B-movies saw the birth and rise

THE GOLDEN AGE OF SPANISH B-MOVIE HORROR

Figure 6.1 Christopher Lee reprised his emblematic Hammer role for Jess Franco's faithful yet financially compromised adaptation of Bram Stoker's novel, *El conde Drácula* / *Count Dracula* (1970)

of such emblematic figures as the Polish werewolf Waldemar Daninsky, the face-grafting crazed surgeon Dr Orloff or the spectral knight Alaric de Marnac. While it is useful to group these icons together as national Gothic gems, I find it more productive to explore different monsters according to the type of cultural adaptation that was required in marketing them to Spanish and international audiences. In order to do this, I propose a separation into 'expanded glocal myths' and 'intrinsic national developments'. Although the borders between the two categories are not always straightforward – Waldemar Daninsky has been considered a national myth (Prada 2003, 141), but Paul Naschy drew heavily on the Larry Talbot character of the Universal werewolf films – this initial separation will help me identify the innovative aspects of Spanish B-movie Gothic. These range from subtle changes to well-known characters like Count Dracula to the fleshing out of the blind zombie-like Knights Templar in *La noche del terror ciego* / *Tombs of the Blind Dead* (Amando de Ossorio, 1972).

The term 'glocal', as I use it in this chapter, indicates texts 'that ha[ve] international status in [their] global spread but at the same time express . . . local identities' (Pakir 2014, 55). This can 'represent a turn towards an intense engagement with the particular as retaining some autonomy from global currents', yet simultaneously 'mark[s] a renewed awareness of how local and global are ... intermeshed in ways we are still struggling to understand' (Brydon 2010, 112). While the glocal, strictly speaking, is more obviously linked to the contemporary global period, especially as a result of the rise of neoliberalism from the 1980s onwards, Spanish (and European) horror cinema of the exploitation era was already partaking of the dynamic transcultural flows motivated by market drives. I therefore read the Spanish Gothic, and its monsters, as inherently Spanish – even if only by virtue of the nationality of the film crews and actors that were a part of B-movies made or scripted by Spanish directors – and as eminently inter- and transnational.

Expanded Glocal Myths

Horror in the late 1960s and 1970s in Spain was strongly coloured by financial constraints and industry growth. Some art-house directors such as Eloy de la Iglesia or Juan Antonio Bardem may well have turned to horror because it offered a powerful vehicle of expression for their anti-establishment views (Willis 2003), but for the most successful directors, such as León Klimovsky and Jacinto Molina, horror was as much a business as it was a personal passion. Horror, although never a true sensation, nor the dominant filmic genre in the 1970s (1972 being the key year, as this is when the most Spanish horror films were made), was nevertheless, for a time, a relatively safe affair, where the recouping of investments was very probable. The low budgets of most Spanish horror films and the nature of the co-production system, under which a large number of titles were financed, meant that profit, albeit modest, could be made. An obvious corollary of this landscape of economic caution was that films had to be sufficiently familiar and recognisable that they could be easily sold to foreign markets, one of the main buyers being North America. The use of de facto dubbing and international casts can thus be explained as more than a coincidence or intrinsic Spanish touch; the intention was for productions to be readily consumable by non-autochthonous audiences. What interests me here is the effect this had on the development of certain sure-fire monstrous figures: in the context of a shaky risk-averse industry, the most transnationally marketable creatures were those that already existed and could be given a 'twist' or have their narratives expanded.

Since copyright fees for the use of patented names and characters (the Frankenstein monster, Count Dracula) presented significant economic challenges, an alternative was to borrow aesthetic markers and simply alter names. The best example of a type of film that tried to have its cake and eat it too was *Los monstruos del terror / Assignment Terror* (Tulio Demicheli, Hugo Fregonese, Antonio Isasi-Isasmendi and Eberhard Meichsner, 1970), a Spanish co-production with West Germany and Italy. This monster mash clearly draws on films like *Dracula* (Tod Browning, 1931), *Frankenstein* (James Whale, 1931), *The Mummy* (Karl Freund, 1932) and *The Wolf Man* (George Waggner, 1941) in its character design, but refers to its creatures by different – sometimes ludicrous – soubriquets: Count Janos de Mialhoff, the monster of Farancksalan or the mummy of Tao-Tet. Another alternative was to accept the costs of copyright licensing and shoot a straightforward adaptation. Hence, Jesús Franco's *El conde Drácula / Count Dracula* (1970), which, despite its artistic ambition to be the most faithful treatment of Bram Stoker's novel, suffered from its small budget and a confusing plot. Interestingly, Franco asked Christopher Lee to reprise his Dracula role (which he had played up to three times by this point) for it, a decision that speaks both to the endemic connection between the actor and Stoker's vampire outside Britain and to Spanish Gothic's desire to exploit already popular cinematic series and figures. Similarly, Vicente Aranda adapted Sheridan Le Fanu's *Carmilla* (1872) in his surreal *La novia ensangrentada / The Blood Spattered Bride* (1972), a film that shares its lesbian love interests with other more exploitational vampire flicks of the period, such as *Vampyros Lesbos* (Jesús Franco, 1971) and *Las hijas de Drácula / Vampyres* (José Ramón Larraz, 1974). These more overtly sexual films were also influenced by Hammer's Karnstein trilogy, especially the colourful Ingrid Pitt-led *The Vampire Lovers* (Roy Ward Baker, 1970). Other films featuring female vampire figures as the main leads include *Malenka, la sobrina del vampiro / Fangs of the Living Dead* (Amando de Ossorio, 1969), *La tumba de la isla maldita / Hannah, Queen of the Vampires* (Julio Salvador and Ray Danton, 1973) and *La noche de los brujos / Night of the Sorcerers* (Amando de Ossorio, 1974).

Parodies were yet another way to engage with foreign cinematic traditions, although these date back to the early twentieth century. Eduardo García Maroto's *Una de miedo / A Horror Film* (1935), for example, was an early short that mocked the conventions established by Universal Horror and referenced the German expressionist *Nosferatu, eine Symphonie des Grauens / Nosferatu* (F. W. Murnau, 1922), and his *Una de monstruos / A Monster Film* segment in the anthology film *Tres eran tres / Three Were Three* (1958) poked fun at Whale's *Frankenstein*. Particularly popular in the fantaterror cycle were vampire parodies. *Un vampiro para dos / A Vampire for Two* (Pedro Lazaga, 1965), Spain's first vampire film, borrowed superstitious myths developed from the Anglo-American Gothic tradition – more specifically, from films like Browning's *Dracula* or Terence Fisher's 1958 adaptation – and mixed them, to great effect, with Spanish folklore and humour. Others soon followed, especially after the international successes of Gothic parodies from America and Europe such as *The Fearless Vampire Killers* (Roman Polanski, 1967), the blaxploitation masterpiece *Blacula* (William Crain, 1972) and *Young*

Frankenstein (Mel Brooks, 1974). The most notable is *Las alegres vampiras de Vögel / Vampires of Vögel* (Julio Pérez Tabernero, 1975), where Transylvanian vampires are combined with Spanish rumba dancers, but *Tiempos duros para Drácula / Hard Times for Dracula* (Jorge Darnell, 1976) and *El pobrecito Draculín / Poor Dracula Junior* (Juan Fortuny, 1977), which track the hardships of the Count's descendants in modern times, also deserve a mention. However, these Gothic B-movie parodies were, in most cases, intended for the national market and were, at most, sold to Spanish-speaking countries like Mexico. This means that, while the films may still be productively thought of as part of fantaterror, their impact outside Spain was limited. They are, however, valuable and original in that they show how foreign myths were culturally adapted so they could resonate with Spanish audiences. Much is made, for example, of the contrast between the Spanish love of garlic and the vampire's endemic fear of it in *Un vampiro para dos*.

More generic fare, such as Klimovsky's *La orgía nocturna de los vampiros / The Vampires' Night Orgy* (1974) and *El extraño amor de los vampiros / Night of the Walking Dead* (1975), was more exportable, if certainly more derivative. There are two particular fantaterror films that stand out in their inspired expansion of well-known myths: *La saga de los Drácula / The Dracula Saga* (León Klimovsky, 1972) and *El gran amor del conde Drácula / Count Dracula's Great Love* (1973). The former, in which a pregnant couple mistakenly end up in Dracula's castle and are forced to give birth to a demonic child who may perpetuate the dying Dracula lineage, was very radical in its anti-natality message. It must be remembered that abortion was a very controversial topic during Francoism and that it remained illegal until 1985, ten years after the end of the dictatorship. *Count Dracula's Great Love*, in its narrative investment in a Count Dracula who prefers staking himself to vampirising his beloved, is a clear predecessor of other more sensitive and romance-driven European Draculas like *Blood for Dracula* (Paul Morrissey, 1974) and John Badham's *Dracula* (1979), and ends in a rare example of vampiric suicide. All in all, vampires were by far the most ubiquitous Gothic figures in fantaterror, a result of their versatility and the relative simplicity of their recreation (the main requirement are fangs), as well as the fact that the myth itself had circulated widely thanks to its long celluloid history. Vampires were transnational monsters in Spain because they do not have deep roots in peninsular literature and therefore had to be adapted from Anglo-American texts.

A lot less common were mummies and zombies, two different varieties of the lumbering undead. The main problem with mummies was the difficulty involved in staging a convincing Egyptian *mise-en-scène*, something neatly resolved in the main Spanish title to centre on this figure, *La venganza de la momia / The Vengeance of the Mummy* (Carlos Aured, 1975). *Vengeance* emulates Hammer's *The Mummy* franchise, especially the Terence Fisher-directed 1959 film, to the point of setting the action in Victorian England. Although *Vengeance* is not particularly original in plot, its colour is one of the most striking in the history of fantaterror, and the film was a perfect fit for Gothic enthusiast Jacinto Molina, the scriptwriter, with its dual focus on horror and romantic engagement. After George A. Romero's surprise hit *Night of the Living Dead* (1968) zombies began to come out of their graves assiduously. To middle-of-the-road and z-budget titles such as *La orgía de los muertos / Terror of the Living Dead* (José Luis Merino, 1973), *El pantano de los cuervos / The Swamp of the Ravens* (Manuel Caño, 1974) and the late *La tumba de los muertos vivientes / Oasis of the Zombies* (Jesús Franco, 1982), one must add the exceptional Spanish-Italian co-production *No profanar el sueño de los muertos / The Living Dead at Manchester Morgue* (Jorge Grau, 1974), a professed attempt to re-imagine Romero's film in colour. Apart from its ecological message about the danger of pesticides, *Living Dead* is an effective take on the modern zombie myth set largely in the Peak District (standing in for the Lake District), and features a really tense scene in a derelict monastery that very specifically harks back to the Gothic tradition. Critics have often praised the film and even seen it as the type of high-quality product that could have flourished in Spain, had the financial circumstances been different (Pedrero Santos 2008: 313).

Although surprising examples of alternatives exist, such as the she-wolf film *Las garras de Lorelei / The Loreley's Grasp* (Amando de Ossorio, 1974), the werewolf sub-genre was almost completely dominated during the fantaterror years by the Paul Naschy phenomenon. Despite my discussion of his most famous character, the Polish Waldemar Daninsky, as an expansion of the myth – of Larry Talbot in particular, as mentioned above – the complexity of the character is such, and the narrative was continued for so long, that he may also be understood as a national and original myth in his own right. Daninsky made his first appearance in *Frankenstein's Bloody Terror*, incidentally Spain's first 3D horror film and one of the key texts associated with the rise of fantaterror, and his story spanned eight sequels from 1968 to 1980 (with another three following between 1983 and 2004). Customarily pitted against evil monsters, such as the Yeti, Countess Wandessa Dárvula de Nadasdy and Mr Hyde, the Pole Daninsky was original in his similarities to another Gothic figure, the wandering Jew, with whom he shares a sad life of unrest that must end in tragedy: the only thing that may kill the werewolf is a silver bullet fired by the woman he loves. In many respects, Daninsky is the prototype of the B-movie Spanish Gothic monster – appropriated, adapted and expanded, libidinous, violent and good value for money.

New National Monsters

Daninsky's borderline example aside, there were a number of native Gothic myths developed by Spanish directors and scriptwriters. As might be expected, national horror figures were not as popular because they were harder to sell to external markets which would not be familiar with them. Cinema has always catered to ready-made audiences – hence the popularity of sequels, prequels and remakes – so risk-averse Spanish filmmakers often sacrificed originality of concept in favour of more certain returns. This is famously the reason why Amando de Ossorio originally struggled to find financial backing for what turned out to be one of the most quintessential figures of the fantaterror cycle: the Knights Templar of *Tombs of the Blind Dead*. The interstitial nature of these Gothic monsters, with traits borrowed from the mummy, the zombie and the religious tyrant, did not seem recognisable enough a formula. An example of how intrinsically Spanish ideas were destined to remain of interest to Spain alone was *El bosque del lobo / The Ancines Woods* (Pedro Olea, 1970), a psychological horror film based on the 1945 novelisation of the nineteenth-century Manuel Blanco Romasanta case, where a serial killer pleaded innocence on account of being under a lycanthropic curse. The ambiguity of the film, as well as its reliance on 'costumbrismo' (a national form of social realism) in the many scenes depicting rural life, are both national markers and what potentially makes the film difficult to view and/or understand for foreign viewers. All this means is that, with the exception of the Blind Dead and Alaric de Marnac, both of which I consider in more detail below, new national Gothic myths were largely isolated cases and did not lend themselves to the serialisation typical of the more transnational myths.

One of the most celebrated of the fantaterror films is *Pánico en el transiberiano / Horror Express* (Eugenio Martín, 1972), a co-production with the UK which featured Christopher Lee and Peter Cushing as two of its three male leads. The film is a well-executed train mystery, its signature image being its monster's glowing eyes, which indicate the beginning of the process of possession. What initially appears to be the missing link between humans and their ancestors, an ape-like figure found frozen in Manchuria, is soon revealed to host an incorporeal alien capable of travelling between hosts. The creature can also drain humans of their feelings and memories, effectively turning them into zombies, and is eventually described as an intergalactic energy from antediluvian times. *Horror Express* thus manages to evoke motifs from zombie and body-snatching films, but, since it is set in 1906, also has a strongly Edwardian (if not Victorian) Gothic feel about its *mise-en-scène* and cinematography that distances it from the science fiction genre to which it more obviously belongs. Its monster, a Gothic remnant of the past and older than humanity, echoes H. P. Lovecraft without feeling derivative of his Elder Gods pantheon (cosmic entities who inhabited the Earth before humans did). The film, although financially successful and popular in Spain, did not lead to further sequels.

Perhaps the most interesting case of a single attempt at developing a 'born-and-bred' Spanish Gothic film was *Cross of the Devil* (1975), which, although it ended up being controversially directed by the Brit John Gilling, had been penned by Jacinto Molina. Adapting three legends from Spanish post-Romantic writer Gustavo Adolfo Bécquer, 'El monte de las ánimas' / 'The Forest of the Souls in Purgatory' (1861), 'El miserere' / 'The miserere' (1862) and 'La cruz del diablo' / 'The Devil's Cross' (1860), the film fails in many respects – in its pace, most notably – but it is worth singling out the potential the source material had, and still has, for the development of an autochthonous Gothic. The monster in *Cross of the Devil* is the spirit of a local baron who, killed by the peasants he long exploited, manages to come back to life through his armour. The latter is eventually captured, molten and cast into the shape of a Christian cross, so its evil may be exorcised via religious imagery. As it turns out, the cross still possesses traces of the baron's energy, and its haunting presence has affected the area where it was planted. Mixing European folklore (the tyrant nobleman) with Spanish superstition and locales (the cross of the devil tale is Catalan in origin, although the story is set in Soria in the film), Bécquer's legends are the foremost manifestation of a type of Spanish Gothic that harks back to the oral tradition and the 'cuento de vieja' (old wives' tale). Strongly Catholic yet stemming from a myriad of sources – to this day, the origins of Bécquer's legends are hotly debated – the transnational potential of Bécquer's oeuvre seems evident, seeing as it appealed to a British director who had worked assiduously for Hammer.

While *Horror Express* and *Cross of the Devil* are significant as national explorations of the Gothic, interested in reaching out to a well-known tradition with new figures that were not steeped in mimicry, the two most iconic original monsters were, without a doubt, the Blind Dead and Alaric de Marnac. The Blind Dead in particular have had a healthy life outside Spain, with releases of the tetralogy in various VHS prints and then in DVD box sets in 2005 and 2014. The novelty of the myth was such, as I have mentioned, that there was some initial scepticism on the producers' part regarding the viability of the project when first proposed by de Ossorio. The Blind Dead are Knights Templar, a medieval Christian military order that existed throughout Europe and was instrumental in the development and maintenance of a European/Christian hegemony during the Crusades. In the first film in the series, *Tombs of the Blind Dead*, their background story is narrated, and their blindness accounted for: they were hung for their Satanic practices in search of immortality, which included the drinking of the blood of innocents, and their eyes were pecked out by birds. This means that their reanimated corpses cannot see and thus mainly react to sound, an innovative aspect that brings the skeletal, hooded figures allegorically close to the grim

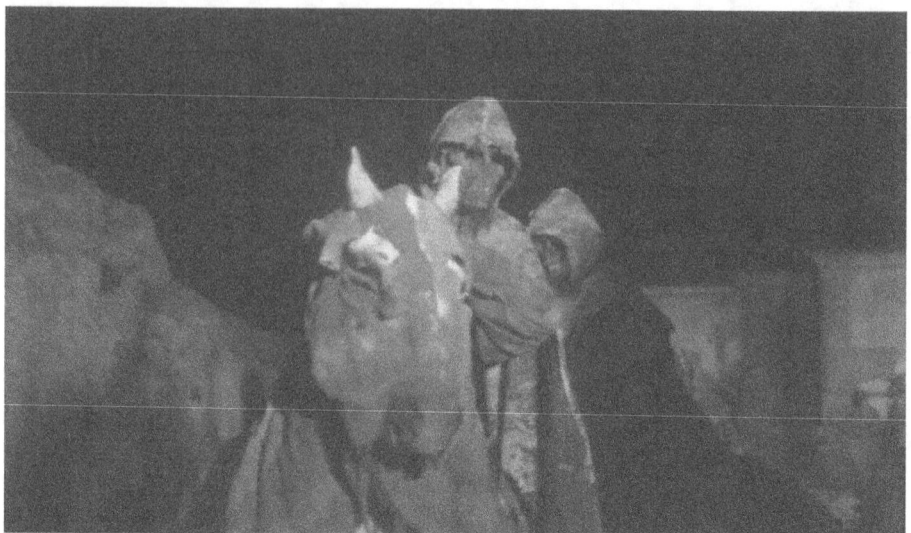

Figure 6.2 Amando de Ossorio's Blind Dead, from the co-production *La noche del terror ciego / Tombs of the Blind Dead* (1972), are a quintessential example of Spain's production of national Gothic myths

reaper. Although some elements are borrowed from zombie and vampire cinema (the scene where the Templars escape their tombs in a desolate cemetery), Spanish film critic Gómez Rivero (2009, 268) has suggested that de Ossorio took inspiration from Bécquer's 'The Miserere'. Although I have not found any factual evidence to confirm or disprove this suggestion, the Templars' chant, a recurring element in the chase scenes, does thematically link these creatures with those of the resurrected dead in Bécquer's tale. Their popularity saw the film spawn three sequels, but dwindling budgets and excessive repetition, including the reusing of footage, led to the series' decline.

The last Gothic monster I want to consider in this chapter is Jacinto Molina's second great character after Daninsky, the knight Alaric de Marnac. Inspired by the misdeeds of the historical Gilles de Rais, murderer of children and occultist, Alaric's first appearance was in *El espanto surge de la tumba / Horror Rises from the Tomb* (Carlos Aured, 1973). The film tells the tale of a fifteenth-century sorcerer and his mistress who, accused of witchcraft, curse the executioners and their descendants. The dead are eventually invoked back to life, and they proceed to commit new crimes in contemporary France. Interesting for their reliance on more obviously Gothic motifs (medieval times, the damning of future generations, Satanism and black magic), the Alaric films are also unusual for their lack of sequentiality. The two sequels do not tell a linear story; instead, the main character is developed in different, if connected, ways. *El mariscal del infierno / Devil's Possessed* (León Klimovsky, 1974) is not technically linked to *Horror Rises from the Tomb*, as its main character is called Gilles de Lancré. However, the character's interest in the philosopher's stone and virginal sacrifices (as well as his first name) directly connect him to de Rais and de Marnac. *Devil's Possessed* is more of a historical melodrama, however, so that the psychology of the character has the chance to evolve in ways it had not in *Horror*. *Latidos de pánico / Panic Beats* (Jacinto Molina, 1983) returns to Alaric, and combines the medieval Gothic with the modern; the main action takes place in a medieval-style modern villa, where the spirit of the knight returns in full armoured regalia to punish the mischievous women in the family's lineage. Intergenerational doubling between characters is key to a film that twists and turns in unexpected ways and provides one of the most original (if convoluted) plots of any Spanish B-movie Gothic ever. Alaric, like the Blind Dead, has clear predecessors – Gilles de Rais, Bluebeard – but his development over the three instalments and quintessential occult background (characteristic of the sword and sorcery genre Molina also championed) distinguishes him from more traditional Gothic monsters.

Overall, the production of Gothic films, with Gothic monsters, during the golden age of Spanish horror was very substantial and, if sometimes poorly executed, was as original as it was derivational. Yet, the country's preference for a different nomenclature and for a focus on the supernatural elements of this cinematic cycle, rather than on the transnational origins of the myths expanded or developed in them, means that the horror films covered throughout this chapter are rarely ever considered an inherently Spanish achievement in the Gothic mode. At best, they constitute their own cycle, fantaterror, of interest from a primarily industrial point of view. As Ann Davies (2016, 115) concisely summarises it, the problem is that 'Spanish culture was able to create a Gothic context but unable to recognize it as such'. As I hope to have shown, the tribute that films like *Count Dracula's Great Love* or *Frankenstein's Bloody Terror* paid to Hammer Horror and Universal monster features is such that the former needs to be recognised as Gothic, if only by extrapolation. As a natural result of an industrial context in which profit and the recouping of financial investments were crucial, the logic of the market, which demands originality as well as tried-and-tested formulas, ushered forth a body of B-movie films that are only now beginning to be studied with the seriousness and rigour they demand. As well as being valuable in their own right, especially as unlikely survivors of a cinema produced under heavy censorship laws, they are more broadly a testament to the intrinsically transnational and glocal aspects of the Gothic as a cinematic mode.

Bibliography

Brydon, Diana (2010), 'Cracking Imaginaries: Studying the Global from Canadian Space', in Janet Wilson, Christina Şandru and Sarah Lawson Welsch (eds), *Rerouting*

the Postcolonial: New Directions for the New Millennium (Abingdon and New York: Routledge), 105–17.
Byron, Glennis (ed.) (2013), *Globalgothic* (Manchester: Manchester University Press, 2013).
Davies, Ann (2016), 'Spanish Gothic Cinema: The Hidden Continuities of a Hidden Genre', in Elena Oliete-Aldea, Beatriz Oria and Juan A. Tarancón (eds), *Global Genres, Local Films: The Transnational Dimension of Spanish Cinema* (London and New York: Bloomsbury), 115–26.
Diego, José de (2014), *Cine bizarro: Los clásicos del 'cinéma bis'* (Madrid: Torres de Papel).
Elbert, Monika and Bridget M. Marshall (eds) (2013), *Transnational Gothic: Literary and Social Exchanges in the Long Nineteenth Century* (Farnham and Burlington, VT: Ashgate).
Gómez Rivero, Ángel (2009), *Cine zombi* (Madrid: Calamar Ediciones).
Jacobs, Edward H. (2000), *Accidental Migrations: An Archaeology of Gothic Discourse* (London and Cranbury, NJ: Associated University Presses).
Luque Carreras, José A. (2015), *El cine negro español* (Madrid: T&B Editores).
Mathijs, Ernest and Xavier Mendik (eds) (2004), *Alternative Europe: Eurotrash and Exploitation Cinema since 1945* (New York: Columbia University Press).
Pakir, Anne (2014), 'Glocal English in Singapore? A Re-exploration of the Localization of English', in Neil Murray and Angela Scarino (eds), *Dynamic Ecologies: A Relational Perspective on Languages Education in the Asia-Pacific Region* (London and New York: Springer), 49–58.
Pedrero Santos, Juan A. (2008), *Terror Cinema! Cine clásico de terror* (Madrid: Calamar Ediciones).
Prada, Juan Manuel de (2003), 'El ciclo de Waldemar Daninsky', in Paul Naschy (ed.), *La marca del hombre lobo: La licantropía de la leyenda medieval al cine de nuestros días* (Madrid: Imágica Ediciones, 2003), 20–41.
Shipka, Danny (2011), *Perverse Titillation: The Exploitation Cinema of Italy, Spain and France, 1960–80* (Jefferson, NC: McFarland).
Willis, Andrew (2003), 'Spanish Horror and the Flight from "Art" Cinema, 1967–73', in Mark Jancovich, Antonio Lázaro Reboll, Julian Stringer and Andy Willis (eds), *Defining Cult Movies: The Cultural Politics of Oppositional Taste* (Manchester: Manchester University Press), 71–83.

FILMOGRAPHY

Las Alegres vampiras de Vögel / Vampires of Vögel (Julio Pérez Tabernero, 1975)
Blacula (William Crain, 1972)
Blood for Dracula (Paul Morrissey, 1974)
El Bosque del lobo / The Ancines Woods (Pedro Olea, 1970)
Ceremonia sangrienta / The Legend of Blood Castle (Jorge Grau, 1973)
El Conde Drácula / Count Dracula (Jesús Franco, 1970)
Countess Dracula (Peter Sasdy, 1971)
Cross of the Devil (John Gilling, 1975)
Dracula (Tod Browning, 1931)
Dracula (John Badham, 1979)
El Espanto surge de la tumba / Horror Rises from the Tomb (Carlos Aured, 1973)
El Extraño amor de los vampiros / Night of the Walking Dead (1975)
The Fearless Vampire Killers (Roman Polanski, 1967)
Frankenstein (James Whale, 1931)
Las Garras de Lorelei / The Loreley's Grasp (Amando de Ossorio, 1974)

THE GOLDEN AGE OF SPANISH B-MOVIE HORROR

El Gran amor del conde Drácula / *Count Dracula's Great Love* (1973)
Gritos en la noche / *The Awful Dr. Orloff* (Jesús Franco, 1962)
Las Hijas de Drácula / *Vampyres* (José Ramón Larraz, 1974)
Latidos de pánico / *Panic Heartbeats* (Jacinto Molina, 1983)
Malenka, la sobrina del vampiro / *Fangs of the Living Dead* (Amando de Ossorio, 1969)
La Marca del hombre lobo / *Frankenstein's Bloody Terror* (Enrique López Eguiluz, 1968)
El Mariscal del infierno / *Devil's Possessed* (León Klimovsky, 1974)
Mil gritos tiene la noche / *Pieces* (Juan Piquer Simón, 1982)
Lost Monstruos del terror / *Assignment Terror* (Tulio Demicheli, Hugo Fregonese, Antonio Isasi-Isasmendi and Eberhard Meichsner, 1970)
The Mummy (Karl Freund, 1932)
The Mummy (Terence Fisher, 1959)
Night of the Living Dead (George A. Romero, 1968)
No profanar el sueño de los muertos / *The Living Dead at Manchester Morgue* (Jorge Grau, 1974)
La Noche de los brujos / *Night of the Sorcerers* (Amando de Ossorio, 1974)
La Noche del terror ciego / *Tombs of the Blind Dead* (Amando de Ossorio, 1972)
Nosferatu, eine Symphonie des Grauens / *Nosferatu* (F. W. Murnau, 1922)
La Novia ensangrentada / *The Blood Spattered Bride* (Vicente Aranda, 1972)
La Orgía de los muertos / *Terror of the Living Dead* (José Luis Merino, 1973)
La Orgía nocturna de los vampiros / *The Vampires' Night Orgy* (León Klimovsky, 1974)
Pánico en el transiberiano / *Horror Express* (Eugenio Martín, 1972)
El Pantano de los cuervos / *The Swamp of the Ravens* (Manuel Caño, 1974)
El Pobrecito Draculín / *Poor Dracula Junior* (Juan Fortuny, 1977)
La Residenciaa / *The House That Screamed* (Narciso Ibáñez Serrador, 1968)
El Retorno del hombre lobo / *Return of the Wolf Man* (Jacinto Molina, 1980)
La Saga de los Drácula / *The Dracula Saga* (León Klimovsky, 1972)
Tiempos duros para Drácula / *Hard Times for Dracula* (Jorge Darnell, 1976)
Tres eran tres / *Three Were Three* (1958)
La Tumba de la isla maldita / *Hannah, Queen of the Vampires* (Julio Salvador and Ray Danton, 1973)
La Tumba de los muertos vivientes / *Oasis of the Zombies* (Jesús Franco, 1982)
Una de miedo / *A Horror Film* (Eduardo García Maroto, 1935)
The Vampire Lovers (Roy Ward Baker, 1970)
Un Vampiro para do / *A Vampire for Two* (Pedro Lazaga, 1965)
Vampyros Lesbos (Jesús Franco, 1971)
La Venganza de la momia / *The Vengeance of the Mummy* (Carlos Aured, 1975)
The Wolf Man (George Waggner, 1941)
Les Yeux sans visage / *Eyes without a Face* (Georges Franju, 1960)
Young Frankenstein (Mel Brooks, 1974)

TV Series and Documentaries

Historias para no dormir / *Stories to Keep You Awake* (TVE, Narciso Ibáñez Serrador, 1966–8)
Horror Europa with Mark Gatiss (BBC, John Das, 2012)
Zarpazos! Un viaje por el Spanish Horror / *Claws! A Journey through Spanish Horror* (Víctor Matellano, 2014)

7. AUSTRO-TRASH, CLASS AND THE URBAN ENVIRONMENT: THE POLITICS OF *DAS DING AUS DER MUR* AND ITS PREQUEL

Michael Fuchs

Produced on a combined budget of less than 2,000 Euro, *Das Ding aus der Mur* ('The Thing from the River Mur'; 2012) and its prequel, *Das Ding aus der Mur: Zero* (2015), were obviously not made with a mass market in mind. Indeed, after a brief stint in select Austrian theatres and screenings at some small Austrian film festivals, *Das Ding* was uploaded to YouTube, where it has amassed fewer than 12,000 views in the four years between its uploading in March 2013 and the time of writing of this chapter. Like its predecessor, *Zero* was screened in a few theatres and at a couple of small festivals before it was released on DVD, in which format it is directly available from the films' producer and director, David Hehn.

Narratively, the films are highly fragmented, extraordinarily trite and extremely clichéd. The two movies tell the story of Police Chief Alois Ratzinger and his fight against a monster which slays human beings in the vicinity of the river Mur in the Austrian city of Graz. The titular creature is an unnatural hybrid whose DNA combines the genetic information of various species, including humans, while Ratzinger is an alcoholic, indifferent policeman constantly tired of work (not only his work, but work in general). Still, he somehow not only ends up battling the monster, but in fact succeeds in defeating the creature in hand-to-hand combat towards the end of *Das Ding*. *Zero* makes it clear that Ratzinger had, in fact, defeated the creature (or, rather, its ancestors) previously.

However, the story provides little more than the pretext for scenes of violence. In this respect, the movies do not particularly diverge from standard horror fare, since, as Stephen Prince has noted, in horror movies 'narrative structure per se is less significant than the creation in viewers of states of fright, anxiety, even disgust' (2004, 8). Typically, these emotions are projected onto and/or triggered by the monster, which 'threatens normality' (Wood 2003, 72) and points at 'an array of societal, political and sexual threats' (Halberstam 1995, 23). Monsters, in short, are political. However, 'within the Gothic', David Punter has argued, 'we can [only] find a ... displaced ... engagement with political ... problems' (1980, 62). This displacement of political questions has led scholars such as Andrew Smith and William Hughes to question whether 'the Gothic ... can be used for radical or reactionary ends' (2009, 2).

In this chapter, I will suggest that the Ding is, indeed, used 'for reactionary ends', as the monster functions as a critique of capitalism which speaks to two interrelated political concerns. The first of these issues is that the two *Das Ding* films address environmental questions through the monster. In this context, Elisabeth Grosz has argued that the monster 'is an ambiguous being whose existence imperils categories and oppositions dominant in social life' (1996, 57). Monsters, she continues, 'occupy the impossible middle ground between the oppositions dividing the human from the animal ... one being from another ... nature from culture ... and the living and the dead' (Grosz 1996, 57). The Ding is such a liminal being: On the surface, it appears non-human, but its DNA is in part human. Since its biological set-up includes the genetic information of different life forms, the Ding belongs to several species and at the same time occupies a netherworld between these species. The monster is an amphibian creature, living in the water and on land – neither one, nor the other. Finally, neither the characters nor the viewers ever truly understand where the Ding comes from. Is it a *lusus naturae* (i.e. a freak of nature) or is it – consciously or unconsciously – a techno-cultural product created by humans?

In addition, the films provide political commentary through the symbolism surrounding the river itself. The Mur is positioned between the natural and the cultural, as it is a seemingly 'natural' element in the cityscape of Graz. However, human beings have shaped the river for thousands of years. Indeed, the region's earliest settlers in the Palaeolithic Age had probably already sought to shape the river and control its forces (Habsburg-Lothringen 2015, 36). While large-scale measures to regulate the river's flow were not implemented until the nineteenth century, starting in the 1820s, entire floodplains were removed, the riverbed was dramatically lowered and the river's course stretched. The introduction of electricity towards the end of the nineteenth century exacerbated the anthropogenic impact on the Mur ecosystem, as hydroelectric power plants went into service along the river. Until the late 1960s, ecological questions were ignored when installing these power plants, causing water temperatures to rise, resulting in decreased aeration levels and, consequently, decimating non-human life in the river (Bernhart et al. 1973, 52).

While counter-measures against the river's pollution were slowly introduced in the wake of the environmental awakening in the latter half of the 1960s, in the 1980s the Mur was one of the most polluted rivers in Europe. In 1994, Wolfgang Windisch, then nature conservation representative of the city of Graz, pleaded for tightening the 'human–water relationship' (1994, 25; my translation), which led not only to the restoration of the river (acknowledged in 2014, when the Styrian government received the International River Foundation's European Riverprize for its conservation efforts), but also, particularly in Graz, to the project of literally bringing the people closer to the Mur by developing a promenade, biking routes, and so on.

However, these measures have introduced new problems. Like the redevelopments of (former) port areas across the Western world, residential development projects have been mushrooming along the Mur's riverbanks in Graz since the late 1990s. Whereas, up until the late 1980s, Murside developments consisted primarily of industrial and lower-income residential areas (apart from the heart of the city), apartments and houses close to the river have been in high demand in recent years, resulting in prices skyrocketing. Until thirty years ago, the river traversing the city from north to south functioned as a relatively clear line of demarcation between the labourers' districts in the west and the city's middle- and upper-class areas in the east. The redevelopment of the river – along with other urban development measures – has moved the

Figure 7.1 The Mur about two kilometres north of the old town/city centre of Graz. Photo taken by the author

labourers' residential areas further west, while upper-class real estates have been moving from the city's outskirts towards the city centre, putting pressure on the (formerly) lower-class areas of the city.

Accordingly, indefinable though the monster may be in some respects, the Ding is also clearly rooted in early twenty-first-century Graz, interconnecting the movies' ecological critique with a layer of social consciousness. However, the movies do not present this satire of the city, its political environment and its socio-cultural climate in an in-your-face way. Instead, viewers are slowly introduced to the satirical impulses guiding the movies and are thus invited to approach the movies in their entirety in a particular, knowing way in order to decode the films' meaning. Typical of horror and the Gothic, the monster plays an extremely important role in this context.

Laughing at the Monstrous Body

In both horror and the Gothic, the monster is the central character. Traditionally, the monster is thought to produce 'fear, anxiety, terror, horror, disgust and revulsion' (Botting 2013, 6). However, the *Das Ding* films do not quite operate in the ways one would accordingly expect, as their visual effects suffer from miniscule production budgets (although one must acknowledge the production team's commitment and workmanship). Repeatedly, scenes in which viewers might expect moments of shock and disgust become moments of laughter. In

Figure 7.2 The Ding in all its glorious ridiculousness. Image taken from *Das Ding aus der Mur: Zero*. © Hianbliata Productions, 2015. Screenshot used by permission of Hianbliata Productions

particular, the movie's monster simply looks ridiculous. While its visual design draws on the Creature from the Black Lagoon, the monster is obviously played by a man in a suit who wears rubber boots in the first film and flippers in the second. As a result, the Ding looks less convincing than the Creature, despite sixty years of technological progress between the motion pictures.

Although the Ding's bodily presence in the diegetic world counteracts the expected effects of typical monsters, Mary Y. Hallab has pointed out that while '[h]orror movies are rarely *intended* to be comic', many iconic horror monsters 'are innately ridiculous' (2016, 138; italics in original). This '[u]nintentional humor', she continues, may, in fact, 'reinforce . . . the creepy effect of scenes such as Nosferatu rising straight up from his coffin' (Hallab 2016, 138). Similarly, in his early discussion of *The Texas Chain Saw Massacre* (1974), Robin Wood diagnoses the centrality of 'the sense of grotesque comedy, which in no way diminishes but rather intensifies its nightmare horror' (2003, 84), to the film. Indeed, silly though the Ding may be, the ludicrous costume results in material reality's constant invasion of the films' fictional world, as the bargain costume and cheap – yet at the same time overdone – special effects draw viewers' attention to the constructed nature of the diegetic world. Tellingly, Sigmund Freud remarked that 'an uncanny effect is often and easily produced when the distinction between imagination and reality is effaced, as when something that we have hitherto regarded as imaginary appears before us in reality' (2001, 244). Accordingly, the monster's amateurish design in fact reinforces the uncanny effect established by its genetic hybridity.

Beyond generating uncanny effects, the Ding's look elicits affective responses. In his book *Body Gothic* (2014), Xavier Aldana Reyes rightfully points out that 'the gothic is . . . inherently somatic and corporeal' (2014, 2). Yet whereas Aldana Reyes' interest lies in how the graphic display of wounded bodies (re-)activates recipients' 'awareness of their own bodies, particularly of their vulnerability' (2014, 2), the Ding generates a different kind of bodily response – laughter. Indeed, in their introduction to the anthology *The Laughing Dead* (2016), Cindy Miller and Bow Van Riper explain that '[t]he emotional affects of horror and comedy may be radically different, but the mechanisms by which they operate are strikingly similar', for 'both comedy and horror depend on the shock of the unexpected' (2016, xiv).

Whereas horror generally offers a 'shared experience of projected pain through vicarious feelings' (Aldana Reyes 2014, 2), the Ding's weird look causes a cacophony between (inculcated) affective expectations and the affects actually experienced when watching the movies. This discord invites viewers to engage in what Jeffrey Sconce has called 'paracinematic reading'. At the heart of this alternative viewing mode is 'a pitched battle between a guerrilla band of cult film viewers and an elite cadre of would-be cinematic tastemakers' (1995, 372). While Sconce is quick to point out that 'the politics of social stratification

Figure 7.3 The movies' amateurish special effects invite what Jeffrey Sconce has called 'paracinematic reading'. Image taken from *Das Ding aus der Mur: Zero*. © Hianbliata Productions, 2015. Screenshot used by permission of Hianbliata Productions

and taste . . . is more complex than a simple high-brow/low-brow split' (1995, 372) would suggest, he still conceives of paracinema as always-already political. After all, paracinema is defined 'in opposition to a loosely defined group of cultural and economic elites, [the] purveyors of the status quo who . . . rule the world' (1995, 374). Viewed from this perspective, the Ding emerges as a vehicle which critically addresses the status quo, in particular in relation to ecological questions and class politics.

Environmental Politics

The movies' ecological subtext begins to surface as early as *Das Ding*'s opening sequence. As two unnamed young women enjoy the sun at the Mur promenade close to the centre of Graz, they catch a glimpse of a small greenish creature, which looks like a hybrid between a fish and an amphibian. The animal's mere presence terrifies the two women, who run off screaming before the critter quickly disappears again. The credits following this cold opening are displayed against the backdrop of images of waste in the river, which are contrasted with rather calm images of 'pristine' nature and panorama shots of the city. When the film's title shows up, the music – which had been relatively slow up to that point – suddenly becomes faster and more aggressive. The punk-style music accompanies images of DNA strands and the metamorphosis of a tadpole into a frog. These visuals are followed by depictions of dead fish, a newspaper announcing an incident in a nuclear power plant in Graz, different kinds of underwater life, demonstrations in various cities, and toxic waste. The opening montage concludes with some more images from the newspaper reporting on fishermen disappearing in the Graz area and the nuclear power plant's possible 'impact on the ecosystem', since 'experts caution against the endangerment of the Mur and all the animal and plant life inhabiting the river' (Hehn 2012; my translation). Here, the audiovisual text is evidently meant to 'help to counteract the destruction of the natural world' (Ross 1994, 81) not only by confronting viewers with the manifest consequences of pollution, but also by showcasing that there are ways in which to protest against – and implicitly to also counteract – these developments.

The visual constant in the opening credits (aside from the omnipresence of death and decay) is the digital images of DNA strands, which move and create connections, introducing the horrors of genetic change and mutation right away. Indeed, while both movies visualise the ambiguous threat in the form of the creature, neither film makes explicit what the actual source of the danger is. This lack of an easily and clearly definable threat has haunted the environmentalist movement. Al Gore observed as early as 1992 that the most serious problem conservationists have to face resides in the realm of the imagination, as the large-scale and long-term effects of anthropogenic actions cannot be experienced. As a result, 'most people do not yet accept the fact that this crisis is extremely grave' (Gore 2013, 36).

While the reason for the Ding's appearance remains a mystery, a scientist featured in *Das Ding* mentions that the Graz Nuclear Power Plant (NPP) may have caused the mutation. *Zero* delves further into the history and role of the power plant and makes clear that not even all of Graz's inhabitants are aware of its existence. Indeed, in a brief exchange between Alois and his unnamed fisherman buddy, the latter wonders whether Alois knows about the Graz NPP. Alois is flabbergasted: 'We have a nuclear power plant?' (Hehn 2015; my translation). These references to the Graz NPP draw on the audience's awareness that Austria is an anti-nuclear-power country and play on the lack of transparency of, and resultant lack of interest in, Austrian politics (where else could you fund and build a power plant without anyone noticing?). In addition, these allusions point about 120 miles northwards in Austria's geography (and around forty years back in time), to a place where the Austrian government had an NPP built. Famously, although the Zwentendorf NPP was finished, as a result of numerous demonstrations, public sentiment against nuclear energy and an eventual national referendum, which vetoed the NPP, the power plant never began operations. Zwentendorf was thus the only NPP built in Austria.

In the world of the films, however, the Graz NPP does exist. Ratzinger's friend has even been to the place and has witnessed some 'very strange things' (Hehn 2015; my translation) happening there. In a flashback, viewers can see him sneaking around the NPP. As the fisherman gets closer, he can hear screams of terror and pain. He enters the building. Inside, he can see a medical professional opening the chest of a nearly (after some seconds truly) dead man. The doctor removes some internal organs, yet the surgery's purpose remains unclear. However, the brief scene emphasises that covert operations take place in the NPP. These covert operations, additionally, are connected to the monster when one of the guards expresses his fear that the public will, sooner rather than later, come to understand what truly happens in the NPP because of the human bodies piling up. Not coincidentally, the monster nests close to the pile of corpses.

However, the environmental problems caused by the NPP far exceed the mere emergence of the Ding. In *Zero*, Alois's fisherman friend repeatedly complains about the strange non-human animals he has pulled out of the Mur in recent weeks – whales, three-eyed fish and various creatures that elude verbal description. When he comes across an adolescent Ding on the riverbank, the fisherman wonders, 'Hey, what kind of fish are you? You disgusting thing!' (Hehn 2015; my translation). At this moment, Ratzinger turns up, which triggers the following dialogue:

Ratzinger: Hey, what have you got there?
Fisherman: I told you that the fish are getting bigger and bigger!
Ratzinger: But that's no fish!
Fisherman: Well, but it's no crawfish, either.
Ratzinger: Yes. I've noticed that it doesn't have any pincers.
Fisherman: Shall we notify anyone?
Ratzinger: Well, I'm the police, anyways. So, it's all the same. Is it still alive? (Hehn 2015; my translation)

When the fisherman pokes the creature with a stick in order to verify it is dead, it jumps up. Ratzinger responds by instantly shooting it. Apparently, in the world of the *Das Ding* movies, the creature primarily exists to be exterminated. When the fisherman wonders what to do with the dead body, Alois's conclusion is simple – 'Well, we'll put it where we dump everything into . . .' – and the two men finish the thought in unison: '. . . into the Mur!' (Hehn 2015). In this way, the movie satirises a practice which has defined the relationship between the Styrian population and the Mur. Indeed, the river was (mis)used as a dumpsite for centuries, if not millennia. While it proves impossible to ascertain when human beings did, in fact, begin dumping large amounts of waste into the Mur, documented human practices in Graz include the disposing of human bodies and the dumping of animal carcasses and scraps into the river until well into the eighteenth century (Leitgeb 1994, 9). In fact, it took until the Gössendorf sewage treatment plant started operations in

1974 for the city's wastewaters to be processed before being emptied into the river. Although the river's water quality has dramatically improved in the past three decades, the water's hygiene levels still make it dangerous for humans to kayak, surf or swim in the river, let alone eat (from) the organisms inhabiting it (Müller 2012). Politicians, of course, seek to keep this information secret, in particular because there are plans in place to further develop the riverbanks into urban recreational areas – and aquatic sports are a big selling point in this context.

Although Alois and his buddy's inconsiderate 'waste management' is played for laughs, the naïveté with which they treat the Mur and the life forms living in the river point to the dangers of the Mur embodied by the Ding. For these characters, the Mur – and its bacterial contamination levels – pose a threat of which they are blissfully ignorant. In a way, this attitude is understandable because the river is part of their lives. They live close to the river; the river nourishes them – the river (and whatever is in the river) is a part of them.

The fictional Mayor of Graz, Willi Arndt, epitomises a different understanding of the river. When asked about the disappearances of people in the vicinity of the Mur in a televised interview featured in *Zero*, he attributes the disappearances to 'a minor flood'. Arndt's logical conclusion is that the people thus 'simply drowned' (Hehn 2015; my translation). By referring to the flood, the politician identifies a 'perpetrator' the city's inhabitants cannot blame for its actions; it is a 'perpetrator' existing outside the legal system. In fact, Arndt explicitly stresses that the flood is 'legally incomprehensible' (Hehn 2015; my translation), not only creating an easy excuse for not taking any serious reactive measures, but also indicating that human beings are helpless when confronted with the forces of nature.

Yet beyond these more basic points, constructing the flood as 'legally incomprehensible' locates the natural disaster outside the human domain and thus supports the idea that 'the human is entirely outside the natural' (Cronon 1996, 17). As William Cronon has explained, 'nature' has been discursively constructed as the binary counterpart to the human sphere. Placing the pristine and wild natural world in opposition to the cultured, artificial and controlled world of the human is deeply entrenched in our Western way of thinking. However, cities are places where the interrelations between nature and culture become lived reality. This aspect becomes evident not only in the monster, which, due to its unspecific origins, bridges the divide between the chaotic design of nature and the (purportedly) controlled ventures of techno-science, but also in the interplay between the socio-cultural sphere and interventions in 'nature'.

Class Politics

While the fictional mayor implies the separation of the domain of nature and the human sphere, Wolfgang Windisch's 1994 plan to re-unite the people of Graz with the river flowing through the city was driven by the idea that urbanites needed 'the contact with pristine nature' (1994: 25; my translation). This contact, he believed, could most easily be established at the Mur's riverbanks. Tellingly, this is where the Ding snatches its victims – and it doesn't just kill anyone. Indeed, radio news in *Zero* stresses that the vast majority of people going missing in the vicinity of the Mur are people from Graz. As the reporter explains, the perpetrator's obvious preference for locals 'can probably be attributed to the fact that practically only the inhabitants of Graz and hillbillies from nearby municipalities use the Mur and its surroundings for recreational purposes' (Hehn 2015; my translation). On the surface, the reporter's scornful tone characterises her as a touchy woman who tends to look down on other people. On a deeper level, however, the contempt is directed not so much at the inhabitants of Graz and its surroundings, but rather at the politicians who (try to) keep the bad water quality a secret in an attempt to launch ever-new recreational development projects along the river.

On the basic level of content, both movies support the reporter insofar as the monster primarily preys on rather simple-minded people from the (lower) working class. For example, *Zero*'s second half focuses on a group of friends who end up partying on the river's shores – 'close to the nuclear power plant' (Hehn 2015; my translation), as one of the characters clarifies. They drive through the city in an older Chevrolet SUV model, unfazed by its gas consumption. Ignorant of the dangers of the Mur (despite radio broadcasts and television news reports), they plough through the greenery on the top of the riverbank before starting to drink beer, listening to music and chilling close to the river. A few minutes later (in terms of runtime), the entire group except pseudo-final girl Pia is dead. Pia manages to escape the monster, but she is trapped in the sewer system as the movie concludes.

While one could argue that the monster punishes the group's ecological transgressions, the fact that Pia simply tricks the creature by hiding in its food stash made of human bodies underlines that the Ding literally feeds on human beings. Accordingly, the creature becomes the symbolic stand-in for a man-made system which shamelessly exploits its throwaway sources – whether non-human or human is of little relevance in this context. Just as the creature mauls and consumes humans, the medical professionals in the NPP strip the human body of its assets. The first movie implies that one of these assets is the human genetic code, which was combined with other species' genetic information to form the Ding.

Beyond connecting its titular monster to the largely invisible class struggle raging in the streets of Graz, *Das Ding* raises the question of how the exploitation of human beings is even possible in the (post-)enlightened world of the early twenty-first century. The answer, the movies suggest, proves rather simple: politicians, whose thinking is still anchored in the twentieth century (if not earlier). More importantly, politicans do not want to rouse the public and change the status quo, which, after all, assures their existence. Following a horror tradition established by *Jaws* (1975), the public figure most explicitly attacked is the mayor. In his televised interview, Arndt's most frequently used expression is 'äh' (the German equivalent of 'umm'), which indicates that he is not that rhetorically gifted and/or that he tries to conceal the truth, causing him to constantly fumble for words. Revealingly, at the end of the interview, a kind of Freudian slip occurs, as he remarks that 'the people simply drowned. And what about politics? Drowned, too' (Hehn 2015; my translation).

The parodying of the city's mayor highlights not only the vacuity of politicians' speeches, but also the extreme differences between what linguists might call the surface and the deep level of language – that is, what Mayor Nagl's fictional stand-in actually says and what he means. Beyond stressing these differences between (rhetorically) performing the role of the mayor of Graz and taking serious political action, the mayor's parody also displays the different perceptions of what politicians consider essential policies for the city's imagined well-being and what the city's inhabitants deem important on the ground level.

The first film, especially, addresses these different perspectives in its audiovisual language. Repeatedly, panorama shots of the city are brightly lit during daytime and offer impressive vistas during the night, with the interplay of electric light, moonlight and the darkness of the night. Upbeat Styrian folk music usually accompanies the daylight images, while soothing sounds accompany the night-time scenes, evoking an idealised view of the city. At the street level, on the other hand, the picture is dominated by little to no musical accompaniment and focused on the grisly murders (and the investigations into them).

The opposing views of the city also become manifest in the movies' depiction of the middle class. One of the first scenes in the original movie, for example, shows a middle-class urbanite stomping into the sewer systems of Graz, prattling, 'Where is the party?' (Hehn 2012; my translation). Once he has found the party, he celebrates life at a rave. This scene highlights the fact that the middle class has conquered the sewers, liminal spaces on the fringes of the 'civilised' world, where it hosts parties. This development was facilitated by the measures to 'bring humans closer to the water', which has – the movie implies – sanctified even the dirtiest places of the city and accordingly allowed the middle class to invade spaces they traditionally did not move in. For example, the instalment of a promenade along the river has been accompanied by conflict, as locals and tourists increasingly encounter the homeless people who had occupied the areas closer to the river (for example, living in tents on the riverbanks and under bridges) for decades before the redevelopments started in the 1990s. The mere presence of these homeless people in what are supposed to be recreational areas brings the middle class face to face with dimensions of post-industrial capitalism most people prefer not to be confronted with.

However, one (sub-)group of the middle (and, possibly, upper) class merits special attention in the first film: hipsters. Hipsters play a tension-laden role in contemporary Western capitalism: This group claims to shun consumerism and to perform an alternative lifestyle to the triviality of mass culture. However, their difference from mainstream culture largely depends on an ironic understanding of consumer culture while still embracing capitalist practices. Hipsters may highlight problems in capitalist cultures, but, in the end, they are what Michel Foucault might call 'docile bodies' (1995, 135–69) operating in support of the system. In the movie, these would-be individualists, who (purport to) act in environmentally sound ways and cling to the idea of individualism in sameness, support the monster (i.e. support the exploitation of human beings). First, they stage a public protest in front of the city hall with little approval from passers-by. Later, a handful of hipsters can see the creature swimming in the Mur. Armed with signs asking the public to 'save the monster', they begin cheering for the Ding, which sets in motion the only scene in which the creature goes after a group of middle-classers, as if to punish them for their lack of understanding of the world and their concomitant idealised and naive lifestyle, made possible by exploitative practices.

Splatstick and the Mur

In the end, *Das Ding aus der Mur* and *Das Ding aus der Mur: Zero* symbolically connect the creature to the Mur. As a result, the monster reflects the recent anthropogenic changes to the river and reflects on how these changes have affected the city. In particular, similar to how the Ding preys on local 'hillbillies' (as the news report in *Zero* has it), Murside developments in the recent past have not only displaced the lower classes and further dispossessed those people already stricken by poverty, but have also introduced a 'natural' part into the cityscape that is anything but 'natural' – in the traditional sense.

While the *Das Ding* films follow the long-established practice of (especially) B-movies in critiquing the establishment, they draw most explicitly on the Troma tradition, highlighted by the appearance of iconic producer and director Lloyd Kaufman in the second movie. In view of the intertextual connections between the *Das Ding* movies and Troma, it seems significant that in a chapter on the ecological messages of select Troma films, Robin L. Murray and Joseph K. Heumann conclude that '[i]n spite of their sometimes overpowering campy humor and horrifying violence, these Troma films show the consequences of disturbing a pristine ecosystem and offer a viable solution to greedy humans' exploitation of the natural world' (2016, 105).

However, the *Das Ding* movies do not hark back to an idealised conception of nature. Set in the second-largest city of Austria, the movies seem well aware of the incompatibility of urban life and the idea of 'pristine' nature. Indeed, no matter whether it is the monstrous result of nuclear radiation, a genetic experiment gone awry or the outcome of water pollution, the titular creature is caused by anthropogenic actions. While the movies display fictionalised ways in which humans intervene in the Mur ecosystem, the Ding simultaneously represents the Mur and how humankind has shaped the river. The creature accordingly emphasises the interconnectedness of contemporary (techno-capitalist) culture and 'natural' worlds through a monster which simultaneously represents the potential outcome of genetic engineering and embodies the river flowing through Graz. The Ding accordingly merges these two semantic fields and highlights that the seemingly 'pristine' natural world surrounding the Mur is as much shaped by human beings as our human existence is shaped by non-human forces beyond our control.

BIBLIOGRAPHY

Aldana Reyes, Xavier (2014), *Body Gothic: Corporeal Transgression in Contemporary Literature and Horror Film* (Cardiff: University of Wales Press).
Bernhart, Leopold et al. (1973), *Wärmebelastung steirischer Gewässer* (Graz: Amt der Steiermärkischen Landesregierung).
Botting, Fred (2013), *Gothic*, 2nd edn (London: Routledge).
Cronon, William (1996), 'The Trouble with Wilderness; Or, Getting Back to the Wrong Nature', *Environmental History* 1/1, 7–28.
Foucault, Michel (1995), *Discipline & Punish: The Birth of the Prison* (trans. Alan Sheridan) (New York: Vintage).
Freud, Sigmund (2001), 'The "Uncanny"' (trans. James Strachey, Anna Freud, Alix Stracey and Alan Tyson), in James Strachey (ed.), *The Standard Edition of the Complete Psychological Works of Sigmund Freud, Vol. 17: An Infantile Neurosis and Other Works* (London: Vintage), 217–54.
Gore, Al (2013), *Earth in the Balance: Forging a New Common Purpose* (New York: Earthscan).
Grosz, Elisabeth (1996), 'Intolerable Ambiguity: Freaks as/at the Limit', in Rosemarie Garland Thomson (ed.), *Freakery: Cultural Spectacles of the Extraordinary Body* (New York: New York University Press), 55–66.
Habsburg-Lothringen, Bettina (ed.) (2015), *Die Mur: Eine Kulturgeschichte* (Graz: Universalmuseum Joanneum).
Halberstam, Judith (1995), *Skin Shows: Gothic Horror and the Technology of Monsters* (Durham, NC: Duke University Press).
Hallab, Mary Y. (2016), 'Humor in Vampire Films: The Vampire as Joker', in Cynthia J. Miller and A. Bowdoin Van Riper (eds), *The Laughing Dead: The Horror-Comedy Film from* Bride of Frankenstein *to* Zombieland (Lanham: Rowman & Littlefield), 138–53.
Leitgeb, Franz (1994), 'Wie es mit der Mur einmal war', in *Ideen für eine Stadt am Fluss: 1. Murenquête* (Graz: Amt für Stadtentwicklung und Stadterhaltung), 7–13.

Miller, Cynthia J. and A. Bowdoin Van Riper (2016), 'Introduction', in Cynthia J. Miller and A. Bowdoin Van Riper (eds), *The Laughing Dead: The Horror-Comedy Film from* Bride of Frankenstein *to* Zombieland (Lanham: Rowman & Littlefield), xiii–xxiii.
Murray, Robin L. and Joseph K. Heumann (2016), *Monstrous Nature: Environment and Horror on the Big Screen* (Lincoln: University of Nebraska Press).
Müller, Walter (2012), 'Mur-Surfen in Graz auf Wellen voller Fäkalbakterien', *Der Standard*, 6 July, <http://derstandard.at/1341526709134/Gesundheitsgefaehrdung-Mur-Surfen-in-Graz-auf-Wellen-voller-Faekalbakterien> (last accessed 15 August 2016).
Prince, Stephen (2004), 'Introduction: The Dark Genre and Its Paradoxes', in Stephen Prince (ed.), *The Horror Film* (New Brunswick, NJ: Rutgers University Press), 1–11.
Punter, David (1980), *Literature of Terror: A History of Gothic Fictions from 1765 to the Present Day* (New York: Longman).
Ross, Andrew (1994), *The Chicago Gangster Theory of Life: Nature's Debt to Society* (London: Verso).
Sconce, Jeffrey (1995), '"Trashing" the Academy: Taste, Excess, and an Emerging Politics of Cinematic Style', *Screen* 36/4, 371–93.
Smith, Andrew and William Hughes (2009), 'Introduction: Defining the EcoGothic', in Andrew Smith and William Hughes (eds), *EcoGothic* (Manchester: Manchester University Press), 1–14.
Windisch, Wolfgang (1994), 'Über Natur an der Mur', in *Ideen für eine Stadt am Fluss: 1. Murenquête* (Graz: Amt für Stadtentwicklung und Stadterhaltung), 25–6.
Wood, Robin (2003), *Hollywood from Vietnam to Regan . . . and Beyond: Expanded and Revised Edition* (New York: Columbia University Press).

FILMOGRAPHY

Das Ding aus der Mur (David Hehn 2012)
Das Ding aus der Mur: Zero (David Hehn 2015)

8. WITHER THE PRESENT, WITHER THE PAST: THE LOW-BUDGET GOTHIC HORROR OF STOCKHOLM SYNDROME FILMS

Johan Höglund

DE-PARADISING NORDIC HISTORY AND THE WELFARE STATE

Since the turn of the millennium, a number of historical, cultural and sociological investigations have participated in a systematic critique of Nordic history. This has included the nations' colonial histories, their welfare projects, and the systems and discourses that organise contemporary Nordic societies. Magdalena Naum and Jonas M. Nordin show, in the Introduction to *Scandinavian Colonialism and the Rise of Modernity: Small Time Agents in a Global Arena* (2013), how the Nordic nations were active partners in early colonial enterprises such as the transatlantic slave trade and the colonisation of North America, India and Africa. Special attention is also given to how the nations that make up contemporary Scandinavia colonised the northern territory referred to as Sampi and inhabited by the indigenous Saami. Kristín Loftsdóttir and Lars Jensen's collection *Whiteness and Postcolonialism in the Nordic Region: Exceptionalism, Migrant Others and National Identities* (2012) discusses the function of racist discourse and the centrality of whiteness both during the colonial era and in the present postcolonial moment. In *Complying with Colonialism: Gender, Race and Ethnicity in the Nordic Region* (2009), Keskinen and others observe that while the Nordic nations may have perceived themselves as 'outsiders in relation to colonial power relations', they are still 'marked, both culturally and economically, by colonial relations' (Keskinen et al. 2009, 1). In addition, Witoszek and Trädgårdh argue, in

Culture and Crisis: The Case of Germany and Sweden (2002), that while Germany and Sweden certainly took different paths in the 1920 and 1930s, powerful actors within the Nordic nations aided the invention of eugenics and the construction of racist ideologies, as well as the rise of Fascism and Nazism in the twentieth century. Thus, Sweden cannot be said to inhabit the position of 'the moral summit of the western world' (Witoszek and Trädgårdh 2002, 2) as has sometimes been claimed.

The image of Sweden as existing outside the destructive historical and ideological mechanisms of the West is also being dismantled in critically acclaimed literature such as Mattias Hagberg's *Rekviem för en Vanskapt* (2012), Ola Larsmo's *Swede Hollow* (2016) and Torbjörn Flygt's *Underdog* (2001), and in Scandinavian arthouse cinema such as Amanda Kernell's *Sami Blood* (*Sameblod*, 2016), Lukas Moodysson's *Lilja 4 Ever* (2002) and Roy Andersson's *Songs from the Second Floor* (*Sånger från andra våningen* 2000). These novels and films rethink and rewrite Nordic history, the Nordic nations' relationship to the global and the understanding of the Nordic welfare project. All in all, they question a general faith in what can be termed Nordic Exceptionalism.

The critical investigation of Nordic history and society that the academic scholarship, literature and arthouse cinema mentioned here engage in has been widely disseminated also by the genre known as Nordic Noir or Nordic Crime. Since the 1970s, this genre has questioned the image of Scandinavia as a socialist welfare utopia relatively free of the organised crime and the erratic psychopathic violence that haunt other countries and regions. Importantly, Nordic Noir rarely collapses into invasion narratives that attribute brutal criminality to outside influences. Even though Eastern European mafias and fundamentalist terrorism feature in Nordic Noir, the genre typically locates the criminal threat in the Nordic nation's own history and welfare project. In the words of Daniel Brodén, Nordic Noir highlights the 'dark aspects of the welfare state model' by portraying 'violence and human darkness as "normal" parts of contemporary life' (Brodén 2008, n.p.).

The identification of, and narrative focus on, modernity's dark aspects are, of course, central to Gothic. In *Empire and the Gothic*, Smith and Hughes describe the early Gothic novel as characterised by an anti-Enlightenment fervour (2003, 3). This fervour makes visible, albeit in twisted and metaphorical ways, how Enlightenment societies have aided in the production of terror by casting the human as a disposable cog in a machine tasked with furthering modernity through industrialisation, capitalism and colonialism. This potential of Gothic to interrogate modernity as both process and discourse is arguably one of the most important reasons why the form has grown in stature over the years, why it has reached far beyond the geographical confines of Britain, and why it has infiltrated a plethora of other genres and media, including Nordic Noir as discussed above.

Understanding Gothic as a mode capable of detecting and dismantling an uncritical faith in modernity and the modern state, this chapter argues that new low-budget Nordic horror film is a form of Gothic horror cinema engaged in an interrogation of Nordic history that is similar to that conducted by contemporary literature, film and scholarship. Indeed, it is horror film that has made the most provocative, disturbing and visceral use of the Gothic mode. As discussed in the introduction to this book, horror cinema can be said to grow out of a number of seminal Gothic narratives through influential films such as *Nosferatu* (1922), *Dracula* (1931) and *Frankenstein* (1931). At the same time, horror cinema, especially of the mainstream variety, tends to defend, rather than dismantle, modernity, the nation state and normative constructions of gender and race. It is through returning to Gothic's refusal to uncritically embrace modernity and normativity that (in particular low-budget) horror cinema has been able to revitalise itself during the past century. Thus, movies such as *Night of the Living Dead* (1968) and *The Texas Chainsaw Massacre* (1974) tell Gothic stories precisely because they bring into focus the violence inherent in normative, capitalist society.

The material studied in this chapter is the violent low-budget horror movies from the Swedish production company Stockholm Syndrome Film and co-directors Sonny Laguna, Tommy Wiklund and David Liljeblad. The argument is that the terror that rises to rend bodies asunder in Stockholm Syndrome Film's productions must be understood in relation to a complex and suppressed Swedish historical past. However, that does not mean that these films simply follow in the provocative path of *Night of the Living Dead* or *The Texas Chainsaw Massacre*. As I will discuss, these films do not necessarily offer a sustained critique of colonialism, racism and the patriarchal discourses, even if they enable such a critique. It is thus possible to read these films in two divergent ways. The first reading understands these films as deeply conservative celebrations and a commodification of the spectacle of violence that arises when the core values of Nordic exceptionalism are declared void. The second reading positions these values as part of an inquisitive and provocative Gothic tradition that insists on displaying the abject death and destruction that has always accompanied modernity. In this way, these movies straddle the border that tentatively separates Gothic from normative horror.

As of early 2017, Stockholm Syndrome Film has released four feature-length productions: *Madness* (2010), *Blood Runs Cold* (2011), *Wither* (*Vittra*, 2012) and *We Are Monsters* (2014). Although these films use Swedish actors and were filmed in Sweden, only *Madness* and *Wither* engage directly with Nordic characters and geographies. *Madness* takes place in Minnesota and involves a small Swedish community that lives there, while *Wither* is entirely set in Sweden. *Blood Runs Cold* and *We Are Monsters* also employ Swedish actors, but because the locations are international and the scripts are in English, the connection to the Nordic region and society is more tenuous. Thus, this chapter focuses on *Madness* and *Wither* and discusses the other films only in passing.

A SHORT HISTORY OF NORDIC HORROR FILM

Whereas Nordic Noir has received significant and international scholarly attention, low-budget Nordic horror cinema has been subjected to scarce but enthusiastic critique. The existing body of work on this genre in Scandinavia includes work by Yvonne Leffler (2014), Tommy Gustavsson (2015), Gunnar Iversen (2016), Pietari Kääpä (2014) and Jo Sondre Moseng and Håvard Vibeto (2011). Most of these scholars discuss Nordic low-budget horror film as growing out of a local cinematic tradition. However, this very tradition, as well as low-budget horror is general, is perceived as being in constant conversation with a growing body of English-speaking films.

To turn first to the development of local, Scandinavian cinema, Victor Sjöström's *Körkarlen* (*The Phantom Carriage*, 1921), based on Nobel prize laureate Selma Lagerlöf's novel of the same name, is commonly understood as its auspicious beginning. As Yvonne Leffler observes in 'The Devious Landscape of Scandinavian Horror', both Lagerlöf's original novel and Sjöström's adaptation are fundamentally Gothic narratives that revolve around confrontation with past wrongs in the face of immanent death (2013, 143). *The Phantom Carriage* has also served as inspiration for a number of successful horror films, including Stanley Kubrik's *The Shining* (1980). However, it is most often discussed in Scandinavian film studies for having influenced director Ingmar Bergman early work (Cinquegrani 2015, 130). Bergman's own medieval sagas *Det Sjunde Inseglet* (*The Seventh Seal*, 1957) and *Jungfrukällan* (*The Virgin Spring*, 1960) are certainly also a type of bleak and notably Gothic horror cinema, containing powerful, graphic and violent scenes of death, rape, murder and revenge. As Bergman continued his career, he did not drop his interest in the horrific and his *Persona* (1966) and *Vargtimmen* (*The Hour of the Wolf*, 1968) have been described as commanding works of modernist horror (Michaels 2000, 17). Both the practical horror of Bergman's early films and the psychological horror of his later productions constitute an internationally acclaimed, well-funded, artistic and provocative body of films that lack the popular address associated with Gothic, but which converge on the same disturbing explorations of the human psyche and critique of modern society. However, Bergman's oeuvre did not form a foundation for a growing horror tradition in Scandinavia. It was arguably not until Lars von Trier's provocative and deeply psychological *Antichrist*, a movie recognised for its affinities with Gothic (Murphy 2013), was released in 2009 that this particular tradition was effectively continued in the Nordic region.

If the cultured and critically acclaimed horror that finds its most authoritative voice in Bergman's modernist cinema is one beginning for Nordic horror film, the other has fewer ties to Scandinavian culture and cinematic tradition. This looks westward, towards the less artful, but more normative and commercially viable and sensational, B-movie Gothic horror produced in the USA for large youth audiences. The first such movie is *Rymdinvasion i Lappland (Invasion of the Animal People, Terror in the Midnight Sun*, 1959), and it takes its cue from the post-Second World War wave of creature feature and alien invasion films that brought huge crowds to the drive-in theatres in the USA. As with many movies after it, the script and some of the actors are English in order to reach beyond the relatively small audiences of Scandinavia. This first Swedish horror B-movie ticks all the boxes with flimsy alien props, a gigantic destructive monster, a lurid shower scene and a square-jawed, white, male hero, but it spawned very few followers. Another attempt to introduce the US low-budget paradigm into Sweden occurred in the 1980s when the slasher and gore genres were popular, the most notable being *Blödaren* (*The Bleeder*, 1983). However, the absence of powerful private film studios, the reluctance of the Scandinavian film institutes to fund genre movies, and, as argued by Tommy Gustavsson, film censorship, made nation-wide production and distribution of violent horror movies difficult. The costly apparatus needed to film, edit and distribute film during the pre-digital era prevented the production of all but a few Nordic horror movies. As Gustavsson also observes, the ones that did get produced generally avoided taking themselves very seriously and are intentionally or unintentionally comical (2015, 191).

The end of film censorship in Scandinavia in the late 1990s and early 2000s, along with the revolution in digital filmmaking, paved the way for a renaissance of Nordic horror cinema (Gustavsson 2015, 191). Despite small budgets, the digital format made it possible to create movies with reasonably high production values. The digital revolution thus gave rise to a new generation of filmmakers who started to create horror films at the beginning of the new millennium. This has resulted in a major rise in the number of low-budget, horror feature films produced in Scandinavia. Of the 139 Swedish feature films labelled as horror by IMDB, only 26 were made before the year 2000, and a total of 60 were produced before 2010. More than half of all Swedish horror movies have thus been produced since 2010.

A studio that has taken advantage of the opportunities of the new format is Stockholm Syndrome Film (SSF). Its four full-length horror movies to date have been made on microscopic budgets and they rarely stray from the inspiration supplied by classic B-movie horror films such as *The Texas Chainsaw Massacre* (1978), *I Spit on Your Grave* (1978) and *Evil Dead* (1981), films that have sometimes been labelled as sadistic and misogynist celebrations of violence, and, as argued by Robin Wood, sometimes as troubling Gothic sagas about the sadism and misogyny inherent in contemporary capitalist society (Wood 1984, 189). In addition to this, SSF clearly pays homage also to a more recent horror genre which has been termed 'torture porn' by its detractors and 'spectacle horror' by its supporters and which includes films like *Saw* (2004) and *Hostel* (2005). While the first efforts of SSF, *Madness* and *Blood Runs Cold*, make some use of the comic relief common to the low-budget slasher or gore movie, the studio's latter efforts *Wither* and *We Are Monsters* revolve around much more realistic and bleak scenes of horror. The focus on the visual destruction of the human body that characterises these later films prompts the characterisation of these movies as either spectacle horror or torture porn. These two terms in themselves signal the precarious nature of modern low-budget film. If described as torture porn as defined by film critic David Edelstein, these films are simply exercises in explicit violence catering to a cynical audience that gets off on the abject suffering of others (Edelstein 2006). If understood as spectacle horror as defined by Adam Lowenstein (2011), these films can be viewed as an extreme form of what Xavier Aldana Reyes has called body Gothic (Aldana Reyes 2014; Lowenstein 2011). As described, this article will discuss SSF's movies as both spectacular, micro-budget body Gothic in conversation with a certain vision of Swedish history and as deplorable and fundamentally misogynist torture porn to which history serves as mere background.

Madness: The Swedish Emigrant Myth Eviscerated

SSF's first full feature horror film, *Madness*, was made on a tiny budget and massive enthusiasm. In the hopes of some kind of distribution in the USA, the film purportedly takes place in the USA but was actually shot in Sweden with Swedish actors who awkwardly deliver the English script. Few reviewers of the film failed to notice the imperfect accents and observe that they create an unintentional comic effect. The reviewers also complain that the general storyline has already been rehashed by hundreds of horror films since seminal low-budget Gothic horror movies such as Wes Craven's *The Hills Have Eyes* (1977) and Hooper's aforementioned *The Texas Chain Saw Massacre*. Like many micro-budget imitations of Craven and Hooper's films, *Madness* revolves around a group of young, white people who are taken prisoners, mutilated, tortured and murdered by a group of incoherent, rural psychopaths. While several people are either killed or seen as dead bodies in the film, the main victims are two cheerleaders and two young men. The cheerleaders are travelling to a competition in their costumes and with no luggage other than their pompoms. At a gas station, a site that typically serves as the entryway into horror in low-budget horror film, they meet the young men whose car has broken down. Squeezed into a small Volkswagen, the only vehicle with a US licence plate in the film, they take off down Swedish country roads posing as US highways. Before the four people can move beyond a first causal flirtation, the car is brought to a sudden halt when one of the villains throws a small animal onto the windscreen of the car. The group is brought to the farm and the film then ticks off a series of obligatory low-budget movie horror scenes, including the sometimes brutal abuse of the captured men and women, the disposal of dead bodies incidental to the plot, the confused escape of the victims from their strangely inept captors, a number of seemingly un-choreographed fight scenes, and the killing of both victims and perpetrators until the survivors (in this case the remaining boy and girl) are free to limp back towards civilisation.

What sets this movie apart from the countless other low-budget horror films is, most importantly for this chapter, that the action is located somewhere 'near Minneapolis, May 3rd, 1994', and that the film's villains, three of whom are played by the film's three co-directors, often drop English and speak a growly but otherwise perfect and un-subtitled Swedish to each other. This may simply be a way for the directors to appeal to a general xenophobia in its audience. However, the Minnesota setting and the villains who speak Swedish also connect the film to a particular sequence of Swedish and Nordic history, and to the myths that the writing of this history has encouraged.

This history and its mythologies revolve around the great exodus from Sweden to the USA that occurred between 1841 and 1920. Impoverished by King Charles XII's unsuccessful bid for Swedish dominance of northern Europe in the early eighteenth century, as well as by underdeveloped industry and years of mismanaged and failed harvests, Swedish farmers began leaving for the USA in the early 1840s with hopes of a better future. At least 1.3 million Swedes travelled across the Atlantic in the years that followed. The Swedish emigrant experience was similar to that of many other non-Anglophone, white, protestant European migrants, but in Swedish popular history, the Swedish emigrant was given a particular shape through the hard-working characters of Vilhelm Moberg's *Emigrant* novels published between 1949 and 1959.

The four novels that make up this series, *Utvandrarna* (*The Emigrants*, 1949), *Invandrarna* (*The Immigrants/Unto a Good Land*, 1952), *Nybyggarna* (*The Settlers*, 1956) and *Sista brevet till Sverige* (*The Last Letter to Sweden*, 1959), have sold 2 million copies in Sweden and *The Emigrants* was voted the greatest Swedish novel of the twentieth century. The story is rugged and realistic, and does not shy away from describing scenes of abject violence, including brutal confrontations between Native Americans and Swedish farmers. At the same time, the series still provides an image of the emigrant Swede as a brave traveller as well as a morally just and masculine worker. The central characters are the poor farmers Karl-Oskar and Kristina, who decide to abandon their native Sweden for the USA when their strenuous efforts at farming the arid land fail to provide for their growing family. Settling with other Swedes in

STOCKHOLM SYNDROME FILMS

Figure 8.1 Promotional poster showing the Swedish villains of *Madness* (2010). Image courtesy of Stockholm Syndrome Film

Minnesota, they manage to make a new life for themselves, working hard, struggling to keep their own culture alive while at the same time integrating with Anglo-US society. In the 1970s, the novels were turned into a number of state-sponsored films featuring major Swedish actors of the period. Since then the myth has acquired a life of its own, encouraging a national understanding of the Swedish emigrant as somehow exceptional and in many ways unrelated to other forms of migration out of, or into, Sweden. In their most recent and very successful incarnation, *Kristina från Duvemåla*, the novels take the form of a musical with a score written by Benny Andersson and Björn Ulvaeus of ABBA.

There are several notable similarities between *Madness* and Moberg's fiction. The film is purportedly set in rural Minnesota, the same location as *The Emigrants*. Because the villains speak Swedish it is easy to assume that they are descendants of Swedish migrants. In addition to this, one of the Swedish villains in the film is named Aaron, which is also the name of a sadistic farmer in Moberg's first novel in the series. In view of these similarities, it is significant that the film's action tells an anti-Moberg narrative that destroys the myth of the Swedish migrant as diligent farmer and nation builder. The film begins with the suggestive warning that 2,000 people disappear in the USA every day and that not all are found. In the film, the five Swedish-speaking farmers seem accountable for a large share of those unresolved disappearances. They torture, abuse and kill people with a strange determination combined with baffling incompetence. They are sexual predators who prey on men as well as on women (the film features a rare scene of male rape censored for the US DVD release) and in a few scenes it is suggested they eat their victims, even if most dead bodies seem to be thrown haphazardly into a nearby lake.

The film's connection to Swedish migrant history mostly likely developed out of necessity. One of the few ways to make sense out of Swedish-speaking actors in a film purportedly set in the USA is to place the action in Minnesota with its large Swedish heritage. Even so, the film remains an attempt to evoke an image of the North American Swede as a serial-killing, brutal, rural monster who is similar to the degenerate Hillbilly of *Deliverance* (1972) or *The Hills Have Eyes*. The fact that the Swedish clan prefer to speak Swedish to each other suggests an unwillingness to assimilate into the US community represented by the victims. Moreover, the villains' Swedishness is linked to their brutality and violent natures, something that negates the understanding of the Swedish migrant as morally just and hard-working.

The myth of the Swedish emigrant in the wake of Moberg's fiction is, in fact, being contested by current historical research and in new fictions about the Swedish exodus to North America. Swedish writer Larsmo's novel *Swede Hollow* describes the destinies of several Swedish migrants living in a shantytown located in a ravine outside St. Paul, Minnesota. The Swedes of *Swede*

Hollow are at the bottom of, or even outside of, society. They struggle to keep their lives together, and while they have personal dreams not entirely dissimilar to those of the thrifty migrants of Moberg's fiction, their dreams are not realised. Poor and without prospects, they violently attack other migrant groups and the disenfranchised black population. One of the most horrific scenes of the novel is a lynching sequence. At the same time, the migrant Swedes of the story are also subjected to violence.

Madness and *Swede Hollow* are widely dissimilar texts made for very different audiences. The violence conducted by and on Swedish immigrants in *Swede Hollow* is realistic and historically documented and aimed at a socially and historically conscious reader. By contrast, the brutally violent attacks by the Swedish-American farmers in *Madness* are absurdly hyperbolic. Even so, the violence on display in *Madness* and that described in *Swede Hollow* serves a similar purpose. In these two texts, the depiction of the Swedish migrant collapses the myth of the hard-working, productive and morally exceptional individual and thus challenges one of the central mythologies of Swedish history. It can even be argued that *Madness* accidentally offers the most radical critique of this myth by replacing Karl-Oskar and Kristina not simply with social outcasts, but with monsters.

Wither: Underground Gendered Pasts

Madness's spectacularly low budget is seen in all aspects of the film, but it is most apparent in how the Swedish actors struggle to overcome their Swedish/British accents when delivering the script's English dialogue. SSF's third film, *Vittra* or *Wither*, departs from this first effort by being set in Sweden and by allowing the Swedish actors to speak their native language. In addition, *Wither* includes the well-known Swedish actor Johannes Brost, dramatically increasing the star power and production value of the film. While *Wither* is certainly still a micro-budget film, it is a significantly more polished work and succeeds in being frightening and gruesome in ways that *Madness* and SSF's second film *Blood Runs Cold* do not. At 5.0, the film also has the highest IMBD rating of all SSF's movies, including *We Are Monsters*.

Wither (a.k.a. *Cabin of the Dead*) opens with a prologue showing a man in hunting gear and armed with a rifle, shouting and disorientedly walking through a wet forest. He suddenly comes across a woman bent over a shivering young girl, apparently feeding off the girl's bleeding throat. He shouts at the woman to stop and eventually shoots her in the head, only to see her body rise again from the moss. In the next sequence, seven young friends drive out to spend the weekend in an old cabin in the woods. Because they have no key, one of the young women must climb in through the window. Inside, she discovers a light emanating from a hatch in the floor. She opens the hatch, which leads down into a low-ceilinged, dusty stone basement, a familiar setting in low-budget horror. At first, she is excited and explores the small space: tools and jars sit on a work bench, an axe is covered in white grime, a light bulb casts a harsh glare. The young woman then hears a noise from a strangely dark corner of the room and walks cautiously towards it. What she encounters is shown a few minutes later as she has begun drinking with her friends: an impossibly wrinkled and haggard visage materialises out of the blackness and hisses at her. This creature, we are told later in the movie, is a Vittra (a.k.a. Vættr or Weight), a being from Nordic folklore. In this movie, she serves the same purpose as the Babylonian Book of the Dead in Sam Rami's *Evil Dead*, a film which *Wither* joyfully cannibalises.

The Swedish word 'Vittra' has two meanings. As discussed, it is a name long used for a creature of Nordic folklore. However, the word also means 'wither', as in the English title, and this word expands into a plethora of possible readings. After the first girl has been infected by the stare of the Vittra, her body withers, she begins to bleed from her mouth, eyes and scrotum. Her psyche withers in similar ways; she loses her speech and intellectual faculties and, as in the typical low-budget zombie flick, becomes little more than a voracious, flesh-eating carrier of the strange, supernatural contagion she now carries. Those bitten by her soon display the same deterioration of body and mind.

In addition to this, what withers in this film is also the notion that Sweden's history has been characterised by a stable and controlled movement from rural primitivism towards an exceptionally modern, democratic welfare state. In relation to this, the film lets wither the idea that the welfare state is capable of saving the nation and its citizens from the many horrors that have haunted global society, as well as the US cinematic imagination, for decades. Finally, and most importantly, the film withers the notion that Sweden is a gender-equal society that is not plagued by violent misogyny.

The Vittra, hiding in the cellar of the forgotten cabin in the woods, is the primary instrument of this withering. According to Nordic legend, the Vittra is a female creature of the forest living close to people and sometimes interacting, or even cohabiting, with humans. While this creature could spread disease and misfortune if treated poorly, it is typically not a violent and aggressive entity. In many stories, its shape is remarkably beautiful (Bane 2016, 155–6). According to legend, it is possible to live in harmony with the Vittra as long as her needs, and the needs of the nature she protects, are respected. *Wither* rewrites this myth of a human–nature balance, which is also the myth of a displaced male–female balance. The Vittra emerges from the cabin to curse and destroy the people who have invaded her territory. Perhaps the rural Swedish community was never capable of living close to these indigenous creatures, or perhaps something has been irretrievably lost so that this is now impossible. In any case, the humans who intrude are not people with whom the Vittra

Figure 8.2 Poster for *Wither/Vittra* (2012). Image courtesy of Stockholm Syndrome Film.

can coexist; they are forced to destroy each other. Thus, the girl who has been bleeding on the toilet rises with the milky-white eyes of the zombie, walks out to the group and proceeds to bite off a section of the face of one of her friends.

The sight of the transformed girl, the dark blood covering her face and body, the mutilated friend who has fainted from the pain and shock, solicit screams from the rest of the group. For a few seconds, nobody seems to know what to do. Then, one of the young men in the group reacts by furiously beating the infected girl to the ground, straddles her body and proceeds to pound her face in a disturbing display of frantic violence. This is one of many scenes where women are brutalised in the film and several of the reviewers have reacted to the constant violence that the men in the film perpetrate. In the words of the reviewer Malachi at Cinapse.co:

> *Wither* is 95 minutes of males brutalizing females for the delight of ... who the fuck knows. The misogyny on display here is hostile and deeply seeded. There is nothing during the entirety of the film's runtime to suggest that the acts committed were done with any sort of reflection upon the brutality within. Here, we get emotionally complex men dying with dignity, while the women around them are subject to profoundly violent savagery, severed limbs, face smashings, decapitations and a hearty wrought-iron skull fucking. (Malachi 2013)

There is certainly some merit to this harsh judgement of the film. However, violence against women in horror movies need not be thought of as automatically a ritual in misogyny. Carol J. Clover has influentially argued in *Men, Women and Chain Saws: Gender in the Modern Horror Film* (1992) that in the slasher or gore movie, the person termed the 'final girl' by Clover often succeeds in vanquishing the serial-killing male by the end of the film. Thus, Clover argues, these movies record the destructive epistemological and ontological violence practised by patriarchal society, but they conclude with a reversal of this social order, for the female heroine destroys, at least temporarily, the monstrous symbol of male power.

However, it can be argued that this model does not apply to *Wither*. In this film, the monster is not the grotesque male serial killer of *Halloween* (1978), *The Texas Chainsaw Massacre* or *The Girl with the Dragon Tattoo*. Instead, what rises from the basement of the movie's supremely oneiric house is an ancient female creature. This female climbs out of her refuge only to be knifed to death by the only person left standing: the boy who has just killed the final girl by dropping a large bookshelf on top of her. The presence of a female killer and the survival of a final boy, rather than a final girl, thus deprive the film of the ending that Clover understands as potentially liberating. Even so, the male violence of the film can be perhaps be read as an attempt to disturb patriarchy precisely by putting its destructive force on display. In such a reading, the survival of the final boy is a further indictment of the destructive power of male-dominated society; it is a tragic and revelatory culmination in contrast to the forced happy ending of a final girl survivor.

Regardless of whether *Wither* is understood as a sadistic fantasy of male power or a uniquely subversive narrative that displays the enduring and monstrous violence of patriarchy, it graphically and repeatedly portrays extreme violence against women. It can even be argued that women have never been exposed to such graphic violence in any previous Swedish-language film. Thus, *Wither* disturbs one of the central myths of Sweden and the Nordic nations: that Sweden is one of the most gender-equal nations and that misogyny is not allowed the free rein that makes extreme violence against women generally representable. In other words, *Wither*'s portrayal of gruesome violence against women identifies in itself an important representational rupture. Regardless of whether it is misogynist or not, the film constitutes a challenge to the image of Sweden as a refuge from misogynistic violence in practice and in representation.

The depiction of violence against women in *Wither* also casts a deep and troubling shadow over the Swedish welfare state (often referred to in Sweden as the 'people's home' or '*folkhemmet*'). Since the 1920s, this socialist 'people's home' has been tasked with the duty to educate, take care of and protect its citizens. The violence in the film thus also indicates a general failure of this vision of society. When the first infected girl has been violently subdued and sits tied to a door, bleeding, growling and frantic with aggression, the other members of the group debate what they should do with her. The obvious resolution seems to be to call the authorities and thus to enlist the assistance of the welfare state. However, the hunter who has entered the cabin explains that calling an ambulance is not an option. His grandfather has explained that the illness that the Vittra spreads is sudden and violent, and that they may all be infected. In addition to this, he has just seen his wife feed off the bleeding throat of his daughter and then shot her repeatedly. 'A doctor cannot do anything about this', he shouts at the infected girl's desperate friends. This is a horror that the welfare state cannot prevent or fix. They have to 'get rid of' the frantic, bleeding girl, he explains, preferably by burning her body. The friends refuse, of course, and insist on calling the authorities, but they never arrive. If they did, they would in any case be helpless against this particular eruption of violence. The only remedy, within the film's universe, is the primitive and savage solution associated with pre-modernity: to kill everyone and everything. To burn the house to the ground and to thus obliterate both the present threat and the history from which it has arisen.

Sweden Withered

In *Culture, Health, and Religion at the Millennium: Sweden Unparadised* (2014), editors Marie Demker, Yvonne Leffler and Ola Sigurdson observe that the 'reader or cinephile who has long associated Sweden with images of an affluent, complacent, and homogeneous society' will be surprised when confronted with stories of 'corruption, sexual violence, bureaucracy in the service of corrupt powers, and revenge' found in Larsson's *Millennium Trilogy* (2). The book is an attempt to discuss how 'the image of Sweden has undergone a transformation from that of a well-functioning but existentially bland economic wonder into a more pluralistic, fragmented, and – perhaps – gloomy society' (2014, 2). The chapters that make up the collection investigate a general sense of melancholia and gloom which pervades much Swedish culture in recent years and which can be related to both a radical rethinking of the premises of Swedish modernity and to the current state of the Swedish welfare model.

Madness and *Wither* should be related to the same disillusionment with homogeneous narratives of Sweden's past and present as those investigated in *Culture, Health, and Religion at the Millennium*. However, these films take this sense of social collapse to new extremes. The violence that forms the impetus to restore order in Nordic Noir is the constant focus of Stockholm Syndrome Film's productions. The cinephile perhaps captivated by Lisbeth Salander's righteous attempt to find the male serial killer who has tortured and murdered women in his basement in *The Girl with the Dragon Tattoo* is, in all of SSF's films, distracted by the prolonged representation of the abuse that has taken place in that locale. Rather than being asked to reflect on how to understand and perhaps amend a collapsing society, the audiences of *Madness* and *Wither* are encouraged to enjoy the collapse as such.

It is unlikely that SSF is aware of its challenge to the myths of Swedish social coherence or of its part in the rewriting of Swedish and Nordic history. No interview or close reading of SSF's films suggest such an awareness. Rather, the studio is motivated by a need to place its narratives within a historical and discursive context that allows the graphic violence the producers are interested in showcasing to make sense. Set against a Sweden free from historical guilt and devoid of socially grounded evil, the violence does not make any sense. However, if the violence is located not outside but within the historical and discursive border of patriarchy, and if this violence is seen as part of a cruel project of modernity that is not very different from that which enabled, and was enabled by, the slave trade, the scrambles for Africa and Asia and the genocide indigenous populations, the violence can be contextualised and understood.

From this perspective, what makes *Madness* and *Wither* important is not that they are able to effectively theorise this relationship, but rather that the violence that they depict, and commodify, makes the most sense when understood in relation to a general rethinking of Swedish and Scandinavian history and social relations. *Madness* and *Wither* are intuitive narratives about a region in historical and social flux. These films are a combination of several competing and concurrent desires, one of which is to have SSF's work received as a form of independent US horror. This aspiration creates a connection between *Madness* and *Wither* and the interrogation that independent US Gothic horror is involved in; an interrogation that highlights through gothic allegory the nation's long history of violence against its own and other indigenous populations, against the slaves brought from Africa, and against the nations that resisted and resist the spreading of US capitalism. It is by retelling such stories as *The Texas Chainsaw Massacre* in Swedish, for a Swedish audience, and within a Swedish or partly Swedish context, that these films, perhaps accidentally, show Sweden and Swedish history as also plagued by destructive violence and by the discourses that make such violence legitimate. Thus, *Madness* and *Wither* understand horror as arising out of Sweden's historical past and social present, out of the nations' forests and mythologies, even out of the welfare state itself.

BIBLIOGRAPHY

Aldana Reyes, Xavier (2014), *Body Gothic: Corporeal Transgression in Contemporary Literature and Horror Film* (Cardiff: University of Wales Press).
Bane, Theresa (2016), *Encyclopedia of Giants and Humanoids in Myth, Legend and Folklore* (Jefferson, NC: McFarland).
Brodén, Daniel (2008), *Folkhemmets Skuggbilder: En Kulturanalytisk Genrestudie av Svensk Kriminalfiktion i Film och TV*, doctoral diss. (Göteborg: Ekholm & Tegebjer Förlag).
Clover, Carol J. (1992), *Men, Women and Chain Saws: Gender in the Modern Horror Film* (Princeton, NJ: Princeton University Press).
Cinquegrani, Maurizio (2015), 'Shadows of Shadows: The Undead in Ingmar Bergman's Cinema', in Murray Leeder (ed.), *Cinematic Ghosts: Haunting and Spectrality from Silent Cinema to the Digital Era* (New York: Bloomsbury Academic).
Demker, Marie, Yvonne Leffler and Ola Sigurdson (2014), *Culture, Health, and Religion at the Millennium: Sweden Unparadised* (Basingstoke: Palgrave Macmillan).
Edelstein, David (2006), 'Now Playing at Your Local Multiplex: Torture Porn', *New York Magazine*, 39/4, <http://nymag.com/movies/features/15622/> (last accessed 3 November 2017).
Gustavsson, Tommy (2015), 'Slasher in the Snow: The Rise of the Low-Budget Nordic Horror Film', in Tommy Gustafsson and Pietari Kääpä (eds), *Nordic Genre Film: Small Nation Film Cultures in the Global Marketplace* (Edinburgh: Edinburgh University Press), 189–202.
Iversen, Gunnar (2016), 'Between Art and Genre: New Nordic Horror Cinema', in Mette Hjort and Ursula Lindqvist (eds), *A Companion to Nordic Cinema* (Chichester: Wiley Blackwell).
Keskinen, Suvi, Salla Tuori, Sari Irni and Diana Mulinari (2009), 'Introduction: Postcolonialism and the Nordic Models of Welfare and Gender', in Suvi Keskinen,

Salla Tuori, Sari Irni and Diana Mulinari (eds), *Complying with Colonialism: Gender, Race and Ethnicity in the Nordic Region* (London: Routledge).

Kääpä, Pietari (2014), *Ecology and Contemporary Nordic Cinemas: From Nation-building to Ecocosmopolitanism* (London: Bloomsbury).

Leffler, Yvonne (2013), 'The Devious Landscape of Scandinavian Horror', in P. M. Mehtonen and Matti Savolainen (eds), *Gothic Topographies: Language, Nation Building and 'Race'* (London: Routledge), 141–52.

Leffler, Yvonne (2014), '"Nature is the Church of Satan": The Gothic Topography in Contemporary Scandinavian Horror Novels and Films', in Agnieszka Łowczanin and Dorota Wiśniewska (eds), *All that Gothic* (Frankfurt am Main: Peter Lang), 110–23.

Loftsdóttir, Kristin and Lars Jensen (2012), 'Nordic Exceptionalism and the Nordic "Others"', in Kristin Loftsdóttir and Lars Jensen (eds), *Whiteness and Postcolonialism in the Nordic Region* (London: Routledge), 1–12.

Lowenstein, Adam (2011), 'Spectacle Horror and Hostel: Why Torture Porn Does Not Exist'. *Critical Quarterly* 53/1, 42–60.

Malachi (2013), 'Wither, or: Actual Misogyny, Not a Comment Thereupon', *Cinapse. co*, <http://cinapse.co/2013/09/05/wither-or-actual-misogyny-not-a-comment-thereupon/> (last accessed 3 November 2017).

Michaels, Lloyd (2000), 'Bergman and the Necessary Illusion: An Introduction to Persona', in Lloyd Michaels (ed.), *Ingmar Bergman's Persona* (Cambridge: Cambridge University Press), 1–23.

Moseng, Jo Sondre and Håvard Vibeto (2011), 'Hunting High and Low: Notes on Nazi Zombies, Francophiles and National Cinema(s)', *Film International*, 9/2, 30–41.

Murphy, Bernice M. (2013), *The Rural Gothic in American Popular Culture: Backwoods Horror and Terror in the Wilderness* (Basingstoke: Palgrave Macmillan).

Naum, Magdalena and Jonas M. Nordin (2013), 'Introduction: Situating Scandinavian Colonialism', in Magdalena Naum and Jonas M. Nordin (eds), *Scandinavian Colonialism and the Rise of Modernity: Small Time Agents in a Global Arena* (New York: Springer), 2–16.

Smith, Andrew and William Hughes (2003), 'Introduction: Enlightenment Gothic and Postcolonialism', in Andrew Smith and William Hughes (eds), *Empire and the Gothic: The Politics of Genre* (Basingstoke: Palgrave Macmillan), 1–12.

Witoszek, Nina and Lars Trädgårdh (2002), 'Introduction', in Nina Witoszek and Lars Trädgårdh (eds), *Culture and Crisis: the Case of Germany and Sweden* (New York: Berghahn).

Wood, Robin (1984), 'An Introduction to the American Horror Film', in Barry Keith Grant (ed.), *Planks of Reason: Essays on the Horror Film* (Metuchen, NJ: Scarecrow Press).

9. TURKISH B-MOVIE GOTHIC: MAKING THE UNDEAD TURKISH IN *ÖLÜLER KONUŞMAZ Kİ*

Tuğçe Bıçakçı Syed

B-movies were once considered 'the Hollywood stepchild, the underbelly of the double feature' and 'the scrambling rat of cinematic innovation' (Sterritt and Anderson 2008, xi). Nevertheless, they constituted the backbone of Turkish cinema from the 1950s onwards and had their heyday in the 1970s. The main sources of B-movies in Turkey were adaptations, or more precisely exploitations, of American and British productions, as copyright law was then non-existent in Turkey. During the adaptation process, the films were *Turkified* in the sense that they were adapted to be culturally relevant for Turkish audiences. The settings would be Istanbul, the characters' Anglophone names would be replaced with Turkish names, and Anglo-American references would be replaced with Turkish equivalents. Also known as *Turksploitation* films worldwide, these movies were shot within a day or two with very low budgets, in limited locations, with unknown actors, using poorly written scripts, ill-assorted costumes and hastily made sets. Although filmmakers used almost no visual effects, genres such as fantasy, science fiction, superhero and Gothic horror were the most popular genres for Turkish B-movies. Technical deficiencies pervaded the industry, and there were often commercial concerns about the cultural and religious differences between Western Gothic conventions and Turkish culture, which made Gothic B-movies the most difficult genre to produce. Yet, perhaps owing to the growing global interest in the genre, Turkish production companies still made films in this genre, though they were limited in number.

From the 1950s up until the 1990s, Gothic tropes were utilised by many genres in Turkish cinema, including sci-fi, parody and melodrama, but four films in particular achieved the classic Gothic atmosphere in Turkish contexts and established a foundational cinematic aesthetic for the Turkish Gothic tradition. As with other B-movies, the common element of these four Gothic films is the emphasis given to the *Turkification* process; that is, the ways in which the filmmakers make the Gothic conventions *Turkish*. *Çığlık* (*The Scream*, 1949) was the first Gothic horror film of Turkish cinema, and, although the film did not survive, the process of Turkification is seen in *Çığlık*'s posters and newspaper advertisements (which I discuss below). In *Drakula İstanbul'da* (*Dracula in Istanbul*, 1953), Turkification is engendered through the shift in time, place and religion; moreover, Mina is depicted as a showgirl who dances in front of an oriental palace setting. In the 1970s, another adaptation, *Şeytan* (*The Devil*, 1974), follows the same pattern: it relocates the plot of William Friedkin's *The Exorcist* (1973) to Istanbul and tailors the themes of the original film to the context of 1970s Turkey when discussions of reinstating traditional Islamic values – which were once suppressed by secular ideologies – escalated.

Ölüler Konuşmaz Ki (*The Dead Don't Talk*, 1970), a fairly unknown Gothic horror film which was found on a dusty shelf in an old film studio in 2001, sheds more light on Turkish B-movie Gothic and the processes of Turkification. This chapter focuses on *Ölüler Konuşmaz Ki* as a quintessential illustration of Turkish Gothic. It is a fascinating example because, although it draws on Western Gothic conventions, it is not based on an Anglo-American plot or story. Rather, it attempts to create a native Gothic atmosphere by reinventing classic Gothic tropes in a Turkish context and hybridising the 'undead' creature by drawing on Turkish and Balkan folklore. *Ölüler Konuşmaz Ki* introduces the earliest scene of Islamic exorcism in a Gothic horror film, developing a motif later which was used in *Şeytan* and which became central to many Turkish Gothic narratives in the twenty-first century. Despite several academic studies of *Drakula İstanbul'da* and *Şeytan*, the absence of detailed analyses of *Ölüler Konuşmaz Ki* indicates a gap in the literature and points to the film's unique place in studies of Gothic in Turkey.

Turkish Film Production: A Very Brief History

Cinema was first introduced to the Ottoman Sultan Abdülhamit II by a French illusionist, Monseigneur Bertrand, in a private screening in the Yıldız Palace in Istanbul in 1896 (Özgüç 1990, 7). For many decades, cinema was controlled by North American and Western European nationals in Turkey and mainly screened for the non-Muslim population in the Pera district of Istanbul (Dönmez-Colin 2008, 22). The first film directed by a Muslim-Turkish Ottoman citizen was a short documentary funded by the military: *Aya Stefanos'taki Rus*

Abidesinin Yıkılışı (The Demolition of the Russian Monument at St Stephan, 1914) (Mutlu 2006, 75–86). During the First World War, the military became involved in film production, making adaptations of early Turkish literature such as *Mürebbiye* (The Governess, 1919) and *Binnaz* (1919) adapted from novels by Hüseyin Rahmi Gürpınar, a popular novelist of the time (Dönmez-Colin 2008, 23). After the foundation of the Republic of Turkey in 1923, film production became a propaganda tool for modern, westernised Turkishness envisioned by the governing elite. Under Muhsin Ertuğrul's one-man leadership, this vision was promoted through films about nationhood, the War of Independence and depictions of heroic military leaders (25). In 1948, the law changed so that municipal revenues reduced taxation on Turkish films, which protected and promoted a national film industry, and cinema quickly became a lucrative investment driven by large audiences (Süner 2010, 3). Accompanied by the 'economic growth, industrialisation and urbanisation' of the 1950s, the Turkish film industry expanded, providing many new opportunities for production companies, directors, scriptwriters and actors (3). The film production companies were mostly located in the Yeşilçam (Green Pine) street of Beyoğlu district in Istanbul, which became an important haunt for new filmmakers and engendered the rise of Yeşilçam (the Turkish Hollywood).

The 1950s also saw the rise of Turkish B-movies. Unlike in the USA, where B-movies emerged out of an industry that was struggling through the Great Depression, Turkish B-movies were a direct result of the over-expansion of the industry (Kuhn and Westwell 2012, 39). The doors of the cinema industry were open to everyone, so films were made with very little equipment. Few people were skilled in lighting or editing, which led to poor production values. (Scognamillo 2010, 111–15). During the 1950s, 553 films were made (mostly melodramas) and twelve of them were genre B-movies, the most popular being Turkified productions such as *Tarzan İstanbul'da* (*Tarzan in Istanbul*, 1952) and *Drakula İstanbul'da* (the first Turkish vampire movie). Visual effects were experimented with for the very first time in *Görünmeyen Adam İstanbul'da* (*The Invisible Man in Istanbul*, 1955) and in the sci-fi B-movie *Uçan Daireler İstanbul'da* (*Flying Saucers in Istanbul*, 1955).

Between the coup d'états of 1960 and 1980, Yeşilçam experienced a golden age despite the political and social problems throughout the country. The progressive constitution of 1961 paved the way for a more hopeful atmosphere within the industry and provided a new experimental platform for many filmmakers (Dönmez-Colin 2008, 36). Some directors took advantage of this freedom and moved towards 'social realism' by discussing previously taboo issues which, according to Gönül Dönmez-Colin, 'reflected the search for identity in a period of rapid transition from traditionalism to modernism' (38). In the meantime, countless B-movies were shot with the 'pile them high, sell them cheap' attitude that engendered 'a cinematographic inflation' (Scognamillo

2010, 160). Some directors were shooting more than one film at the same time and were using scenes from various films interchangeably, which is best illustrated in *Kilink İstanbul'da* (*Killing in İstanbul*, 1967) and *Kilink Uçan Adama Karşı* (*Killing vs. Superman*, 1967). Inspired by an Italian photo comic series, the Turkish Kilink series was a commercial success, earning its makers three times its low budget. The films became the most popular B-movies of the 1960s, resulting in six sequels.

The advent of frequent TV broadcasts in 1968 and the ongoing rise of colour film productions from the mid-1960s had tremendous effects on the films of the subsequent decade. The tension between right-wing and left-wing politics in Turkey, fuelled mainly by university students, moved to the streets, which led to a perception that the streets were unsafe for women and children. TV was then perceived as a safer form of entertainment for families and the film industry was forced to rethink its target audience. This is one reason why Turkish B-movies of the 1970s gravitated towards superhero films and sex comedies that appealed to single working men. The most popular American superhero of the period was Superman, and this was exploited in films such as *Süper Adam* (*Superman*, 1971), *Süper Adam Kadınlar Arasında* (*Superman Among Women*, 1972), *Süper Adam İstanbul'da* (*Superman in Istanbul*, 1972), *Süpermen Dönüyor* (*Superman Returns*, 1979), *Süpermenler* (*Supermen*, 1979) and *Üç Süpermen Olimpiyatlarda* (*Three Supermen in the Olympics*, 1984). While superhero films sexualised women via revealing superhero costumes or by sexually victimising women at the hands of the super villains, the sex comedies included nudity and generated serious controversies among the pro-Islamists, which led to them being suppressed eventually.

In retrospect, the most influential, and globally best-known, B-movie of Turkish cinema is *Dünyayı Kurtaran Adam* (*The Man Who Saved the World*, 1982), also known as *Turkish Star Wars*. Directed by Çetin İnanç, the film combines features of science fiction, adventure and Gothic genres, telling the story of two spaceship pilots who find themselves on a planet governed by an evil wizard. In order to return to Earth, the two pilots wage a battle against the wizard and fight numerous fantastic creatures including ninjas, mummies, skeletons and zombies. Not surprisingly, as an exploitation film *Dünyayı Kurtaran Adam* steals scenes and soundtracks from, among others, *Star Wars: Episode IV – A New Hope* (1977), *Raiders of the Lost Ark* (1981), *Flash Gordon* (1980) and *Moonraker* (1979)(Glaser 2016). Although some footage from the film remained to the present day, the entire film was recently discovered by a cinema enthusiast and producer, Ed Glaser, and will be restored for a DVD release. *Dünyayı Kurtaran Adam* is the 'holy grail of cult films', as Glaser (2016) remarks, and certainly, the epitome of Turksploitation films.

Turkish B-Movie Gothic

The Gothic dimensions of *Dünyayı Kurtaran Adam* and all other Turksploitation films of Yeşilçam have their origins in Turkish Gothic B-movies. In fact, Savaş Arslan considers that the Turkification process is best represented in the Gothic horror texts of Turkish cinema because of these texts' 'attempt to domesticate themes often nonexistent in Turkish culture' (Arslan 2011, 163). However, not all Gothic B-movies were subjected to the Turkification process in the same way, which certainly contributed to the development of a distinctively *Turkish* Gothic tradition.

Çığlık (directed by Aydın Arakon), for instance, the first Turkish Gothic B-movie, differs from its successors in that its plot is not directly adapted from a Western production but draws on those conventions affiliated with Anglo-American Gothic narratives. The film tells the story of a doctor who is stranded on a stormy night in a mansion, where a man drives his young niece to madness over the question of rightful inheritance. As the name of the film suggests, the screams of the victimised girl reverberate with the mysterious and dark atmosphere of the film's aesthetics. According to Scognamillo and

Figure 9.1   The poster for *Çığlık* (Atlas Film, 1949)

Demirhan, upon release the film failed to create suspense, terror or excitement and was thus considered an unsuccessful first attempt at the Gothic horror genre (2005, 63). *Çığlık* is not available today: it was either lost or destroyed in a fire in the building of the production company. However, the posters and the newspaper advertisements for the film have survived, and they tell us much about its promotion and marketing (63). In the newspaper advertisements composed by Atlas Film for the movie's release, *Çığlık* is described as 'a revolutionary film which will keep its audience under its influence for days' and 'a masterpiece of Turkish film-making' (Figure 9.2). In addition, the poster presents the film as 'the great Turkish film' and emphasises the word 'Turkish' by using bold and capitalised letters (Figure 9.1). Clearly, *Çığlık* was not a masterpiece, but Atlas Film tried to market the Gothic as a new national genre that would appeal to Turkish audiences, and, perhaps unintentionally, laid the foundations of Turkish Gothic.

Another masterpiece of Turksploitation films, *Drakula İstanbul'da* (directed by Mehmet Muhtar), was the only Turkish Gothic film which had a box-office success and a healthy budget compared to *Çığlık* and other B-movies of the time. The producer, Turgut Demirağ, states the following about the production of the film: 'The shooting took seven weeks and all indoor scenes and a few outdoor ones were shot on a set' (Scognamillo and Demirhan 2005, 64). The art director of the film, Sohban Koloğlu, asserts that he and the crew 'made an extra effort for the bats and armour, for Dracula's downhill scrambling, and for the model of Dracula's castle' (66). The movie was adapted directly from Turkish novelist Ali Rıza Seyfi's literary adaptation of Bram Stoker's *Dracula* (1897), entitled *Kazıklı Voyvoda* (*Vlad the Impaler*, 1928), and yet Seyfi's nationalistic subtext in the novel is erased from the film. Nevertheless, *Drakula İstanbul'da* draws on Turkish identity in significant ways, but Mina's bellydancing in front of a palace setting is perhaps the most striking Turkification detail in the film. Inspired by Stoker's novel and Tod Browning's 1931 film version, *Drakula İstanbul'da* includes the classical Gothic aesthetics in an Islamic context for the first time in Turkish cinema and in a worldwide *Dracula* adaptation. Additionally, several critics have pointed out that the historic and aesthetic links between Vlad Tepeş and Dracula in *Drakula İstanbul'da* were unprecedented at its time (Silver and Ursini 1997, 155; Joslin 2006, 47).

Hoping to attain the box-office success of *Drakula İstanbul'da*, Metin Erksan, an acclaimed director of Yeşilçam whose film *Susuz Yaz* (*Dry Summer*, 1964) won the Golden Bear Award at the 1963 Berlin Film Festival, directed *Şeytan*, which would later become known as 'the Turkish *Exorcist*'. *Şeytan* was Erksan's first attempt at making a Gothic horror film, and, working for the Saner Film Production Company, he travelled to London to see William Friedkin's *The Exorcist* (1973) and read William Peter Blatty's novel, which

Figure 9.2   Newspaper advert dating back to 24 April 1949 regarding the release of *Çığlık*

he planned to adapt for his own film (Scognamillo 2010, 221). *Şeytan*'s plot is a homage to *The Exorcist*; however, Erksan changes the religious context and iconography for the Turkish market and, according to Kaya Özkaracalar, the Gothic themes of science vs religion and faith vs doubt are combined in *Şeytan* with the theme of 'the reconfirmation of Islam's power and validity' (Özkaracalar 2003, 214). Considering the political and social intricacies of the 1970s that confronted secular thought with the rising interest in Islamist nationalism, *Şeytan*'s subtextual references are particularly pertinent. Iain Robert Smith remarks accordingly that *Şeytan* 'highlights the failings of the rationalist, secular discourse' that Atatürk's reforms disseminated in Turkey and 'explicitly celebrates Islam for being able to defeat the "evil" forces in the world' (Smith 2008, 10). Although the film is widely considered a poor production technically, the Turkification in *Şeytan* reveals a subtext which corresponds to the social and political context of Turkey in the 1970s. The appearance of the girl and the mother visiting a mosque wearing headscarves concludes the film with a stand in favour of religious ideology.

For many, *Drakula İstanbul'da* and *Şeytan* are representative of Turkish Gothic horror cinema due to their international popularity. Indeed, *Drakula İstanbul'da* demonstrates a genuine effort to develop a Gothic aesthetic in a Turkish film and *Şeytan* focuses on supernatural dimensions of Gothic horror, combining it with Islamic symbols. In order to replace the Christian iconography of Anglo-American Gothic texts with the Turkish Islamic context, both *Drakula İstanbul'da* and *Şeytan* use the Qur'ān instead of the cross and the Bible, and the zam-zam water (water from a well in Mecca believed by Muslims to be holy) instead of Christian holy water. Nevertheless, being exploitations of UK and US productions respectively, *Drakula İstanbul'da* and *Şeytan* lack something crucially necessary for them to be called intrinsically Turkish, and that is the presence of native supernatural motifs.

Ölüler Konuşmaz Ki and the Hybrid Undead of Turkish Gothic

Ölüler Konuşmaz Ki (Figure 9.3), directed by Yavuz Yalınkılıç, is a hidden gem of Turkish Gothic which uniquely combines the Gothic aesthetics of *Drakula İstanbul'da* and the supernatural horror of *Şeytan* using a supernatural creature from Turkish and Balkan folklore. Upon release, the film did not achieve box-office success, which partially explains why there is no archival information about its production details and interviews conducted with anyone involved with the shooting process. Lost and forgotten for almost thirty years, the film was rediscovered in 2001 by a young cinema writer, Sadi Konuralp, in an old depot of Lâle Film studios (Konuralp 2002, 1). Since its rediscovery, *Ölüler Konuşmaz Ki* has been criticised for its convoluted storyline and its assumed misuse of the Gothic horror genre. In one of the few articles that mention the

Figure 9.3   The poster for *Ölüler Konuşmaz Ki* (Objektif Film, 1970)

film, Kaya Özkaracalar describes it as 'uneven' with a 'rather incoherent' plot which 'might be seen as involuntarily adding to the force of the movie, puzzling the audience to such a degree that logic and rationality are abandoned' (Özkaracalar 2003, 212). Indeed, *Ölüler Konuşmaz Ki* suffers from some inconsistencies of plot, which results in moments of confusion. However, the film still conveys a comprehensible narrative using B-movie Gothic aesthetics.

The budget for *Ölüler Konuşmaz Ki* was much lower than those for *Drakula İstanbul'da* and *Şeytan*. Although colour film stock was available in 1970, *Ölüler Konuşmaz Ki* is shot in black-and-white with a largely unknown cast in an old mansion in the largest of the Prince Islands in the Marmara Sea near Istanbul. Shooting a film outside Istanbul on an underpopulated island with a small cast and limited locations is fully consistent with B-movie production values. In fact, the Princess Islands were historically used as a place of exile by disgraced and sick Byzantine royals and have been populated mostly by Greeks, Armenians and Jews. The historical buildings on the Islands are mainly monasteries, churches, convents and orphanages built in the styles of Christian architecture. Thus, the location conveys a Gothic atmosphere: the island is depicted as a small town, secluded, foreign and mysterious. This sense of mystery is represented in the first scene, which resembles Jonathan Harker's journey to Transylvania in Stoker's *Dracula* as well as other European Gothic texts set in foreign and threatening locations.

The film opens with the arrival of a couple, Melih and Oya, on the town. While they walk with their bags on the street, a horse-drawn carriage stops and a mysterious driver invites them into the carriage. He tells the couple that they will not find a place to stay except Mr Adem's mansion, for it is 'the fifteenth of the month', and that he will return home before dark. The emphasis on 'the fifteenth of the month' is reminiscent of 'the fifth of May' mentioned in Stoker's *Dracula*: Jonathan Harker is warned by an elderly Romanian lady that 'It is the eve of St. George's Day. Do you not know that tonight, when the clock strikes midnight, all the evil things in the world will have full sway?' (Stoker 1897, 19). St George's Day is celebrated by many Christian churches around the world as a feast day, but according to Stoker's personal notes, he based his interpretation on the Eastern Orthodox tradition of Transylvania, which he read about in Emily Gerard's *Transylvanian Superstitions* (1885) (Stoker 2008, 121). 'The fifteenth of the month' mentioned in the film has no known referent in Turkish or Islamic cultures and it is simply used for its sinister effect and superstitious implications. In fact, throughout the film, whenever someone mentions the fifteenth of the month, a church bell rings in the background, creating a Gothic effect that portends danger. Oya worries about the driver's fear of 'the fifteenth of the month' and the threatening aspects of their journey, but Melih reassures her that 'superstitious beliefs are outdated in this world' and, at any rate, he carries a gun for protection (*Ölüler Konuşmaz Ki*).

As the film continues, it is revealed that the main setting for the film, Mr Adem's mansion, is haunted – most probably by the recently deceased Mr Adem. The haunting is not explicit but is implied when the mysterious butler, Hasan, welcomes the couple, saying: 'the spirit of Mr. Adem will be pleased' (*Ölüler Konuşmaz Ki*). However, the spirit of Mr Adem is not a spirit or a ghost: he is a *hortlak*. According to Turkish mythology and Anatolian folklore, *hortlak* is the name given to a restless spirit of the dead, a dead person who rises from the grave at night (Yaltırık 2013, 200). The meaning of *hortlak* derives from the Turkish word meaning 'to rise from the dead' or *hortlamak*. The main characteristics of the *hortlak* are similar to those of other undead creatures, including the ghouls of Arabian narratives, the zombies of African diasporic stories and the vampires of Balkan and Russian folklore. In different regions of Anatolia, it is believed that an evil person who dies can rise from the grave as a *hortlak* and haunt people who had angered him during his life. A *hortlak* can sometimes run very fast, ride a horse, use a gun, attack, beat up and abduct people. It has an ugly, horrific face, sometimes carries a stick and is dressed in a burial robe or disguised as an animal (Eyüboğlu 1998, 104–5). The *hortlak* in Turkish folklore, which sometimes resembles a zombie, corresponds to the figure of the vampire in the Balkans; in fact, archival documents and travelogues composed by Ottoman governors and travellers about incidents relating to belief in these creatures go back to the Middle Ages. In the sixteenth century, an Islamic leader of the Ottoman Empire, Shaykh Al-Islam Mehmed Ebusuud, put forward a fatwa on what to do if a corpse should arise from his grave as a *hortlak*. His instructions include staking the corpse to the ground; then, if all else fails, the head should be cut off and the body should be burned (Düzdağ 1972, 197–8).

In *Ölüler Konuşmaz Ki*, the similarities between vampires, zombies and *hortlaks* lead to the figure of the undead as a hybrid form. In the film, the *hortlak* rises from the grave while two townsmen dig grave plots; he walks very slowly, holding his hands up, resembling the American-style zombie of the 1970s. However, the *hortlak* also laughs and constantly speaks (loudly and strangely), thus distancing him from the traditional American zombie narrative. During their first night in the mansion, Melih and Oya are attacked by the *hortlak*. Melih fires his gun at the creature, who simply says, 'I have a scar in my head, right? While they were nailing my coffin, the nails cracked my skull. But my head does not hurt. I won't die. Bullets won't do anything to me' (*Ölüler Konuşmaz Ki*). In Turkish folklore, the *hortlak* can only be kept in the grave when the coffin is opened up and the corpse is nailed to the ground (Beydili 2005, 435). This echoes the *hortlak*'s comment about a nail cracking his skull, but it also reminds us of the necessity of a piercing tool in killing zombies and vampires. We do not see Melih and Oya after this scene, and, despite the absence of any bloodshed, we assume that the *hortlak* killed them.

After the audience is introduced to the haunted mansion and the *hortlak* figure, the film's main character, Sema, arrives in the town. In the background, the audience hears Krzysztof Komeda's infamous song used at the beginning of Roman Polanski's *Rosemary's Baby* (1968). Having established its B-movie standards with the stolen soundtrack, the film introduces Sema's character, who is depicted as an educated young woman who comes to this small tranquil town as the new teacher. Upon arrival at the mansion, she encounters the same peculiarities as Melih and Oya. During her first night, she is frightened by the howling of wolves, and the next day a young hunter, Kerem, tells her that, according to the townsmen, between fifteen and twenty girls have been killed by the *hortlak*. Sema is dismissive: she does not believe in *hortlaks*, djinns or fairies. Later, among friends, Kerem expresses his thoughts on the matter: 'I am surprised to hear such stories in a century when people are going to the Moon' (*Ölüler Konuşmaz Ki*). And when asked if he is afraid of the *hortlak*, Kerem answers: 'I don't believe djinn, fairy, hortlak stories. For me things that I can see with my own eyes and hold with my own hands are important' (*Ölüler Konuşmaz Ki*). Once again, the film aligns Sema and Kerem with rationality; they are dismissive of superstitious belief systems.

Later in the film, Kerem attends a meeting wherein the *hortlak* is described as a vampire-like figure. During the meeting, the imam (Islamic priest) recounts a real-life *hortlak* story, something he experienced during his youth. He says:

> You know, these stories take place in the Balkan countries. We are from Varna. We used to go dove hunting when we were young. Mr. Rüstem was one of the leading persons in the town. But in each hunt, we would come back with one less person. Then we consulted religious authorities. They told us that we have a living dead among us. Crazy Rıza heated up an iron stake and staked Mr. Rüstem's heart with it. So our town got rid of the *hortlak*.

In his speech, the imam refers to his past, and to a town which was ruled under the Ottoman Empire. Under Ottoman rule for almost four centuries, Varna was presented to Bulgaria by Russia after the Russo-Turkish Wars of the late nineteenth century. Referring to his past in Varna, the imam also discusses Turkey's modern history and, by associating this *hortlak* story with the Balkan states, highlights how Yalınkılıç was inspired by the vampire of Balkan folklore.

Furthermore, when the *hortlak* captures Sema for the first time, the creature is scared of the amulet that she wears around her neck. This triangular amulet, which was first used in *Drakula İstanbul'da*, carries prayers from the Qur'ān and is as powerful against the vampire as the crucifix was in Stoker's novel. By using the same motifs as *Drakula İstanbul'da* did, *Ölüler Konuşmaz Ki* reminds the audience of the vampire myth and emphasises the role of religion when confronting the undead. It is important to note that the word '*hortlak*' is also used in *Drakula İstanbul'da* (instead of 'vampire'); and in order to overcome the *hortlak*, Dr Naci (the Turkish Van Helsing) suggests driving a stake through the heart of the creature, cutting off its head and filling its mouth with garlic. This summarises the conclusion of *Drakula İstanbul'da*, but in *Ölüler Konuşmaz Ki* we see a scene of religious exorcism for the first time in a Turkish film (Özkaracalar 2012, 252).

During her second night in the mansion, Sema is once again attacked by the *hortlak*. She goes to the school principal, Mr Nuri, for help but finds that he is under the influence of the *hortlak*. Sema then turns to Kerem, his friend Remzi and the imam to fight the *hortlak*. She traps the creature in Mr Nuri's house and the imam silently reads from holy scripture while Kerem and Remzi hold up the Qur'ān to disempower the *hortlak*. Here, the audience hears the tunes of an Islamic hymn in the background, which reinforces the reading of the scene as an exorcism. Frightened by the holy books that surround him, the *hortlak* exclaims: 'Did you hear? The voice of my friends! They are calling for me. The screams of my friends, the dead! They are burning somebody again. My corpses ...' (*Ölüler Konuşmaz Ki*). These lines echo the famous speech uttered by Dracula in Bram Stoker's novel: 'Listen to them, the children of the night. What music they make!' (Stoker 1897, 52). After the *hortlak* utters his speech, he moves closer to Sema's head, and then he is interrupted by the morning call to prayer from the local mosque. The use of Islamic prayer in a Gothic horror film in Turkey starts with this scene in *Ölüler Konuşmaz Ki*. The exorcism scene is not carried out as dramatically as it is in *Şeytan* (or in other Turkish Gothic horror films of the twenty-first century), yet *Ölüler Konuşmaz Ki* is the first of its kind: the undead is expelled through Islamic ritual. At the end, the *hortlak* melts away, leaving behind his shoes, coat and hat as the sun rises on the horizon. The result is a hybrid undead creature that mixes the attributes of vampires, zombies, *hortlaks* and some Islamic demonology.

Despite its Islamic conclusion, *Ölüler Konuşmaz Ki* takes a more nuanced stand when it comes to the characterisation of Sema. Sema is welcomed to the mansion by the butler, Hasan, who is a character with allusions to Renfield in Bram Stoker's *Dracula* as well as the hunchbacked servant in *Drakula İstanbul'da*. Hasan serves the *hortlak*, but he also tells his own story to Sema, as he did to Oya and supposedly to every woman who came to stay in the mansion. He guides them to the basement and reveals a female portrait from behind a curtain, saying:

> This is you maybe. Maybe not. But it does not matter. She was beautiful too once. But she is soil now. She does not even hear. I, on the other hand, I am living for her . . . I am living for beauties like her. But they are all leaving me. They leave me and go away. (*Ölüler Konuşmaz Ki*)

The use of portraits, pictures and paintings is a common element found in much early Gothic fiction such as Horace Walpole's *The Castle of Otranto* (1764), Matthew Lewis's *The Monk* (1796) and Ann Radcliffe's *The Italian* (1797). The literary critic Kamilla Elliot characterises Gothic fiction as 'the mother ship of literary picture identification'. She suggests that the repeated presence of these portraits signals the social identity and class status of the subject in the pictures and relates directly to the contexts of the novels (Elliott 2012, 6). The function of the portraits in *Ölüler Konuşmaz Ki*, however, pertains to the development of the plot and the characterisation of Sema, for Oya and Sema become linked to the figure in the portrait, identifying themselves with her beauty and death. By showing them the portrait, Hasan prophesies their downfall, and when faced with the portrait the women experience fear, terror, doubt, loss and the repetition of history. Thus, the portrait signals the end of the female characters, and yet Sema refuses to bow to the inevitable and plays a significant role in defeating the *hortlak*. Unlike other female characters who preceded her, Sema manages to run away from the confines of the mansion and lures him out to the ritual that wipes him off the face of the earth. Moreover, in doing so she wears a white night-gown, which conventionally represents the purity of the female character in Gothic fiction. Therefore, Sema acts as the Gothic heroine who escapes from her villain while Kerem becomes the chivalric hero who helps to save her and the town. As Komeda's 'Lullaby' plays in the background, the film concludes with Sema and Kerem walking hand in hand into the future, which signals an appreciation of rational thought rather than a strict praise of religious ideology.

James Morgart has suggested that the first Gothic films are not 'horrific', but 'assist [us] in tracking the evolution of the application and innovation of Gothic horror aesthetics' (Morgart 2014, 376). The Gothic tropes and aesthetics of *Ölüler Konuşmaz Ki* speak to Morgart's argument and extend it to the Turkish context. Following in the footsteps of *Çığlık* and *Drakula İstanbul'da*, the production and release of *Ölüler Konuşmaz Ki* enable us to track a new form of the undead in Gothic: a hybrid figure that mixes Anglo-American Gothic tropes with Turkish and Balkan folklore, as well as an Islamic cultural and religious context. The resolution of the film – which draws on Islamic ritual and the Qur'ān – anticipates the Turkification of Gothic narratives in *Şeytan*, yet avoids taking a firm stand on religious values and ideology. Moreover, the use of portraits and the characterisation of Sema as the Gothic heroine refine the Gothic aesthetics of the film. *Ölüler Konuşmaz Ki* had the lowest budget of all Gothic B-movies in Turkish cinema, but its impact on the evolution of Turkish Gothic has been massive.

Bibliography

Arslan, Savaş (2011), *Cinema in Turkey: A New Critical History* (New York: Oxford University Press).
Beydili, Celal (2005), *Türk Mitolojisi Ansiklopedik Sözlük* (Ankara: Yurt Yayınları).
Dönmez-Colin, Gönül (2008), *Turkish Cinema: Identity, Distance and Belonging* (London: Reaktion Books).
Düzdağ, Mehmet Ertuğrul (1972), *Şeyhülislâm Ebussuud Efendi Fetvaları Işığında 16. Asır Türk Hayatı* (İstanbul: Enderun Kitabevi).
Elliott, Kamilla (2012), *Portraiture and British Gothic Fiction: The Rise of Picture Identification, 1764–1835* (Baltimore, MD: The Johns Hopkins University Press).
Eyüboğlu, İsmet Zeki (1998), *Anadolu İnançları* (İstanbul: Toplumsal Dönüşüm Yayınları).
Glaser, Ed (2016), 'Long-Lost 35mm Print of Cult Film "Turkish Star Wars" Rediscovered', *Neon Harbor*, <http://neonharbor.com/long-lost-35mm-print-of-cult-film-turkish-star-wars-rediscovered/> (last accessed 19 February 2017).
Joslin, Lyndon W. (2006), *Count Dracula Goes to the Movies: Stoker's Novels Adapted, 1922–2003* (McFarland).
Konuralp, Sadi (2002), 'Unutulmuş bir Türk Korku Filmi', *Geceyarısı Sineması* 12/1.
Kuhn, Annette and Guy Westwell (2012), 'B-movie'. in *A Dictionary of Film Studies* (Oxford: Oxford University Press).
Morgart, James (2014), 'Gothic Horror Film from the Haunted Castle (1896) to the

Psycho (1960)', in Glennis Byron and Dale Townshend (eds), *The Gothic World* (Oxford: Routledge), 376–87.
Mutlu, Dilek Kaya (2006), 'The Russian Monument at Ayastefanos (San Stefano): Between Defeat and Revenge, Remembering and Forgetting', *Middle Eastern Studies* 43/1, 75–86.
Özgüç, Agâh (1990), *Başlangıcından Bugüne Türk Sinemasında İlkler* (İstanbul: Yılmaz Yayınları).
Özkaracalar, Kaya (2003), 'Between Appropriation & Innovation: Turkish Horror Cinema', in Steven Jay Schneider (ed.), *Fear Without Frontiers: Horror Cinema Across the Globe* (Godalming: FAB), 205–17.
Özkaracalar, Kaya (2012), 'Horror Films in Turkish Cinema: to Use or Not to Use Local Cultural Motifs, That Is Not the Question', in Patricia Allmer, Emily Brick and David Huxley (eds), *European Nightmares: Horror Cinema in Europe Since 1945* (New York: Columbia University Press), 249–60.
Scognamillo, Giovanni (2010), *Türk Sinema Tarihi* (İstanbul: Kabalcı).
Scognamillo, Giovanni and Metin Demirhan (2005), *Fantastik Türk Sineması* (İstanbul: Kabalcı).
Silver, Alain and James Ursini (1997), *The Vampire Film: From Nosferatu to Twilight* (Montclair, NJ: Limelight Editions).
Smith, Iain Robert (2008), 'The Exorcist in Istanbul: Processes of Transcultural Appropriation Within Turkish Popular Cinema', *PORTAL Journal of Multidisciplinary International Studies* 5.1.
Sterritt, David and John Anderson (2008), *The B List: The National Society of Film Critics on the Low-budget Beauties, Genre-bending Mavericks, and Cult Classics We Love* (Cambridge, MA: Da Capo).
Stoker, Bram (1897), *Dracula* (New York: Grosset & Dunlap).
Stoker, Bram (2008), in Robert Eighteen-Bisang and Elizabeth Miller (eds), *Bram Stoker's Notes for Dracula* (Jefferson, NC: McFarland).
Süner, Asuman (2010), *New Turkish Cinema: Belonging, Identity and Memory* (London: I. B. Tauris).
Yaltırık, Mehmet Berk (2013), 'Ghoul-Witch Beliefs in Turkish Culture', *Journal of History School (JOHS)* 6/16, 187–232.

Filmography

Çığlık (The Scream, Aydın Arakon 1949)
Drakula İstanbul'da (Dracula in Istanbul, Mehmet Muhtar 1953)
Ölüler Konuşmaz Ki (The Dead Don't Talk, Yavuz Yalınkılıç 1970)
Şeytan (The Devil, Metin Erksan 1974)

PART III

AFRICA AND ASIA

10. *FILAMU YA KUTISHA*: TANZANIAN HORROR FILMS AND B-MOVIE GOTHIC

Claudia Böhme

The first Tanzanian horror film, *Nsyuka* (2003), is about an evil ancestor spirit that haunts a young woman and her family. It was shot over three weeks with a tripod made out of tree branches. The actors were forced to walk long distances to get to the set, and amassed their own funding to make the film. It is, to be sure, a low-budget film that has the quality and style associated with an international B-movie tradition. After the film was made, the music production company Wananchi Video Production saw a potential market, so it adapted the model of Nollywood films to the Tanzanian context, thus producing cheap films on VHS very quickly and selling them to local audiences. The Tanzanian video film industry was born. This set the stage for the first stars of the Tanzanian film industry, the director Mussa Banzi and the actors associated with the group White Elephant.

Many young filmmakers followed in Banzi's footsteps, and as a result, the genre of *filamu ya kutisha* (frightening film) developed. The Gothic dimensions of these films are highlighted through the various narratives of witchcraft, ghosts, zombies and violence (such as in splatter films). Through the improvement of techniques and production practices, the Gothic content of *filamu ya kutisha* has undergone major shifts and currents: the clumsily produced movies first made on VHS recorders have evolved into better-quality low-budget films using digital recording devices.

Like other African video films, Tanzanian movies are often judged to have sensational content, low production values and a large commercial market.

Consequently, film critics and many movie-goers do not consider *filamu ya kutisha* to be 'proper' African cinema, and yet Tanzanian video movies are immensely popular and have a massive following in the country. But that does not mean that local audiences are ignorant of other cinematic traditions, for foreign films have long been popular with Tanzanian audiences and local video movies are sometimes discussed as copies of North Atlantic films. This raises important questions. How do we categorise Tanzanian video film? Can we apply the B-movie label to these films? Or do the unique aesthetics of these films require a different way of describing and labelling these productions?

The film critic and scholar Robin Wood offers a very simple formula for Gothic horror films. For him, there are three variables: normality, the monster, and the relationship between the two. 'Normality is threatened by the monster', and, according to Wood, is defined by 'the heterosexual monogamous couple, the family, and the social institutions (police, church, armed forces) that support and defend them'. By contrast, the monster is 'society's basic fears', and it is the third variable, the relationship between normality and the Monster, which constitutes the essential subject of the horror film (1986: 79). These three variables could be applied to the *filamu ya kutisha*. However, normality, monstrosity and the relationships between them have very different meanings in Tanzania. While it is acknowledged that scary Hollywood and Nollywood movies are influential on Tanzanian video films, there is an important distinction to be made. This is because Tanzanian filmmakers mix foreign cinematic forms with narratives that are based on local myths and belief systems. Although some North Atlantic low-budget Gothic films also have connections to folklore, urban myths, 'true stories' and religion, Tanzanian viewers do not always view figures such as ghosts, witches or zombies as supernatural or sensational. Rather, Tanzanian movies with spirits and other such figures are seen as being connected to everyday life, and as a result these dimensions to the video films are viewed as didactic or educational, offering audiences ways of seeing a realm of darkness and the occult so as to gain access to truth and power (Behrend 2005; Meyer 2006). At the same time, however, humour is not negated by the didactic content, for there are also exaggerated and satirical presentations of supernatural beings and audiences are often invited to laugh at and reflect upon local ontologies and beliefs.

To understand the distinct and ambivalent local meanings and functions of the *filamu ya kutisha*, it is important to trace the development of these films in relation to the reception of international B-movie Gothic in the region. How have foreign films been received by Tanzanian audiences? And how have they influenced Tanzanian video filmmakers? Placing the *filamu ya kutisha* alongside North Atlantic B-Movie Gothic movies highlights similarities and differences, foregrounding how Tanzanian filmmakers creatively rework foreign material. To identify the 'Tanzanianness' of these films, it is important to remain sensitive to the filmmakers' appropriations of foreign cinema as well as the unique stylistic and local narrative content that are integrated into these works.

This chapter is based on ethnographic fieldwork that focused on the video film scene in Tanzania between 2006 and 2012. As a participant observer, I became a member of Mussa Banzi's video film art group White Elephant in 2006; I thus took part in the rehearsals, shooting and editing of films. In 2007, I acted in the Gothic horror film *Popobawa*; in this production, I contributed with a White European figure to the film and this led to discussions about authenticity during the production and the film's reception. Through my participation I was able to gain valuable insights into film production and reception in Tanzania and gain a deeper understanding of what Gothic horror films mean to filmmakers and their audiences.

African Video Movies: Viruses or Trash?

African video films are often criticised for their crossover aesthetics: they often mix genres, they contribute to the soap opera tradition of African cinema, and they blur the North Atlantic distinctions between television and cinema. By problematising these classifications, they are usually prevented from entry into the major international film festivals (Haynes 2000: 1 ff.). As Karin Barber has described for popular theatre, they occupy a cultural space which is defined by what they are not: they are neither art nor film; they are not African cinema (Barber 2000: 3). In addition, these video films are often criticised for their focus on opulent urban lifestyles, idealisation of wealth, sexism, racism and the occult. Some critics argue that these films depict Tanzania – and, by extension, the African continent – as primitive, backward and pre-modern (Okome 2010).

The label 'African Cinema' was first used as a political and anti-colonial expression. When filmmakers from West Africa began making movies in the 1960s and 1970s, the films were attempts to decolonise the audience and challenge and counter the North Atlantic hegemonic gaze by articulating post-colonial political views and developing new aesthetics for local narratives. These films were categorised as auteur cinema; as a result, critics often ignored the filmmakers' experimentations with different genres and cinematic styles. But because early West African filmmakers were educated in Western Europe, and because their films were financed by companies based in European metropolitan centres, their films did not always counter the North Atlantic gaze and many African filmmakers found themselves indebted to western production techniques and unable to finance films that could be 'truly' African. Video film production offered an alternative. These filmmakers were free from foreign and state finances, enabling them to make movies for African audiences and experiment with the forms of horror and Gothic that have become so popular with African consumers.

The French ethnographic filmmaker Jean Rouch asserted that 'video is the AIDS of the film industry'. But this assertion is often misunderstood and taken out of context. For instance, Pierre Barrot describes his experience of hearing this statement ironically quoted by a filmmaker from Niger. Barrot writes:

> Now that he is gone, one can only guess at his meaning: was he warning about the viral nature of piracy, which is frequently associated with video, or perhaps he was warning of the dangers of this equipment, since video, as a tool designed for mass consumption, was beginning to replace film, previously the preserve of a small group of specialists? Such purists might fear the process of vulgarization and compare it to a weakening in an immuno-defense system – a virus that could no doubt be considered equally fatal to cinema. (Barrot et al. 2008: 3)

The last point made here is expanded upon by Kenneth Harrow in his recent book on African cinema. Harrow uses the notion of 'trash' to discuss the changing history of African film production: trash, he argues, has always been present in African cinema, for detritus in the narratives constitutes signs and metaphors for a state of being as well as the video film industry itself. Indeed, for Harrow, the trash found in Nollywood cinema can be understood through Achille Mbembe's description of postcolonial African nations in his work *On the Postcolony* (2001). Harrow writes:

> The trailers that run endlessly before each part of Nollywood VCDs give us all the above, in voices filled with the apprehension and excitement that preceded viewing all trashy film, all images of trashy people who behave in the trashiest way. If, as Mbembe mildly concludes, it is true that Africa is not an 'incomparable monster' of a 'mute place of darkness', he has evoked this untruth in ways that speak in loud decibels, as befits the gothic ruins of thundering detritus. All we need are the titles – 'Blood Sisters', 'Dangerous Sisters', 'Jezebell', 'Formidable Force', 'Mark of the Beast', or 'Witches.com' – and we are prepared to enter into the 'mute places of darkness of the heart' that the beast will feed upon. This is the side of Lagos that hosts Djibril Diop Mambety's 'hyenas', the beasts of today's urban streets where 'saignantes' strut and the rich race through the night in their Mercedes, dressed to kill. (Harrow 2013: 5)

Here, Harrow points to the 'trashy' dynamics of Gothic and links them to the popular Nollywood videos that sensationalise, among many other things, witches, beasts and Jezebels. But Harrow is not suggesting that these films have no worth; on the contrary, he finds in the trash a dark side to life in postcolonial Africa, a depiction of places that challenge metanarratives and dominant discourses (Harrow 2013).

The same can be said of Tanzanian video films, which often include narratives about taboo subjects related to sexuality, violence and terror that are by-products of the postcolonial nation (not the result of a colonial oppressor or a foreign agent). Such topics were seldom depicted in popular Swahili theatre; this is because drama has often been used as a tool for fighting superstition and promoting the idea of modern health care in socialist Tanzania (Lange 2002: 225–6).

The first Tanzanian video films were also criticised by some viewers as being derivative of Nollywood films, focusing too much on sex, crime, witchcraft and horror. Despite this criticism, the films were extremely popular and successful: they replaced Nigerian films in the market-place and the video film industry continues to grow. The low production values are offset by the appeal of the local stories, the use of Swahili and the Tanzanian stars (Böhme 2014). This popularity has led to a situation in which hundreds of directors and thousands of Tanzanian actors are involved in the industry and new DVD productions are released every day and distributed throughout East Africa, watched in thousands of small cinemas, libraries and homes. And the recent development of the satellite programme *Africa Magic* has enabled access to these films throughout the continent and across the globe.

Filamu ya kutisha: A Brief History

The distribution of foreign Gothic horror films in Tanzania began in the early colonial period. As early as 1954 the classification category 'H' (horror films) was added to the list used by the Film Censorship Board (Brennan 2005: 502). By the end of the 1970s, the classic Gothic horror films, such as Todd Browning's *Dracula* (1931), were shown in Tanzanian cinemas. In the 1980s, video films began circulating in Tanzania and movies from Hollywood, Hong Kong and India were among the most watched. According to Arjun Appadurai, these transnational flows can be seen as part of the emergence of a new media-scape and the basis for new 'imagined worlds' (1996: 33). With the rise of Nigerian Gothic horror film imports in the early 2000s, the genre's popularity increased (see also Krings 2007, 2010). In 2017, foreign horror movies are sold in the local markets; they are usually pirated copies from China and include horror collections with up to forty movies on one DVD. Easy access to these films has influenced Tanzanian filmmakers, enabling them to remain up to date on foreign productions and contributing to the development of local stories. These collections carry lively titles like 'Terrorist Dismembered Killing', 'Vampire Zombie Brutal War', 'Hollywood Vampire Zombie', 'Vampire and Corpse' or 'Terrorist Ghost Killing'. For example, the

Canadian horror film *The Wrong Turn* (2003) from the collection 'Terrorist Dismembered Killing', became a model for a Tanzanian film titled *The Brown Coat* (2008).

Like the German *Schauerroman* and the British Gothic novel, which formed a basis for North Atlantic Gothic horror films, the popular Gothic literature of Tanzania is woven into the scripts of the films. Novels with first-hand narrative reports of witchcraft and supernatural beings pervade popular Tanzanian literature, many of them marketed with book covers that include images relating to Gothic and horror which are part of both local and global contexts.

Mussa Banzi, who sparked the Tanzanian horror film genre, was inspired by *hadithi ya kutisha*, the Gothic horror stories which were told to him by his aunt, as well as by Tanzanian horror and crime authors (such as Ben R. Mtobwa, C. G. M. Mung'ong'o or Aristablus Elvis Musiba). Nigerian and US Gothic horror films are also profoundly influential on Banzi's work, and he founded the Tamba Arts Group in 2001 with the express intent of making larger-scale productions similar to those produced in other countries. When his first film, *Nsyuka*, was completed in 2003, the music production company Wananchi Video Production distributed the movie, and this marked the beginning of the video film industry in Tanzania.

In these formative years, a handful of directors produced no less than one movie a month. The Indian-owned companies Wananchi and GMC (which specialised in local music and pirated foreign movies) established a distribution network in the market area of Kariakoo (smaller production networks can now be found in the cities of Mwanza, Tanga, Arusha, Mbeya and Kigoma). Within five years, the industry expanded so that at least five DVD movies were released each week, an industry driven by demand and the increasing number of DVD players in Tanzanian homes. This initiated two more distribution companies, Kapico and Steps Entertainment Ltd (the latter has become the most successful in the country).

Filamu za kutisha ('frightening films') are designed to inspire fear in the viewer, and fans rate each movie according to its fear factor. Yet this genre also blurs boundaries, and there are various expressions for classifying the types of 'frightening films': *filamu ya kusisimua* is a scary movie that includes suspense, and *filamu ya kichawi* is a terrifying film about witchcraft. Regardless of the classification, in the early years, *filamu za kutisha* were so popular that they guaranteed financial success and, as a result, many first-time directors embraced the form. But at the start only two directors made frightening films, Mussa Banzi, who set his films in the city, and Sultan Tamba, who made films about ghosts in small villages. They paved the way for newcomers like Haji Dilunga and Shariff Jumbe, who began making films in 2006. Shariff Jumbe is open about his debt to foreign movies and freely mixes this influence with local spirit stories, as exemplified in his first film, *Bwawa la Shetani* (*Swamps of the Devil*,

2007), which mixes *Predator* (1987) with local vampire stories. This hybridity is consistent with the history of Gothic horror. According to Linda Badley, the form is defined by its trans-mediality and is articulated by Edgar Allan Poe in his 'Philosophy of Composition' (1846) as a text that functions like a 'technological apparatus' that triggers intense reactions in the audience (Badley 1995: 2 ff.). This mixture of forms is significant for Tanzanian filmmakers, who develop ideas and images from Hollywood, Bollywood, Nollywood, local folklore and Gothic literature, as well as theatre.

When I asked Mussa Banzi about his idea for a certain *mise-en-scène* he replied '*Nimeitunga tu!*' ('I have just created it!'). Several plastic bags full of notes, scripts, storyboards, comic sketches, newspaper articles might serve as inspiration for a film. While the narrative basis is mainly taken from local stories, the monster is often created according to globally recognisable Gothic figures such as ghosts, vampires or zombies. The soundtracks are usually taken from Hollywood films and rearranged by musical 'sampling', which, according to Tobias Wendl, is the matrix of the films, and results in 'a highly original, hybrid cocktail'. In this respect, 'the current video production can aptly be conceived as a "local address" for reconfiguring and re-articulating the global flow of images for new local audiences' (Wendl 2004: 266).

But Tanzanian filmmakers of Gothic horror are distinct from their Hollywood counterparts. This is because the figures of monstrosity in the films – ghost, witches, zombies – are not just understood as fictional beings. They are also part of a belief system that incorporates witchcraft and spirit beings so the films have an educational component, teaching the audience how to cope with magical powers. Many filmmakers draw on beliefs linked to their cultural heritage, including the myths and folklore of the Zaramo people of the coast near Dar es Salaam. These stories often focus on witches and their evil powers; others focus on the *mganga* (the healer), who is a figure that appears in most *filamu za kutisha*. Although these figures are rooted in the local culture, they adopt character traits and contribute to the plot in ways similar to North Atlantic Gothic horror films. According to Tobias Wendl, the character of the healer or witch doctor or jujuman shares traits with the mad scientist. He writes:

> What, from a structuralist point of view, makes the jujumen resemble the 'mad scientist' ... is that both attempt to transgress normality and manipulate the natural reproductive cycle. The jujuman operates in his shrine, the mad scientist in his laboratory. Generally they both over-estimate their powers and their creations (or transformative acts) go out of control ... A significant difference between the two is that the mad scientist is largely inspired and motivated by his own mad dreams, whereas the jujuman does not act out his own dreams, but those of his clients. (2004: 275–6)

A corollary to this are Tanzanian comics, *katuni za miujuza* (miracle comics), which the cultural critic Jigal Beez describes as works that draw on local stories to frighten, shock and educate their readers (2004, 153). By using local stories, Tanzanian filmmakers make their films more 'real' in that they sometimes function as quasi-documentaries for local audiences.

From Dracula to Nsyuka

The idea for Mussa Banzi's *Nsyuka* came from his friend Askofu, who told him about the ancestral myth of the Wanyakyusa, who live in southern Tanzania (Banzi 2006). According to the myth, the dead enter the underworld *ubusyuka* as *abasyuka*, and sometimes, during the night, the *abasyuka* rise up and gather around their graves, near fires lit for them. If their descendants do not pray for them, the *abasyuka* become angry and punish those who remain alive (Busse 1998, 8–9).

In line with the aesthetics of North Atlantic horror movies, the opening sequence of *Nsyuka* is a tracking shot that moves over the cemetery at night as the soundtrack for *Friday the 13th* (1980) plays in the background. After a cut, the viewer first glimpses the monster Nsyuka, who digs his way out of a grave with long fingernails. Then the title suddenly blazes across the screen in a red font that drips with blood. As Nsyuka emerges, the viewer sees he is a small and strange figure with long dreadlocks; he is wearing rags, and the camera follows his feet, focusing on his long claw-like nails, as he walks slowly through the graveyard and disappears into the darkness.

The story begins with the nightmare of the young woman Dorlin, who, returning home from a drive with her fiancée, finds her housemaid and her dog brutally slaughtered. The evil Nsyuka appears: he laughs and haunts her until she wakes up. The dream leaves her restless and she sees it as a bad omen, for she has had trouble getting pregnant. She decides to visit a local healer, *mganga*, who tells her that her mother took a forbidden trail near Nsyuka's homestead while she was pregnant with her. The only way to break the spell is to have intercourse with the *mganga* while being possessed by the spirit. Shocked by his advances, Dorlin decides to visit a female *mganga*, who is able to bring Nsyuka into her fiancé's body. The ritual is successful and Dorlin gets pregnant; she then forgets the trouble and marries. But when the *mganga*'s guiding charm is removed from her in the hospital, her pregnancy becomes complicated and the doctor discovers an animal-like form in her body. Nsyuka then appears and warns her against having an abortion. Dorlin eventually has a baby boy, but while he is growing up her son develops a hunger for raw flesh and shows magical abilities. He is the monster's son and Nsyuka takes him home.

'*Nimeongeza*' ('I have added some things'), says Banzi when explaining the outward appearance of Nsyuka, who is played by the Rastafarian actor

Emmanuel Kasoga (a.k.a. Bob Kijiti), a Reggae musician who has become an actor (Interview 2006). When I asked Bob Kijiti to draw me a picture of Nsyuka he titled it 'Nsyuka-Tanzania's first Dracula movie'. Nsyuka certainly shares features with Dracula, as well as the *abasyuka*, but he is a revenant hybrid with roots in both cultures (Krings 2007). Although Nsyuka was a big success, Mussa Banzi left the Tamba Arts Group over disputes regarding the distribution of finances. He took half of the actors with him and founded a new group, *Shumileta*, and with them he created a new horror figure for the genre of *filamu ya kutisha*.

Female Vampires: *Shumileta – Queen of the Devil*

At the beginning of the film, we hear the repetitive sound of the soundtrack of *Predator* and we see an object flying towards the Earth. Under a full moon on the beach, a white goat is transformed into a woman in a white wedding dress; blue flashes emanate from her eyes as she looks up to the moon. A voice off-screen gives her orders: 'Go and find the husband of your choice!' She slowly rises and walks away in the dark.

The woman is Shumileta. The command comes from her father, king of the underworld, who sends his daughter to Earth. She then walks along Tunisia Road in Dar es Salaam wearing a glittering short dress and waiting for customers with her fellow prostitutes. After she manages to attract the first man, she leads him to the nearby cemetery where we see a dispute about money and safe sex; the man pays more for sex without a condom and he receives a consuming bite from Shumileta. As in many vampire narratives, the spectre of a life-threatening epidemic lies in the background of *Shumileta*. The symbolic logic of the film conjures the HIV/AIDS crisis in the region and Banzi seeks to educate his audience about the dangers of the illness. In the context of HIV/AIDS, the 'kiss of death' is not the result of local spirits who force their victims to love them.

Like Nsyuka, Shumileta turns into an evil vampiric monster; after her feast, she raises her arms and laughs diabolically before vanishing into darkness. She then meets Mack, a young man who gives her a ride home at night. Shumileta leaves her red shoes in the car and Mack's fiancée, Monte, gets jealous. Monte and Mack go to confront Shumileta, but they only find her sister, who tells them Shumileta died many years ago. To follow the spirit of Shumileta, Mack and Monte consider consulting a *mganga*, but Shumileta transforms Monte into a chicken and kidnaps Mack. She then flies with him to the underwater world.

In the second part of the film, Monte's mother tries to get her children back with the help of Mganga Ndele, who uses a screen on the wall to see what is happening. But he is not powerful enough: he and Mack are dying. Another *mganga* is able to catch Shumileta in a box which they bury, but it is eventually found and opened. Shumileta escapes and takes Mack from out of his grave back to the underwater world. Later, Shumileta's spirit sister becomes jealous; she wants Mack for herself and the sisters fight. Shumileta's father intervenes and ends the 'human business'; Mack is set free and he reunites with Monte.

In the first part of the film, the female vampire, Shumileta, represents a demonisation of femininity and seduction that is threatening for men (Creed 1993). The vampiresses do not entirely fit the model of femininity attributed to women by their respective societies (Flocke 1999, 7–8). Like other female vampires, Shumileta embodies a mediation and negotiation of the changing conceptions of gender relations in Tanzania. 'We added a little bit of teeth and fingernails', said Banzi, when he spoke about the creation of Shumileta. 'Since we don't know what the spirits or their bodies look like, we made some apposition, so what we did, we created something which could be enjoyable for the viewers, but we are not sure if spirits have long teeth like that.'

Because belief in spirits is common in Tanzania, these stories connect with people's everyday experiences. I watched *Shumileta* with a family in Dar es Salaam and the grandmother remembered a neighbour who was haunted by a love spirit and consulted a *mganga* to rid herself of the unwanted lover. *Shumileta* is a cinematic visualisation of local stories that revolve around water spirits (or love spirits) who seek men. Taxi drivers working through the night are particularly scared of becoming victims.

As Luise White has shown, stories of vampirism were first reported in early twentieth-century colonial Kenya and Tanganyika following rumours of blood-sucking firefighters called *wazimamoto* (White 1993, 31). The Dar es Salaam firefighters were said to suck the blood of innocent men, leaving them impotent and lazy. In women's housing settlements in Nairobi in the 1920s and 1930s, single women and prostitutes were not only victims but also were hired by the *wazimamoto* to access male victims (White 2000, 151 ff.). A more recent story can be found in the Swahili term '*unyonyaji*', meaning 'exploitation', derived from the verb *kunyonya* (to suck). As James Brennan shows in his discussion of national political discourses (Brennan 2006), the Marxist picture of the blood-sucking capitalist has been projected onto businessmen from India, the Middle East, Europe and other African countries. These businessmen have been described by Brennan (2006, 398) as the main enemies of the Tanzanian socialist project. This discourse can also be applied to the video industry when directors and actors accuse the *Wahindi* producers of exploiting local artists.

Splatter Action: *Bwawa la Shetani*

The use of *Predator*'s soundtrack in Shumileta came from Shariff Jumbe, a fan of Banzi's horror movies, and who started the Tsunami Arts Group in 2007.

He released his first film, *Bwawa la Shetani* (Swamps of the Devil), in 2007, a story about a mysterious water well in Msanga Kisarawe that he had heard about from his grandfather, a Mzaramo. The story revolves around an ancestor spirit named *Mwingila* who puts a spell on the well: people who use it fall ill and sometimes die. The curse originates from a deadly attack on a young couple who were raped and beaten as they sought water at the well.

The other source of inspiration for the movie is *Predator*, one of Jumbe's favourite Hollywood action movies. He states:

> So I have made it like the mixing of ideas. I mixed the true story of that place [Msanga, Kisarawe] with *Predator*, because if people start thinking about the true part of the story the movie gets more interesting for them. But like in *Predator* they [the characters] are strangers in this forest. So somebody transforms and afterwards swallows one after the other.

Bwawa la Shetani starts like many other horror movies: a group of happy young people travel to a national park. Their car breaks down when the engine overheats. One of them goes to a nearby swamp and dives into the water; blue lightning appears and he is transformed into a creature with long teeth and nails. Blood drips from his mouth. He starts hunting his friends. He slaughters them until only three remain. He pursues them to a nearby village, where an old woman tells them the story of the swamps. The story continues in *Bwawa la Shetani 2* (which follows the plot of *Predator 2*) when a monster (the infected young man) goes to the city (Dar es Salaam) and continues his killing. The city is transformed into an American-style cityscape through the insertion of images of the New York skyline. But the group of young people who survived join forces with two policemen and return to the village near the swamps. They perform a ritual with a *mganga*, which releases the bewitched people and the dead from the curse.

Popobawa

The North Atlantic Gothic horror aspects of figures like Nsyuka or Shumileta lie in contrast to Popobawa, a figure who is based on a much more local story and not depicted like a Hollywood monster. When I spoke to the filmmaker, Haji Dilunga, in 2008 he told me that he had just begun shooting a movie called *Popobawa* (Bat Wing); he invited me to visit the set. *Popobawa* is the story of an evil sex spirit who rapes and sodomises his victims. Stories of Popabawa began circulating in 1965 on Pemba Island (Parkin 2004, 114), where an angry *sheikh*, it is reported, called upon the spirit to life to take revenge on his neighbours in a dispute over a love affair. In the varying descriptions the spirit is sometimes described as a black, bat-like creature with big wings, one eye, pointy ears and long claws. Most importantly, the victims must report the attack in a public forum to prevent Popobawa's return. While local discussions of Popobawa mainly revolve around whether or not he exists, the story has been studied by Africanists. They explain it in several ways: some see it as a version of the incubus legends and relate it to sleep paralysis (Walsh 2005, 14); others see it as a reflection on the horrors of slavery (Parkin 2004, 115); still others understand it as a narrative related to the political transformative eras of the region, for the rumours began one year after Zanzibar's 1964 revolution and reappeared close to the 1995 elections (Walsh 2005, 19). As Zanzibar hosted Africa's first colour television station and was one of the main centres of cinema business in East Africa, it is also possible to see Popobawa as a reflection of creatures like Dracula or Batman (Walsh 2005, 16).

Popobawa has become a very popular story. It was the subject of diverse newspaper, internet and blog articles and also became part of diverse pop cultural products around the world (Thompson 2017). In 2007, John P. Oscar, a young cartoonist from Dar es Salaam, published a book named *Usiku wa Machungu – Mikononi mwa Popobawa* (*Night of Bitterness – In the Hands of Popobawa*) in the mode of the Gothic novel. As Katrina Daly Thompson has shown in her analysis of collected Popobawa stories from Zanzibar, the circulation of these stories represent ways of talking about sex and sexuality, particularly the violence of rape and sodomy (2011, 13 ff., 2017).

In an interview with Haji Dilunga, he told me that he wanted to make a movie based on a real story and that his audience would have heard rumours of Popobawa in their neighbourhoods. To make the film more attractive, Dilunga made some major changes to the original story. In his version, for instance, it is not a male *sheikh* but the female witch Mamakibibi who tells Popobawa to punish her relatives. Popobawa not only rapes his victims but also kills his enemies (in the style of a splatter movie), including the witch who originally called him into existence. The sodomy, which is hinted at in several scenes, is linked to discourses of hetero- and homosexuality in the region (see also Thompson 2011, 11 ff.; Walsh 2005, 16 f.). For instance, in a side narrative to the main story, a lesbian woman tries to seduce a much younger girl, thus calling attention to non-heteronormative acts. And as in the myth, the film includes explicit references to the spread of HIV/AIDS; in one scene, the victims ask a traditional healer if the spirit can transmit the disease. He confirms that they might be infected. When they later on ask a doctor in a small HIV-testing dispensary (played by me), the white doctor tells them that according to the examination they have neither been raped nor infected but that they should consult a psychiatrist. Finally, Popobawa visits the doctor while she is sleeping, thus shattering her rational explanation of the case. Waking up the next morning with the feeling of having been raped, the

European doctor concludes that Popobawa might be real. The film therefore counters North Atlantic biomedical explanations of HIV/AIDS and denial regarding supernatural beings such as Popobawa.

Conclusion

The appropriation of the Gothic horror film in Tanzanian movies is part of a travelling aesthetics that began in the North Atlantic and eventually found its way into Nollywood and other African video industries. Through a complex process of mediation and remediation, the reception of B-movie Gothic from abroad has also led to the flourishing of scary stories in theatre, comics, books and novels which have been adapted for the screen. These foreign topics, styles and aesthetics are creatively combined with local stories of fear, as the examples of Nsyuka, Shumileta or Popobawa have shown. Through reciprocal interference and intertextuality, the filmmakers have built up a Tanzanian Gothic horror genre with its own aesthetics and language. In the longer tradition of Tanzanian oral and written literature, filmmakers tell their own stories and are able to prompt public debates on formerly hidden issues in Tanzanian society, such as love, sexuality, violence and disease. While often accused of merely imitating foreign film styles, these films are in fact the products of very complex creative and artistic processes. If we look superficially at these films, the titles and their low-budget production values might influence us to classify them as mere trash. But seeing them as just video films or B-movies, we are prevented from a deeper viewing that is needed to understand the complexities of these films. Through a careful viewing of the films and discussions with the filmmakers and their audiences, we can see the nuances in the stories and trace the flow of the narratives, images and discourses across the globe.

Bibliography

Appadurai, Arjun (1996), *Modernity at Large. Cultural Dimensions of Globalization* (Minneapolis, MN: University of Minnesota Press).
Badley, Linda (1995), *Film, Horror, and the Body Fantastic* (Westport, CT: Greenwood Press).
Barber, Karin (2000), *The Generation of Plays. Yoruba Popular Life in Theater* (Bloomington, IN: Indiana University Press).
Barrot, Pierre, Ibbo Daddy Abdoulaye and Lynn Taylor (2008), *Nollywood: The video phenomenon in Nigeria* (Oxford: James Currey).
Beez, Jigal (2004), 'Großstadtfieber und Hexenmeister. Horror- und Fantasy comics aus Tansania', in Tobias Wendl (ed.), *Africa Screams. Das Böse in Kino, Kunst und Kult* (Wuppertal: Peter Hammer Verlag), 153–63.
Behrend, Heike (2005), 'Zur Medialisierung okkulter Mächte: Geistmedien und Medien der Geister in Afrika', in Moritz Baßler, Bettina Gruber and Martina Wagner-Egelhaaf (eds), *Gespenster: Erscheinungen, Medien, Theorien* (Würzburg: Königshausen und Neumann), 201–14.

Böhme, Claudia (2014), 'The Rise and Fall of a Tanzanian Star', in Matthias Krings and Uta Reuster-Jahn (eds), *Bongo Media Worlds. Producing and Consuming Popular Culture in Dar es Salaam* (Cologne: Köppe), 185–210.
Brennan, James R. (2005), 'Democratizing cinema and censorship in Tanzania, 1920–1980', *The International Journal of African Historical Studies* 38/3, 481–511.
Brennan, James (2006), 'Blood Enemies: Exploitation and Urban Citizenship in the Nationalist Political Thought of Tanzania, 1958-75', *Journal of African History* 47/3, 389–413.
Busse, Joseph (1998), *Die Nyakyusa. Religion und Magie* (Bonn: Holos).
Creed, Barbara (1993), *The Monstrous-Feminine. Film, Feminism, Psychoanalysis* (London: Routledge).
Flocke, Petra (1999), *Vampirinnen. Ich schaue in den Spiegel und sehe nichts. Die kulturellen Inszenierungen der Vampirin* (Tübingen: Konkurs).
Haynes, Jonathan (2000), 'Introduction', in Jonathan Haynes (ed.), *Nigerian Video Films* (Athens: Ohio University Press), 1–36.
Harrow, Kenneth W. (2013), *Trash: African Cinema from Below* (Bloomington, IN: Indiana University Press).
Interview with Mussa Banzi, Dar es Salaam, 26.09.2006.
Krings, Matthias (2007), Afrikanische Video-Vampire: Wiedergänger zwischen den Kulturen, in Silke Seybold (ed.), *All About Evil. Das Böse* (Mainz: Zabern), 120–7.
Krings, Matthias (2010), 'Nollywood Goes East. The Localization of Nigerian Video Films in Tanzania', in Ralph Austen and Mahir Şaul (eds), *Viewing African Cinema in the Twenty first Century: Art Films and the Nollywood Video Revolution* (Athens: Ohio Univeristy Press), 74–91.
Lange, Siri (2002), *Managing Modernity. Gender, State, and Nation in the Popular Drama of Dar es Salaam*, dissertation (Bergen: University of Bergen).
Mbembe, Achille (2001), *On the Postcolony* (Berkeley: University of California Press).
Meyer, Birgit (2006), 'Impossible representations: Pentecostalism, vision and video technology in Ghana', in Birgit Meyer and Annelies Moors (eds), *Religion, Media, and the Public Sphere* (Bloomington, IN: Indiana University Press), 290–312.
Okome, Onookome (2010), 'Nollywood and Its Critiques', in Mahir Saul and Ralph Austen (eds), *Viewing African Cinema in the Twenty-first Century. Art Films and the Nollywood Video Revolution* (Bloomington, IN: Indiana University Press), 26–41.
Parkin, David (2004), 'In the Nature of the Human Landscape: Provenances in the Making of Zanzibar Politics', in John Clammer, Sylvie Poirier and Eric Schwimmer (eds), *Figured Worlds: Ontological Obstacles in Intercultural Relations* (Toronto: University of Toronto Press), 113–31.
Thompson, Katrina Daly (2011), 'Zanzibari Women's Discursive and Sexual Agency: Violating Gendered Speech Prohibitions through Talk about Supernatural Sex', *Discourse & Society* 22/1: 3–20.
Thompson, Katrina Daly (2017), *Popobawa. Tanzanian Talk, Global Misreadings* (Bloomington, IN: Indiana University Press).
Walsh, Martin T. (2005), *Diabolical Delusions and Hysterical Narratives in a Postmodern State*. Presentation to the Senior Seminar (Department of Social Anthropology, University of Cambridge).
Wendl, Tobias (2004), 'Wicked Villagers and the Mysteries of Reproduction. An Exploration of Horror Movies from Ghana and Nigeria', in Frank Wittmann and Rose Marie Beck (eds), *African Media Cultures – Cultures de Medias en Afrique. Topics in Interdisciplinary African Studies*, Vol. 2 (Cologne: Köppe), 263–85.
White, Luise (1993), 'Cars Out of Place. Vampires, Technology and Labor in East and Central Africa', *Representations* 43, 27–50.

White, Luise (2000), *Speaking with Vampires. Rumor and History in Colonial Africa* (Berkeley: University of California Press).
Wood, Robin (1986), *Hollywood from Vietnam to Reagan* (New York: Columbia University Press).

Filmography

The Brown Coat (Rashid Mrutu 2008)
Bwawa la Shetani (Shariff Jumbe 2007)
Friday the 13th (Sean S. Cunningham 1980)
Nsyuka I, II (Mussa Banzi 2003, 2005)
Popobawa (Haji Dilunga 2008)
Predator (John McTiernan 1987)
Scream (Wes Craven 1996)
Shumileta-Queen of the Devil I, II (Mussa Banzi 2005, 2006)
Thriller (John Landis 1983)
Wrong Turn (Rob Schmidt 2003)

11. PSYCHOPATHS AND GOTHIC LOLITAS: JAPANESE B-MOVIE GOTHIC IN GEN TAKAHASHI'S *GOTH: LOVE AND DEATH* AND GO OHARA'S *GOTHIC & LOLITA PSYCHO*

Jay McRoy

INTRODUCTION

Since the pillaging of Rome by a combination of Scandinavian and Eastern European warriors (a.k.a. 'the Goths') in the fifth century CE, the 'Gothic' has proven to be a very flexible term infused with a plethora of seemingly contradictory connotations. As Richard Davenport-Hines writes, the 'Gothic has always had the versatility to provide imagery to express the anxieties of historical epochs. It has provided fantasies of dystopia – invoking terror, mystery, despair, malignity, human puniness and isolation – which since the seventeenth century have gratified, distressed, or chilled consumers of paintings, ornaments, buildings, literature, cinema, and clothes' (Davenport-Hines 2000, 1). Invested with multiple paradoxical implications, Gothic art and sentiments have long provided an array of challenges for critics across numerous academic disciplines.

Whereas many critical and popular studies have explored the Western Gothic in its multiple iterations, very few works have sought to explore what might constitute a Japanese Gothic in either a cultural or a cinematic context. Undoubtedly, this lack of sustained scholarship stems from the fact that, in Japan, the term 'Gothic' (*goshikku*) does not carry the same semantic weight or cultural significance as it does in the Western European tradition. This is due to several factors, not the least of which arise from Japan's geographical and historical remove from Rome, medieval Christianity, and the immediate socio-historical influences of Western aesthetic and literary Romanticism. It is perhaps not surprising, then, that critical discourses on Japanese cinema rarely focus on the Gothic as a transcultural style comprising an assemblage of narrative and visual conceits designed to evoke foreboding moods or tonalities. At best, the vast majority of such texts – especially those aimed at a primarily Western readership – draw analogies between Japanese *kaidan* (ghost stories) and similarly striking representations within Western Gothic art.

In recent decades, elements of the Western Gothic clothing style have influenced sartorial fashions among certain Japanese subcultures; the Gothic Lolita (*gosu rori*), for example, is 'one of the most popular costumes' (Kawamura 1998, 29) donned by young women who gather weekly on the Jingu Bridge near the Harajuku subway station. Additionally, dozens of popular *anime* and *manga* titles feature characters sporting Western Gothic attire. As one might expect, these appropriations of Western Gothic elements have also found their way into recent works of Japanese cinema. This is most notable in the horror film, a genre frequently marketed at younger/teenage audiences. Two works in particular stand out in this regard: Gen Takahashi's *Goth: Love and Death* (*Gosu*, 2008) and Go Ohara's *Gothic & Lolita Psycho* (*Gosu Rori Shokeinin*, 2010).

Gothic Japan?

The Gothic is a frequently paradoxical tradition. While some literary and visual artists have historically deployed Gothic tropes as 'emotional, aesthetic and philosophical reaction[s]' against Enlightenment virtues such as 'reason', 'true knowledge', and 'synthesis' (Davenport-Hines (2000, 3), others mobilise Gothic trappings in a reactionary fashion, stigmatising social, cultural and physiological otherness. Thus, even as the monstrous, hybrid bodies of entities like Victor Frankenstein's patchwork creature and Bram Stoker's Eastern European count reveal a cultural fascination with the transgression of perceived boundaries between life and death, human and animal, etc., these same hybrid entities likewise function both as a locus of dread and as a thinly veiled metaphor for a plethora of societal anxieties and fears. Judith Halberstam recognises this latter impulse when she remarks that 'the emergence of the monster within Gothic fiction marks a particularly modern emphasis upon the horror of particular kinds of bodies' (Halberstam 1995, 3). This is accomplished, she argues, by collapsing 'various racial and sexual threats to nation, capitalism, and the bourgeoisie' (3) into a single figure that 'metaphorized modern subjectivity as a balancing act between inside/outside, female/male, body/mind, native/foreign, proletarian/aristocrat' (1).

Modern Gothic fiction's departure from the classic novel's perceived adherence to literalism, a divergence closely linked to the Gothic tale's conspicuous stylistic and narrative devices, directly influences the structure and tone of horror cinema globally. This is especially true of Gothic horror films, where motifs such as decay, dissolution, malignity, impurity, unregulated consumption, hybridity, and depictions of a society under threat circulate widely. In addition, artists like Sidney Sime and Aubrey Beardsley borrowed what they saw as the 'Gothic undertones ... in Japanese art' as 'a reaction against the oppressiveness of Western thought' (Blouin 2012, 12). These appropriations, while illustrative of a desire on the part of Western artists for more expansive and diverse fields of representation, frequently accompanied and, thus, contributed to orientalist discourses by writers as varied as the fantasist Lord Dunsany and journalists like William Randolph Hearst. In such writings, these authors drew upon Asian – and frequently Japanese – settings in order to create an atmosphere of radical ambiguity and supernatural dread, popularising conceptions of the 'exotic Far East' as a realm of other-worldly demons and apparitions. According to Michael Joseph Blouin, 'early attempts to contain the idea of "Japan" in supernatural terms regularly exceeded, on some level, the confines of the artistic form used to do so. It is from this unrest [that many of] the specters of modernity ... are predicated' (19). What's more, these Gothicised conceptualisations of 'Japaneseness' perpetuated xenophobic depictions of 'the Orient' as the locus of potential threats to Western culture in the form of an imagined 'yellow peril'. In keeping with the nineteenth-century Gothic's fascination with and misgivings about the collapse of previously discrete ideas of 'nation' and 'self', these orientalist texts construct Japan as 'monstrous'. The result is the invention of an illusory Japan defined 'as other than the imagined [Western] community' and the Japanese as beings 'that cannot be imagined as community' (Halberstam 1995, 15).

Of course, Gothic tropes – from a preoccupation with death, decay, trauma and grief, to monstrous figures that threaten to unravel the fragile veil of illusions we weave to divide 'self' from 'other' – are by no means exclusive to Western art. Many of the most celebrated works of post-war Japanese cinema, like Kenji Mizoguchi's *Ugetsu Monogatari* (1953), Akira Kurosawa's *Throne of Blood* (*Kumonosu-jô*, 1959), Nobuo Nakagawa's *Ghost Story of Yotsuya* (*Tôkaidô Yotsuya kaidan*, 1959) and Kineto Shindô's *Onibaba* (1964) and *Kuroneko* (*Yabu no naka no kuroneko*, 1968), boast elements reminiscent of the Western Gothic tradition. Lensed over forty years after the Meiji Restoration (1868–1912), and mere decades after Japan's defeat in the Second World War, these films include the supernatural conceits, 'painterly' chiaroscuro lighting schemes, fatalistic undertones, 'dispossessed samurais (*ronin*)' and 'wronged, suffering women' that Japanese film scholar Colette Balmain recognises as constituting what she dubs the 'Edo Gothic' tradition (Balmain 2008, 50). Drawing upon Buddhist and Shinto mythologies, as well as dark tales from Japanese literary and theatrical (particularly *noh* and *kabuki*) traditions, these works resemble Western Gothic films in their compositional and tonal elements. Such similarities may explain the cross-cultural appeal of Edo Gothic films, as well as the continued power of some of their most conspicuous tropes. For example, the figure of the *onryō* – the 'wronged' or 'suffering' woman who returns from the dead to haunt the living – has become, thanks to the international popularity of the Japanese horror film renaissance of the 1990s, one of the most recognisably iconic figures in all of world cinema.

In the realm of contemporary music and fashion, Japan's Goth subculture resembles similar US and Western European scenes in its embrace of Victorian-inflected clothing styles, as well as in the extensive use of cosmetics to sculpt wan yet striking visages. Perhaps the most overt manifestation of this sensibility are Gothic Lolitas (*Gusu-Loli*), young women (and occasionally men) who combine the aforementioned Gothic trappings with attire that fetishises youth through a combination of 'sexuality and cuteness' that, in Japan's 'still largely patriarchal and homogenous culture', can be mobilised as a '"soft" or "nonviolent"' form of rebellion' that allows those who adopt this look to 'empower [themselves] by enhancing [their] sex and gender characteristics' in an overtly performative manner (Kawamura 1998, 113). Such posturing, especially on the part of young women, demonstrates the symbiotic relationship between youth culture and the Japanese fashion industry. Since young people 'are both consumers and producers' of fashion, '[p]rofessionals in the fashion industry rely on the youth, and, as a result, individuals and institutions are in an interdependent relationship in spreading a subcultural phenomenon that comes with specific styles and fashion' (115).

Takahashi Gen's *Goth: Love of Death*

Gen Takahashi's *Goth: Love of Death* draws upon both Otsuichi's 2002 Honkaku Mystery Award-winning novel, *Goth: A Novel of Horror* (*Gosu: Risutokatto Jiken* ['Wristcut Incident']), and the novel's subsequent manga adaptation, *Goth: A Novel of Horror* (Tokyo Pop, 2008), illustrated by Kendi Oiwa. The film tells the story of two alienated high school students, Yoru Morino (Kanata Hongô) and Itsuki Kamayama (Rin Takanashi), who are drawn together by their shared fascination with a series of murders in which pretty, long-haired women are dispatched via injections of potassium chloride. After having their left hands severed at the wrist, their corpses are placed in elegant poses for people to find. In an attempt to forge a relationship with Itsuki, Yoru introduces him to one of her regular haunts, a gloomy café frequented by 'the strangest people'. One rainy evening, while discussing the recent spate of serial 'wristcut' murders, Yoru discovers what she correctly identifies as the murderer's notebook on the café floor. Itsuki is sceptical at first, but after the notebook leads them directly to a yet-to-be-discovered body, it soon becomes clear that they have stumbled upon a piece of evidence that could quickly put an end to the killings were it were to be handed over to the police.

Rather than surrendering the notebook to the authorities, Itsuki and Yoru elect to keep their discovery a secret. When Yoru dresses like one of the serial killer's most recent victims, and is subsequently abducted, Itsuki confronts the café owner. The café owner asks him why he thinks he is the killer, and Itsuki explains that he figured it out when he realised that, out of all of the people in the café, only the owner regularly used a water-based ink that ran on some of the notebook's rain-dampened pages. 'I just don't want anyone getting in the way of my work', the owner explains. 'I totally understand', Itsuki responds. Rather than turning the killer in to the police, Itsuki returns his notebook. In exchange, the owner/killer tells Itsuki where he can find Yoru and then leaves, assuring Itsuki that he will never return. In the apartment above the café, Itsuki finds the walls covered with news clippings about the murders and photos of the murdered women. He also finds a collection of hands in the freezer and a semi-conscious Yoru on the floor of one of the apartment's larger rooms. When asked several days later why he bothered to rescue her, Itsuki explains that he wanted to hear the remainder of Yoru's story about how in childhood her twin sister, Yu, died during a 'hanging' game they used to play. 'It must have been hard', Itsuki tells her, 'keeping your secret for nine years. Yu.' Yoru acknowledges that she is indeed Yu, and that she switched identities with her sister. 'You know', Yoru says moments before Itsuki ends the call, 'I had a feeling. I felt that the first person to call me by my name would be you.'

The English title of Gen Takahashi's *Goth: Love and Death* differs significantly from both the title of the original Japanese novel, *Goth: Wristcut Incident*, and that of its manga revision, *Goth: A Novel of Horror*. With its dual implications of murder and self-harm, *Goth: Wristcut Incident* lends Otsuichi's novel a distinctly violent, bloody and potentially self-destructive resonance. Similarly, the title *Goth: A Novel of Horror* suggests that readers should expect the manga's story line and illustrations to conform to a host of well-established genre conventions. The film's legend, *Love and Death*, not only telegraphs the motion picture's romanticised depiction of the characters' attachment to morbidity and death, but also comes close to acknowledging the connection between 'love' and 'death' that Georges Bataille recognises as existing at the very edge of horror, at the very notion of 'limits':

> There is always some limit which the individual accepts. He identifies this limit with himself. Horror seizes him at the thought that this limit may cease to be. But we are wrong to take this limit and the individual's acceptance of it seriously. The limit is only there to be overreached. Fear and horror are not the real and final reaction; on the contrary, they are a temptation to overstep the bounds. (Bataille 1986, 144)

Itsuki and Yoru repeatedly challenge each other to 'overstep' socially accepted responses to violence and death, a move that distinguishes their blossoming relationship from the more traditional teen romances that occasionally accompany the primary action in contemporary horror films.

Throughout the film's opening sequences, Takahashi frames Yoru and Itsuko as outsiders who seem comfortable in their isolation. Both characters even go so far as to verbally reject the notion of using cell phones because of the inevitable (and frequently unwanted) contact with others that these technologies facilitate. Only when they require these culturally ubiquitous communication devices to maintain close communication do they finally elect to own them, a decision that has unexpected consequences when the serial killer menaces Yoru over her phone. What's more, rather than succumbing to clichéd depictions of young lovers finding solace in each other's company, Takahashi carefully guides his actors through skilfully modulated performances that balance representations of increasing intimacy with portrayals of the intense self-consciousness, precarity and anxiety that underlie many budding human relationships. For instance, Takahashi circumvents the romantic conceit of the 'meet cute', electing instead to provide audiences with a 'meet creepy' as Yoru and Itsuki exchange words and, eventually, books. Yoru gives Itsuki a book entitled *All I Saw Were Dead Bodies*; Itsuki returns the gesture by handing Yoru a collection of works by H. P. Lovecraft. Later, at approximately the film's halfway point, Takahashi similarly avoids conventional depictions of the 'blossoming romance'. Meeting beside a shallow stream where the serial killer's initial victim was discovered, Itsuki asks Yoru to lie in the stream with

Figure 11.1 Yoru (Rin Takanashi) reclines in the stream where the serial killer's first victim was found in Gen Takahashi's *Goth: Love of Death* (*Gosu*, 2008)

her body positioned like the recently discovered victim. As Yoru 'floats' among the stream's iridescent mixture of blues and greens, Itsuki imagines blood blooming out from a large scar on her wrist – an image that recalls the recent murders even as it implies a symbolic consummation of their union. In this sense, although Yoru and Itsuki never touch during this sequence, the film's *mise-en-scène* suggests an emerging intimacy with a beauty and power that few displays of physical contact could convey.

Although drawn to one another by their mutual fascination with the darker sides of human behaviour, Yoru and Itsuki differ pointedly in many regards. Yoru, for example, spends the majority of her time alone, and we never see or hear of her parents. She wears a long-sleeved dark blue school uniform despite the heatwave baking her hometown, a wardrobe choice that enhances her separation from her classmates, who describe her as 'morbid' and 'gloomy'. Her bedroom resembles a Victorian-style library complete with dusty hardcover books, sputtering lamps and candles and flowing black drapery. In contrast, Itsuki 'passes' as a typical high school student. He spends time with his mother and younger sister, hides the macabre texts that most interest him behind a fake bookshelf in his otherwise ordinary-looking bedroom, and is generally amiable around classmates, who view his occasionally dark statements as attempts at humour. Possessed of a seemingly sociopathic lack of empathy, Itsuki wears a mask of 'normality', a deliberate performance rendered especially unsettling in an exquisite tracking shot during which his countenance visibly shifts from melancholic introspection to smiling sociability to – during the shot's final moments – a morose solipsistic brooding.

Itsuki's ability to seemingly shift emotional registers at will is crucial to understanding Yoru and Itsuki's more profound differences. Isuki's ability to 'put on [a] happy face' reveals an important distinction between their characters. As Itsuki points out, their attitudes towards the murders in their community ultimately differ in significant ways. Death and murder are enticing to both Yoru and Itsuki, but whereas Yoru fantasises about dying in romanticised ways, Itsuki's attraction to murder and death is potentially more sinister. As Itsuki warns Yoru, their differing attitudes towards death are analogous to the 'difference between those who kill and [those who] are killed'.

Lastly, although both serial murder and Yoru and Itsuki's shared fascination with death are crucial narrative elements, Takahashi's film plays more like a dark melodrama than a conventional horror film reliant upon jump scares, gore, or supernatural elements. The film's pacing is frequently deliberate, often languorous, which helps shape the film's pervasive melancholic tone. What's more, rather than coding the introverted protagonists as 'monstrous', or in other ways compromising audience sympathies, Takahashi portrays Yoru and Itsuki as complex and introspective. Their brooding demeanours and attraction to the darker aspects of human nature, while certainly atypical, are neverthe-

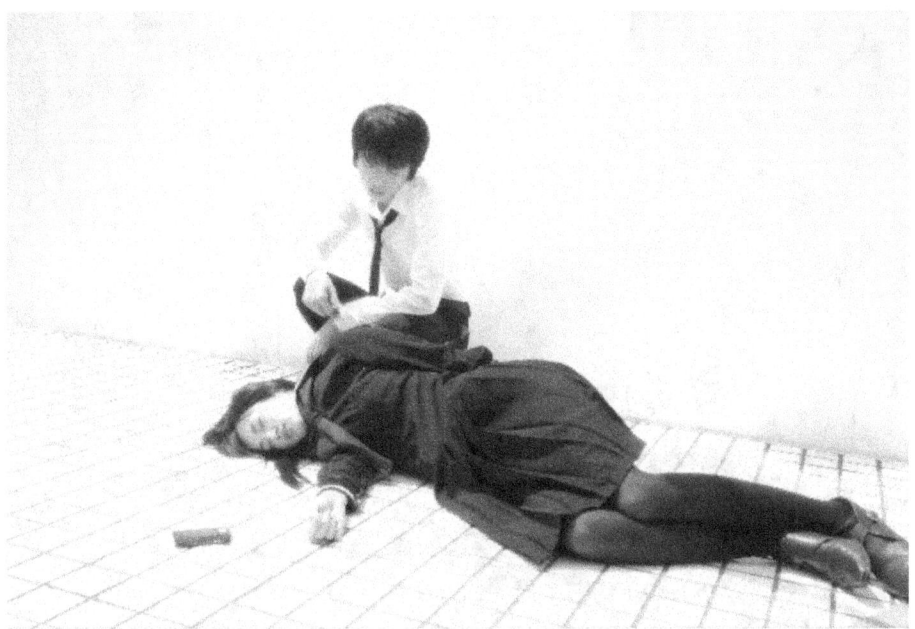

Figure 11.2 Itsuki (Kanata Hongô) crouches over the unconscious Yoru in Gen Takahashi's *Goth: Love of Death* (*Gosu*, 2008)

less depicted as a natural extension of humanity's preoccupation with its own finitude. That *Goth: Love of Death* occasionally traffics in Western Gothic conceits comes as little surprise in an age of increased globalisation. Rather than merely interpolating these Western Gothic elements, however, Takahashi implements them as a means of investigating something far more profound – namely the thanatophilic impulses that draw spectators to cinematic works that, while grim, nevertheless expose what many people recognise as death's ineffable beauty.

Gô Ohara's *Gothic & Lolita Psycho*

Unlike *Goth: Love of Death*'s melancholic tone, dourly introspective protagonists and frequently contemplative pacing, Gô Ohara's *Gothic & Lolita Psycho* is an unrestrained, hyperkinetic exercise in image as/over substance. Written by Hisakatsu Kuroki (*Nightmare Detective 2* [2008] and *Tetsuo: Bullet Man* [2009]) and featuring gore effects by Tsuyoshi Kazuno (*Tokyo Gore Police*, *Tôkyô zankoku keisatsu*, 2008), *Gothic & Lolita Psycho* weaves five elaborate and meticulously choreographed fight sequences around the story of Yuki (Rina Akiyama), a young woman seeking revenge upon five people who attacked her family, killing her mother and paralysing her father

Figure 11.3   The vengeful Yuki (Rina Akiyama) wields her deadly parasol in Gô Ohara's *Gothic & Lolita Psycho* (*Gosu Rori Shokeinin*, 2010)

from the waist down. Clad in tall black leather boots, long black leather gloves, a headdress sporting silk flowers and a lace-fringed black leather dress and corset, Yuki embodies the Gothic Lolita of the film's title. She fights with consummate, almost other-worldly skill, wielding an arsenal of parasols modified to function as deadly weapons ranging from swords to high-powered drills to machine guns with apparently endless ammunition. Expertly choreographed, these skirmishes play out like video game mêlées. Bodies pile up in her wake, and as she draws closer to sating her bloodlust, she discovers not only that her mother was a demon, but that her mother's blood courses through her veins as well. Harnessing her power to defeat the last of her mother's attackers, a self-admitted 'demon hunter' named Masato, Yuki ends the film at the very location in which we see her quest for vengeance commence: a fetish club called The Tokyo Gothic.

Gothic & Lolita Psycho continues a tradition of similarly excessive films, including Noboru Iguchi's *The Machine Girl* (*Kataude mashin garu*, 2008), Yoshihiro Nishimura's *Tokyo Gore Police* (*Tôkyô zankoku keisatsu*, 2008) and Yoshihiro Nishimura's and Naoyuki Tomomatsu's *Vampire Girl Vs. Frankenstein Girl* (*Kyûketsu Shôjo tai Shôjo Furanken*, 2009). Unlike the slow-burning tension and uncanny dread that underlie not only Takahashi's film, but also many defining works of Japanese horror cinema (e.g. Hideo Nakata's

Ring [*Ringu*, 1998], Takashi Shimizu's *Ju-on: The Grudge* [2002] and Kiyoshi Kurosawa's *Pulse* [*Kairo*, 2001]), these more recent films balance extravagant action, slapstick comedy and exaggerated gore effects. Consequently, they do not fit comfortably within the horror genre but, rather, blur the conventions of multiple genres, with extravagant, albeit entertaining, results.

Yuki lacks the psychological depth that Yoru and Itsuki demonstrate in Gen Takashashi's *Goth: Love of Death*. We learn that Yuki is motivated by vengeance; however, we are never told why she decides to adopt the identity of a psychotic Gothic Lolita. Ohara presents us with several brief flashbacks of the assault upon Yuki's family by the assassins she has committed herself to obliterating. Throughout these scenes, a funereal white emerges as the dominant colour scheme. Yuki and her family wear almost exclusively white clothing, and the environment is deliberately over-exposed, further coding the images we see as memories filtered through the haze of trauma. A dark, Gothic-style cross and a framed print of a similar cross bedeck the family's mantelpiece, but the significance of these items is never fully explored. In contrast to the white clothing worn by Yuki and her parents, the armed assailants wear black cloaks and hoods; against the hoary walls, floors and furniture, the blood from the attack (which culminates in Yuki's mother being crucified on the family's living-room wall) takes on an almost opalescent quality.

Figure 11.4   Yuki's mother (Fumie Nakajima) crucified on the living room wall in Gô Ohara's *Gothic & Lolita Psycho* (*Gosu Rori Shokeinin*, 2010)

These fragmentary depictions of the attack on Yuki's family, however, constitute one of the film's otherwise rare attempts at depicting a character's interiority. We revisit the evening of the assault several times, with Yuki steadily recalling details that eventually lead her to question her very humanity. Yuki's brief dialogues with her father likewise provide moments of exposition designed to explain our protagonist's motivation. Since the attack on his family, Yuki's disabled father has further embraced Christianity (as evidenced by his pastor-like attire), and he channels his feelings of guilt and inadequacy at not being able to defend his family into fashioning high-tech weapons for his warrior daughter. In their brief conversation before Yuki's final battle, Yuki's father begs her to give up her quest to destroy the assassins. He claims that having already lost his wife, he does not want to lose his daughter as well. This last-minute call for a change of heart plays out exactly as one might expect; Yuki rejects her father's pleas, a decision that costs her what little family she has left. An opportunity to explore Yuki's emotional and family dynamic is reduced to a simple narrative cliché intended to heighten the stakes of the climactic battle without burdening a thrill-seeking audience with nuanced ethical questions.

Rather than exploring the impetus behind the characters' actions in any substantial depth, *Gothic & Lolita Psycho* is preoccupied with spectacle. Like the film's eponymous hero, each of the assailants, in clothing and action, is a violent variation upon Japanese (stereo)types: Saki (Minami Tsukui) is a katana-wielding yakuza moll; Gerao is a lascivious teacher with psychic powers; Nightwatch is a penitent salaryman who weeps pathetically for forgiveness; Lady Elle is a schoolgirl with a sparking eye-patch and handguns accessorised with knives and a cell phone; and Masato is a charming and handsome gentleman with a talent for dispatching demonic forces. Additionally, in its fusion of physical comedy and intentionally ridiculous gore effects, *Gothic & Lolita Psycho* is a celebration of the human body in all its base materiality. The film's soundtrack intensifies these visuals; the sounds of bodily functions ranging from noodle-slurping mouths to belching and farting are amplified for comedic effect. Similarly, 'levitating' bodies 'float' on clearly visible wires, severed limbs and heads arc through the air in slow motion, and hacked bodies erupt into geysers of blood. In short, the film's *mise-en-scène* deliberately reveals the mechanisms and machinations of the cinematic apparatus.

Capitalising upon its modest budget, Ohara's *Gothic & Lolita Psycho* embraces stylistic affectation as an end in itself. This lends the film's action an intense theatricality. Throughout the protracted fight sequences, low angle framings and minimal set dressing disallow traditional economies of spectator immersion. In foregrounding its bombastic stylistic affectations, *Gothic & Lolita Psycho* continually reminds its audience that they are watching a fiction acted out before cameras on a soundstage. Furthermore, by adopting formulaic

Figure 11.5 Clothed in schoolgirl attire, the dangerous Lady Elle (Misaki Momose) opens fire on Yuki in Gô Ohara's *Gothic & Lolita Psycho* (*Gosu Rori Shokeinin*, 2010)

narrative elements (e.g. revenge) and select visual cues (e.g. emphatic zooms into close-ups, dramatic fonts, etc.) Ohara telegraphs his influences, locating *Gothic & Lolita Psycho*'s narrative and visual style both within a Western cinematic tradition (e.g. Bo A. Vibenius's *Thriller: They Call Her One Eye* [1973] and Quentin Tarantino's *Kill Bill* [2003–4]) and within the context of specific Japanese genre films (e.g. Toshiya Fugita's *Lady Snowblood* [1973]).

Gothic & Lolita Psycho's hyper-stylised aesthetic embraces the performative, 'operatic' and 'theatrical' (Davenport-Hines [2000], 6–7) components of contemporary 'Goth' music and fashion in both its Western and Japanese iterations. Unlike Takahashi's *Goth: Love of Death*, with its focus on the existential implications of its protagonists' behaviours, Ohara's film capitalises upon subcultural 'Goth' fashion and the pop-cultural caché attached to it. Thus, although both Takahashi's and Ohara's films are low-budget 'B-movies' that appropriate Gothic elements, their aims are ultimately quite disparate. Ohara is not interested in immersing his audience within a subtle or compelling drama, nor is he concerned with delving into the emotional depths of complex, richly drawn characters. Boasting a host of melodramatic personages rather than dramatic personae, *Gothic & Lolita Psycho* foregrounds the Gothic as *image* rather than as an artistic and cultural tradition that emerges (and re-emerges) both within and against a rich historical nexus of political and aesthetic concerns. This manoeuvre recalls similar gestures in the work of the popular US director (and international Goth culture icon) Tim Burton, whose alienated protagonists frequently adopt overtly Gothic 'sartorial solutions' (Spooner 2013, 47). Like popular Burton protagonists in films like *Beetlejuice* (1988), *Batman* (1989) and *Edward Scissorhands* (1990), Ohara's deadly Gothic Lolita engages in a process of 'radical self-fashioning', donning attire that directly references one of the most conspicuous *kosupure* (cosplay) figures in Japanese Goth subculture. Consequently, as with many of Burton's characters, Yuki's adoption of the Gothic Lolita persona *as image* broaches the theme of 'self-definition in a mundane [and – for Yuki – absurdly violent] world' (47). For Ohara, as with Burton, a film's 'look', and the tone it engenders, are every bit as important as 'story' (48).

Conclusion

In her recent essay on how one might conceive of an Asian Gothic cinema, Katarzyna Ancuta writes that just because 'Gothic theory has so far been informed exclusively by Western philosophies', scholars should not abandon attempts to explore the Gothic through the critical lenses provided by 'other systems of thought' (Ancuta 2014, 218). Indeed, such scholarship would be a welcome contribution to contemporary Gothic studies. The 'Gothic' has proven a very flexible term which, for well over three centuries, has been used to describe a multitude of aesthetic and cultural features/practices. As I have discussed in the previous pages, although Japan's history and culture differ substantially from those of Europe and North America, many tropes akin to those found in Western Gothic texts frequently inform the works of Japanese genre cinema. In our Internet age, in which more and more works of world cinema are assessable by curious viewers than ever before, motion pictures regularly traverse socio-cultural boundaries that once seemed impenetrable. This radical mobility is exciting. However, as long as contemporary notions of the Gothic remain extensively embedded within a Western historical context, critics will inevitably face limitations when it comes to analysing 'Gothic' elements in Japanese film. New and more expansive conceptualisations of the Gothic will help further illuminate the style's continuing transformations, a critical manoeuvre that will undoubtedly impact the work of film scholars around the globe.

Bibliography

Ancuta, Katarzina (2014), 'Asian Gothic', in Jerrold E. Hogle (ed.), *The Cambridge Companion to the Modern Gothic* (Cambridge: Cambridge University Press), 208–24.
Balmain, Colette (2008), *Introduction to Japanese Horror Film* (Edinburgh: Edinburgh University Press).

Bataille, Georges (1986), *Eroticism: Death and Sensuality* (San Francisco: City Lights).
Blouin, Michael Joseph (2012), *Specters of Modernity: 'Supernatural Japan' and the Cosmopolitan Gothic*, Ph.D. thesis, Michigan State University, <http://etd.lib.msu.edu/islandora/object/etd%3A847/datastream/OBJ/view> (last accessed 3 November 2017).
Davenport-Hines, Richard (2000), *Gothic: Four Hundred Years of Excess, Horror, Evil and Ruin* (New York: North Point Press).
Halberstam, Judith (1995), *Skin Shows: Gothic Horror and the Technology of Monsters* (Durham, NC: Duke University Press).
Kawamura, Yuniya (1998), *Fashioning Japanese Subcultures* (London and New York: Bloomsbury).
Spooner, Catherine (2013), 'Costuming the Outsider in Tim Burton's Cinema, or, Why a Corset Is Like a Codfish', in Jeffrey Andrew Weinstock (ed.), *The Works of Tim Burton: Margins to Mainstream* (New York: Palgrave Macmillan), 47–63.

12. HONG KONG GOTHIC: CATEGORY III FILMS AS GOTHIC CINEMA

Katarzyna Ancuta

In Hong Kong, Category III films are 'approved for exhibition only to persons who have attained the age of 18 years' (Film Censorship Ordinance, section 12). This category was part of a new rating system in Hong Kong under the *Movie Screening Ordinance Cap. 392* implemented on 10 November 1988. It was intended to allow artistic freedom to filmmakers, while protecting children from exposure to inappropriate images in film. In reality, the law created an opportunity for film producers to capitalise on the new-found legitimacy of 'low-budget pornography and gorefests' (Bordwell 2011, 79), leading to an explosion of exploitation films that became characteristic of Hong Kong popular cinema in the 1990s. The films in question, notable for their 'mix of murder and mutilation, large breasts and lesbianism' (Stringer 1999, 362), proved popular with domestic audiences and did well at the box office. They also launched the mainstream careers of stars like Veronica Yip and Anthony Wong, the latter receiving a Best Actor Hong Kong Film Award for his portrayal of a serial killer in *The Eight Immortals Restaurant: The Untold Story* (1993). These films also 'won guarded critical approval, and attracted cult attention from overseas video audiences' (362).

The critic Julian Stringer proposes that we treat Category III films as a distinct genre, albeit characterised by stylistic hybridity. But because the label is used for a variety of local and foreign films, such an all-inclusive generic classification is misleading. The category's diversity is illustrated by the range of films given this classification: Jackie Chan's *Crime Story* (1993), Andrew

Lau's *Young and Dangerous: The Prequel* (1998) and Wong Kar-Wai's *Happy Together* (1997). This category includes crime dramas, erotica, martial arts movies and war films, many of which include violence, racism, misogyny and homophobia, and are unified by their shared 'emphasis on sexuality, class violence, social mobility, the flattening of time, and the imagining of a dystopian postmodern aesthetic' (Stringer 1999, 364).

David Bordwell (2011, 96) notes that 'since ordinary Hong Kong films have a high quota of blood, sex, defecation and vomit, a film has to go far to earn a Category III rating'. Unsurprisingly, then, the first film upon which this honour was bestowed remains one of the most controversial offerings of exploitation cinema, *Men Behind the Sun* (1988). This film is a harrowing account of ruthless medical experimentation carried out by the infamous Japanese Unit 731 in a secret biological and chemical warfare research development facility in Harbin during the Second World War. While the topic may have originated from the director's need to document lesser-known atrocities of war, the film is chiefly remembered for its extreme depictions of mutilated bodies. Indeed, one of the most common discussions related to the film concerns the fate of the cat that dies a terrible death in the movie when it is devoured by thousands of plague-infected rats. Despite the director's claims that the scene was an elaborate special effect, his admission that the film included authentic autopsy footage of a young boy and that local farmers were delighted to see rats burnt alive (IMDb.com) leaves many people doubtful.

Stringer points out that this cinematic turn to sex and violence – motivated by profit – is a common characteristic of film industries that are declining as a result of economic and political changes. He attributes the popularity of Category III films (and their bleak dystopian themes) to the fear of uncertainty associated with the 1997 Hong Kong handover, which gave 'rise to an intense, urgent mass cultural conversation about what Communist rule will bring' (365). This is particularly visible in crime movies, which for Stringer 'represent the displaced political nightmares of those lower-class regional audiences who cannot afford to leave the city or achieve economic independence' (1999, 365). This chapter returns to the discussion of the socio-political tensions portrayed in these films (Stringer 1999; Stokes and Hoover 2003; Williams 2005) and proposes to read Category III crime dramas as part of a Gothic tradition in Hong Kong cinema. I focus on significant films made and released when Category III was at its peak, films that are inspired by true crimes: *The Untold Story* (1993), *The Untold Story 2* (1998), *Ebola Syndrome* (1996), *Daughter of Darkness* (1993), *Daughter of Darkness 2* (1994), *Human Pork Chop* (2001), *Love to Kill* (1993), *Dr. Lamb* (1992), *Taxi Hunter* (1993), *The Underground Banker* (1994), *Run and Kill* (1993), *The Rapist* (1994), *Diary of a Serial Killer* (1993) and *Red to Kill* (1994). Low-budget and following a repetitive stylistic formula of the exploitation genre, these films have been recognised as B-movies made for the thrills of the low-income audience. They engage with the topics of poverty, lawlessness, sexual abuse, family violence and class inequality. They depict crime among underprivileged people who are simultaneously victimised and vilified as monstrous; they also, as Stringer suggests, represent 'violent fantasies of working-class personal destruction' (367).

Misha Kavka (2002) argues that Gothic has never been established as a cinematic genre in its own right but that the term has often been used to describe plots, images, characters or styles within other genres. Kavka goes on to suggest that 'Gothic film brings a set of recognizable elements based in distinct *visual codes*' (210) that constitute the language of these films. She lists, among the key conventions, fear and the manipulation of space (where 'the effect of fear is produced through the transformations, extensions, and misalignments of size and distance'), and the blurring or boundaries (between past and present) that relates to the uncanny return of the abject (or between the masculine and the feminine), thus reconfiguring gender norms and sexuality in terms of monstrosity (210–11). Heidi Kaye (2004) describes Gothic films as having 'strong visuals, a focus on sexuality and an emphasis on audience response' (181); she suggests that their reliance on stylised settings emphasises 'the atmosphere of abnormality' (182). Similarly, Elisabeth Bronfen (2014, 112) posits that the spectral nature of cinema makes it particularly susceptible to Gothic, and she concludes that the 'Gothic film gesture is one of rendering intellectual and socio-cultural crises in excessive visceral, as well as visual terms'.

This chapter offers a Gothic reading of Hong Kong Category III crime films by focusing on the cinematic appropriation of the Gothic conventions and aesthetics woven into the plots, the visual storytelling and the depictions of monstrous characters. I pay specific attention to the representations of class, gender and political ideology, as well as the conflicts brought about by inequality and exploitation. I also explore how these films draw upon Gothic settings and spaces, particularly how they present a dystopian vision of Hong Kong's cityscape.

Gothic Politics, Monstrous Transformations

Category III crime movies reveal a dark side to Hong Kong's economic success and financial prosperity. The low-income heroes of the films live in the world far removed from the imposing skyscrapers, walled residences and luxury malls of the glamorous side to the city. For them, Hong Kong is 'another dimension' filled with 'sweatshops, storefronts, urban pollution, and shantytowns of unrelieved squalor, with too many people and too little land' (Hoover and Stokes 1998, 25). These city dwellers are by-products of the city's 'cutthroat' capitalism and they live out their days with '[n]o minimum wage, no official poverty line, no full employment policy, and a minimal social safety net' (Stokes and Hoover 2003, 47). The class-conscious settings of these films evoke comparisons with American socio-economic horror exemplified by *Henry: The Portrait of the Serial Killer* (1986) and the fiction of Emile Zola, where naturalism is 'an interrogative device often commenting on oppressive social conditions' (Williams 2005, 205).

Fears and anxieties about the 1997 Hong Kong handover (which led to approximately 50,000 people emigrating from the city annually since 1984) were only intensified after news broadcasts of the 1989 Tiananmen Square massacre, which brought 20 per cent of Hong Kong's population to the streets to protest against Communist rule in mainland China (Hoover and Stokes 1998, 26). The heroes of Category III crime films, caught in the downward spiral of poverty and crime, represent those citizens who did not have the privilege of leaving. The films treat crime as endemic in low-income areas and they suggest that the low socio-economic status of the characters leads to their misogyny, homophobia and violence. In *Dr. Lamb*, a taxi driver (modelled on the serial killer Lam Kor-Wan) murders women and then photographs, mutilates and molests their corpses. He chooses victims that he sees as 'bad women', which implies a mission-oriented motive to his murders, but his hatred of women lacks clear motivation. As Tony Williams suggests, Lam's social environment, inclusive of cramped space, uncaring parents and corrupting friends, contributes to the depiction of the character's psychosis (2005, 210) (Figure 12.1). However, his pornographically-depicted sexual attacks on these women can also be read as a 'compensatory mechanism served up to offset the anxieties of political impotence' of the film's male working-class audience (Stringer 1999, 377). In a political and economic system that reduces working-class men to replaceable cogs in the machinery of production, his victimisation of women weaker than him is blindly seen as the only way of reclaiming his power.

Category III crime films demonise the economically underprivileged characters as money-minded, opportunistic, dishonest and uncaring. They drink, gamble, and spend money on prostitutes. They are not particularly intelligent, and they are often unable to comprehend the consequences of their actions. *Human Pork Chop* (inspired by the 1999 'Hello Kitty Murder Case' of Fan Man-yee, whose head was found inside a Hello Kitty doll) tells the story of the torture and abuse of a prostitute who stole money from a local gangster. Her attackers drip molten plastic over her bare legs, lock her inside a refrigerator and force her to eat excrement. Yet the woman's death seems to catch everyone by surprise. Her corpse is stashed in the kitchen refrigerator and the gangsters continue as if nothing has happened, helping themselves to drinks that lie chilled in the fridge under the body. As decomposition begins, they chop her into pieces and boil her body parts to destroy the evidence of the murder. Soon after, they eat soup from the same pot, suggesting that

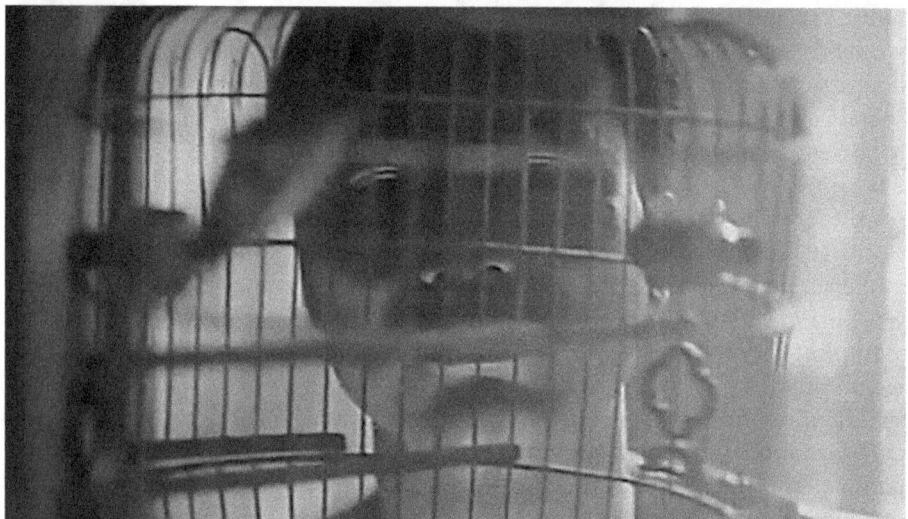

Figure 12.1 Poverty and cramped space contribute to the making of the murderer in *Dr Lamb* (Danny Lee, 1992)

the gangsters consume her or, at the very least, do not care too much about hygiene of the kitchen.

In *Ebola Syndrome*, the character Kai finds himself on the run in South Africa after the murder of four people in Hong Kong. Working as a cook in a Chinese restaurant, Kai is preoccupied with his sexual urges and thinks little of the effects of his actions. His decision to buy meat from the tribe decimated by a mysterious disease and to rape a half-dead tribal woman does not testify to his intellectual prowess. What Kai lacks when it comes to logical thinking he makes up for with his explosive temperament, lashing out against anyone he sees as bullying him. This includes Kai's old boss, who caught him sleeping with his wife, as well as his boss's henchmen and the adulteress herself. But it also extends to Kai's new employers, who exploited him in their restaurant, and the daughter of his girlfriend whom he uses as a human shield when fleeing the police, as well as scores of random people who die infected with the Ebola virus he carries, standing in for the entire system he blames for his failures. Both movies demonstrate that the combination of ignorance and aggression is fatal. Significantly, these qualities are also linked to the low socio-economic status of the characters. They are also used for the further 'othering' of the films' Gothic villains – reclusive, brooding, misogynistic narcissists who indulge in bouts of sadistic violence, portrayed as terrifying and pathetic at the same time (Figure 12.2).

Many of the murderers in these films are depicted as dissatisfied with their lives and driven by the desire for social mobility, often advancing through gambling and extortion. *The Untold Story* begins with Wong Chi-hang (based on a serial killer of that name) burning a man alive in Hong Kong after a dispute over a mah-jong debt. Later in Macau, Wong brutally murders his new boss, as well as his boss's wife, their five kids and his sister in order to claim the ownership of the Eight Immortals Restaurant. He also kills an employee who catches him cheating and a cashier who is too observant for her own good. All the Macau victims end up as delicious 'barbecued pork buns', for which the restaurant is famous. *The Untold Story 2* changes the gender balance, introducing a mentally unstable woman, Fung, who kills her cousin, Kuen, and also processes her into food. Cannibalism is a frequent motif of Gothic texts, not only because it is considered a taboo and often associated with primitivism, but also because it is 'about our participation in a system of exploitation that, in its callous competition and unrestrained aggression, encourages us to consume one another' (Wester 2015, 155). Cannibalism in *The Untold Story* films is portrayed as the ultimate form of economic exploitation.

Before getting eaten, Kuen, who, like Fung, came to Hong Kong from Guangzhou, delivers a lengthy lecture on the Hong Kong lifestyle, which, according to her, prioritises efficiency, stepping on others before they step on you, and finding a rich boyfriend because 'nobody gets rich by working hard'. She scolds Fung: 'You mainlanders are all greedy. There is nothing free in this world. If you want it you should fight for it.' She is unaware that with these words she has just signed her own death warrant. After serving Kuen's barbecued ribs to the restaurant's customers, Fung replaces her in business and in private life, which, Williams argues, represents another type of 1997-related fear: 'What if Mainland interest in Hong Kong did not involve changing it into a Maoist realm but rather in copying its worst practices?' (Williams 2005, 216).

Figure 12.2   Anthony Wong as the Gothic villain. Upper: *Ebola Syndrome* (Herman Yau, 1996); lower: *The Untold Story* (Danny Lee, Herman Yau, 1993)

The phantom of Communist China haunts Category III movies. The mainland as a site of danger is portrayed in *Daughter of Darkness*, a tragic story of Fong, who, after years of domestic violence (which culminates in tortuous sexual abuse by her father), breaks down and brutally slaughters her entire family, for which she is subsequently executed. The sequel, practically a mirror image of the first film, focuses on the murderous revenge of another woman on a family that brutalised her and killed her husband. Although this time she is let off, she takes her own life. Set in a village in southern China neighbouring Hong Kong, which doubles as 'the city of dreams' for the locals, both films continuously oscillate between farce and horror, the former reserved chiefly for the portrayal of the incompetent local policemen who compromise the crime scene, destroy crucial evidence, beat up their suspects, pose for funny photographs with the dead and sexually molest the corpses of female victims. Sexism is rife among the police. The female officer is ordered to undergo a series of gynaecological exams to distract a witness and assist in collective masturbation to obtain semen samples from the villagers. All the nonsensical demands of the commissioner are accompanied by the reminder that good communists are expected to always 'serve the people'. The first film additionally makes a direct reference to the Tiananmen tragedy delivered as a threat to those obstructing the work of authorities. Borderline between abuse and satire, such portrayals remind us of 'the capacity of Gothic formulae to produce laughter as abundantly as emotions of terror or horror' (Botting 1997, 168). They simultaneously offend and provide a comic release, distancing the audience from the characters.

Despite frequent references to communism, China looks quite similar to Hong Kong in Category III films: both places are dominated by greedy opportunists who bully weaker people and profit from the misfortunes of others. Fong's boyfriend, who is a local policeman, is no match for her well-connected father. In the sequel, a 'Northerner' comes to the village to ask his army comrade to impregnate his wife (he is impotent from a war injury). He pleads with his friend that without an heir he will lose his land to his greedy relatives. The arrangement is discovered by a local man, who threatens to report the couple to the authorities; adultery and false claims of parentage are treated severely by the Party. He demands a lot of money from the husband and takes the wife hostage as collateral. The woman is subsequently raped by the man and his son, after which the man's wife brutally inserts a water hose inside the victim's vagina to remove evidence of the rape. Her unwanted pregnancy ends in a self-induced abortion and the husband's feeble attempt at revenge ends in his death. In both films China is the land of danger, extortion, debauchery and lawlessness. The films' settings, limited to unattractive village houses, stand in stark contrast with Hong Kong skyscrapers and luxury residences. Old-fashioned, impoverished and adorned with communist propaganda, these are doubly marked as darkly 'primitive' spaces evoking the traditions of the barbaric 'old country' and the regressive ideology of Communist China that threatens the integrity of capitalist Hong Kong. China functions as the barbaric Gothic borderland here, teeming with monsters about to be unleashed on their neighbours. And yet, most frighteningly, the Chinese 'others' are essentially the same as their Hong Kong counterparts.

The anxiety about the 1997 handover is almost palpable in *Run and Kill*, in which a decadent and corrupt nightclub is named '1997', a direct reference to the year of political change. Fatty Cheung begins the day believing that life is beautiful. But he is shocked when he finds his wife in bed with the grocer, and he wanders aimlessly through the streets until he reaches the '1997' club.

Among the pimps, gangsters, drunks and drug addicts, prostitutes and adulterers, the heavily intoxicated Cheung unintentionally puts a hit on his wife and her lover. The next day they are hacked to pieces by violent thugs described as Vietnamese war refugees. When the Vietnamese burn down Cheung's shop and demand more money he seeks help from a Chinese gang. Things go from bad to worse and he loses the rest of his family and his sanity; he is singled out by a psychotic mercenary, Ching Fung, as the target of revenge for the death of his brother. Portrayed as an indestructible ex-Red Army soldier turned psychotic in the aftermath of (possibly) the Sino-Vietnamese war, Ching Fung is a depiction of a blood-drinking Vietnamese gangster who is a by-product of war and of Hong Kong's hostility to undesired foreigners. The message is clear: war creates monsters. Still, these monsters are only unleashed when Fatty Cheung makes the fateful decision to step through the door marked '1997' (Figure 12.3).

Category III crime films depict their central characters as monsters. Their monstrosity arises out of their class, poverty and ignorance, but these films are also fascinated with monstrous transformations. As Hong Kong mutates from a successful 'Asian Tiger' into dysfunctional 'Asian Gotham', even its most insignificant inhabitants can become beasts. Their monstrous transformations may be triggered by external stimuli like rain (*Dr. Lamb*), or the colour red (*Red to Kill*), or be psychologically motivated, often the result of a mental breakdown caused by grief (*Taxi Hunter*) or abuse (*Daughter of Darkness*). Like shape-shifters in other Gothic movies, such as werewolves and vampires, these characters transform mentally and physically. Lam performs an orgasmic primeval dance to celebrate death (*Dr Lamb*) and Fong becomes possessed as she butchers her family (*Daughter of Darkness*). Ching Fung's killing sprees are preceded by a nosebleed (*Run and Kill*), Fung's behaviour becomes erratic every time she hears the word 'insane' (*The Untold Story 2*), Kai is consumed by a deadly virus (*Ebola Syndrome*), and the rapist Chan transforms from an invisible social worker into a full-blown comic book villain, complete with a ridiculous leotard outfit (*Red to Kill*). In each case, the characters' monstrosity is the result of socio-economic conditions and the dark, dystopian side of the cityscape.

Gothic Appetites: Cannibalising the Oppressed

The final scenes of Brian Yuzna's US satirical horror *Society* (1989) show a cannibalistic orgy during which the rich quite literally feed on the poor. In Category III films, however, it is the impoverished who cannibalise other poor people, often quite literally. The flesh of the victims is frequently processed into barbecued 'pork' buns, ribs, hamburgers, or stews. It is a labour-intensive process and each film involves lengthy scenes of food preparation followed

Figure 12.3 The shadow of Hong Kong handover looms over the characters in *Run and Kill* (Billy Tang, 1993)

by close-ups of unsuspecting customers licking their lips and fingers in delight as they devour human flesh. In *Diary of a Serial Killer*, the murderer mimics the vampire: he drinks his victims' blood and chews on their body parts. In *The Underground Banker*, Anthony Wong (who plays a truck driver whose stable life is ruined by a loan shark) reverts to his *Untold Story* persona; he carries a meat cleaver and threatens to turn the gangsters into pork buns. In these movies, the working-class protagonists are often defined by their obscene appetites.

In *Capital*, Karl Marx warned that 'along with the constantly diminishing number of the magnates of capital, who usurp and monopolise all advantages of this process of transformation, grows the mass of misery, oppression, slavery, degradation, exploitation; but with this too grows the revolt of the working-class, a class always increasing in numbers, and disciplined, united, organized by the very mechanism of the process of capitalist production itself' (1999, Chapter 32, para. 2). Although the representation of violence in these films can be read as 'an irrational bloodthirsty revenge by a low-income proletariat against forces they perceive as oppressive' (Williams 2005, 206), the underprivileged characters of Category III films do not rise up against the rich and powerful. The cannibalistic metaphor of capitalism, which devours living labour 'so long as there is a muscle, a nerve, a drop of blood to be exploited' (Engels, cited in Marx, Ch. 10, s. 7, para. 8), is here understood as eating one's own people. Significantly, it is also a collective experience. Williams suggests that the cannibal motifs in Category III movies are a direct influence of 1970s Italian cannibal films and domestic precursors like Tsui Hark's *We Are Going to Eat You* (1980). But the troubled relationship of Chinese culture to cannibalism goes much deeper.

Zheng Yi's book *Scarlet Memorial: Tales of Cannibalism in Modern China* (1996) is a reportage account of the mass slaughter and collective cannibalism that occurred during the Cultural Revolution in the Guangxi province of southern China (approximately 600 km from Hong Kong). The book includes descriptions of individual cases pieced together from historical sources and conversations with the victims' families, as well as interviews with the killers and cannibals who consumed the 'class enemies' in accordance with the revolutionary directives during spontaneous 'feasts of human flesh' that followed public critiques of revolutionary principles. While some of the former cannibals (like Xie Jingwen) attribute their actions to the spirit of the times when '[a]nything was acceptable as long as it was in the name of class struggle and proletariat dictatorship' (Zheng Yi 1996, 32), others state that is was a political part of the revolution. One of the cannibals, Yi Wansheng, who was 86 years old at the time of the interview, states the following: 'Fear nothing! Will his ghost return to seek revenge? Ha! To engage in revolution, my heart is red! Didn't Chairman Mao say "kill or be killed"? If I live, you must die. Class struggle!' (49).

The core of the investigation focuses on the events in Wuxuan County (between 1968 and 1969), where there were numerous reports of cannibalism. According to Zheng Yi (1996):

> Each criticism rally was followed by a beating, and each death ended in cannibalism ... Not only common people, but everyone, even innocent young boys and girls and teachers, joined in the delirious wave of

cannibalism ... Once victims had been subjected to criticism, they were cut open alive, and all their body parts – heart, liver, gallbladder, kidneys, elbows, feet, tendons, intestines, were boiled, barbecued, or stir-fried into a gourmet cuisine. (111)

Although the official list compiled by the Wuxuan officials mentions over four hundred people who had engaged in acts of cannibalism, Zheng Yi speculates that the number may have been as high as 10,000. Apart from the proletarian zeal for destroying class enemies, at least some of the flesh feasts were also motivated by more self-serving beliefs deeply rooted in Chinese consciousness that certain human body parts like livers or hearts have medicinal properties and can serve as a tonic to improve one's health. Such, for instance, was the case of a teacher in Mengshan County who labelled his 13-year-old student a 'target of dictatorship' to have her killed and consume a 'beauty's heart' supposed to cure diseases (Zheng Yi 1996, 53).

Medicinal consumption of human flesh has a long history in China, and yet the description of a virginal beauty sacrificed to prolong the life of a diseased man of power reads like a classic Gothic narrative invoked by Zheng Yi to condemn the terrors of Cultural Revolution. Such images also anticipate the mechanisms of neoliberal medicine that enable the privileged to 'cannibalise' the organs of poor donors to extend their lives. Maisha Wester invites us to read the metaphor of cannibalism as expressive of racial, cultural and economic anxieties characteristic of 'civilised' societies always weary of the danger of regression into the 'barbaric' and 'primitive' state. For Emilie Yueh-yu Yeh and Neda Hei-tung Ng, the relationship between China and Hong Kong is that of a mother and child, where the 'the mother is "horrific" in the sense of being all-engulfing, primitive' (Freeman, cited in Yeh and Ng 2008, 6) and the source of all horror. Cannibalism in Category III movies thus has a dual purpose – it depicts the exploitative nature of capitalist society characterised by 'rabid consumption' (Wester 2015, 163), but also feeds the racial tensions, a constant reminder that Hong Kong is about to be consumed by its primitive and cannibalistic Communist 'mother'.

Anthropologists make a distinction between hunger and symbolic cannibalism; in other words, eating human flesh because of starvation or for ritualistic purposes. Within the latter category, endophagy (eating one's kin) is often practised as an expression of respect or grief, while exophagy (eating outsiders) is performed to claim absolute victory over an enemy and absorb their strength and virtues (Brottman 1997, 10–11). Occasionally, the Category III depictions of cannibalism are an exertion of dominance over others, but the most striking cases have a practical motivation. Processing human bodies into food serves a double function: it allows the criminal restaurateurs to dispose of incriminating evidence and it provides them with free meat. Nothing goes to waste when

Figure 12.4 The mundane face of cannibalism. Upper: *Human Pork Chop* (Benny Chan Chi Shun, 2001); lower: *The Untold Story* (Danny Lee, Herman Yau, 1993)

waste can also be turned into capital and sold for profit. Interestingly, in all the cases, the murderer-proprietor facilitates rather than participates in the acts of consumption. By forcing customers into unwittingly transgressing a taboo, the killers feel empowered and in control; they demonstrate that, despite their shortcomings and social disadvantages, they are still at the top of the food chain (Figure 12.4).

The dystopian visions of Category III films revolve around those who further their own interests through violence. This is evident through the films' portrayals of individual criminals and organised crime structures, but also the depictions of ordinary families and law enforcement institutions. The protagonist of *Diary of a Serial Killer*, Lam Shiu-bill (modelled on the 'Guanzhou Ripper'

Li Wenxian), seeks to improve the fate of local prostitutes by brutally killing them, for he believes that his actions will ensure their prompt reincarnation. The more horribly they die, he argues, the better their next life will be. The film borrows several scenes from *Dr. Lamb*, for Bill turns the corpses into obscene marionettes, slices off their breasts, and engages in necrophilia. But the film also references the killer's namesake, Buffalo Bill from *The Silence of the Lambs* (1991); pieces of the victims' skin are stitched together to make a skinsuit. The violence is grotesque, but equally disturbing is the silent compliance of Bill's wife, who spends her days slaving in the fields and turns a blind eye to her husband's preoccupation with prostitutes (she even helps him to dispose of a body). Like Buffalo Bill, Lam Shiu-bill is the new breed of a Gothic monster constructed as 'a remarkably mobile, permeable, and infinitely interpretable body' (Halberstam 1995, 21) capable of producing multiple meanings. He exists as an intertextual reference to numerous killers (fictional and historical figures), and his monstrosity bears the markings of a deviant class (he is a low-income provincial lorry driver), race (Chinese mainlander), gender and sexuality (misogynistic womaniser, sexoholic and killer of prostitutes who likes to wear their skin). But perhaps most importantly, he exposes the collapsed boundaries between the monster and the environment that contributed to his making.

In Category III films, violence is not only perpetrated by criminals. Police officers make up for their incompetence by beating confessions out of suspects and terrorising witnesses. In *The Untold Story*, Wong is subject to police brutality and then beaten unconscious by prisoners who act on orders from the guards. After a failed suicide attempt he is transferred to a hospital where a doctor feeds him stimulants and prevents him from sleeping. A nurse also injects water under his skin. While the film generates some sympathy for the ruthless murderer, it also reconfirms the conflation of violence and power in Category III films. Wong even violently kills himself before the case goes to court, thus enabling him to assert his own form of power while incarcerated.

In Category III films, the police and the justice system do not provide law and order. In *Taxi Hunter*, Kin takes the law into his hands and kills taxi drivers after the police stop their search for the driver who killed his pregnant wife. In *The Underground Banker*, Tong chooses to put his trust in the 'reformed' psychotic serial killer, Lam Kor-Wan, rather than seek the help of the police, who often release the gangsters soon after catching them. When the police finally arrive on the scene, they help the boss of the gang and arrest Tong for being a vigilante. Justice is doled out by the serial killer, who intervenes at the right moment and, at the end of the movie, the loan sharks continue to do good business. In *Love to Kill*, Detective Hung, who rescues a woman from her sadistic husband, is told by his supervisors not to get involved in family matters. It is only when the abuser assaults Hung's girlfriend that the police agree to take action, but in the end the battered wife is forced to save herself. Inspector Man's hunt for Ching Fung in *Run and Kill* is a spectacular display of masculine power (with heavily armed special forces units taking over the entire estate), and yet Ching Fung manages to kill Cheung's mother and leave the scene without resistance; he then burns Cheung's daughter alive. In the *Daughter of Darkness* movies, the police fail to protect the first victim; she is taken to a firing squad, and the second victim commits suicide despite being 'forgiven' by the inspector. 'The jars murderer', Lam Kor-Wan, has a deep bond with his investigator (*Dr. Lamb*) and the Tuen Mun Rapist believes that the lead detective 'thinks like a rapist' (*The Rapist*). By exposing the impotence of law enforcement system to prevent the 'terrorist moments' from happening and bring the culprits to justice, these films remind us that Gothic emerges in the moments 'when we find it impossible, with any degree of hope, for our "case to be put"' (Punter 1998, 5).

In the world of Category III movies, the murderer is sovereign. Even if an individual killer is apprehended, the history of violence will be repeated. While most of the films do not explain the pathologies of their villains, the explanations all lead to the same conclusion: the killers are trapped in the cycle of violence where childhood traumas turn victims into future abusers. Chan from *Red to Kill* is an unassuming social worker who runs a workshop for people with special needs and who turns into a monstrous rapist each time he sees something red. This is the residue of a childhood trauma: he witnessed his adulterous mother (dressed in red) murder his father and brother before accidentally killing herself. In *Love to Kill*, Sam miraculously survives a hanging in childhood as he watches his father bludgeon his mother to death and then kill himself. In *The Untold Story 2*, Fong is institutionalised after witnessing the slaughter of her family, but psychiatric treatment worsens her mental state. The never-ending cycle of violence resembles cannibalism, for in symbolic cannibalism the act of consumption is equivalent to the appropriation of the victim's personality. The cannibal symbolically becomes the person he or she eats. In the dystopian world of Category III movies, the victims who become cannibals perpetuate violence and consume the lives of others. Exploring 'traumagothic', Danel Olson observes that the survivors often lose their identity becoming 'possessed' by those who died in the events: 'After the attack, the dead inhabit the living, and they speak. They are not supernatural wisps to be vented like smoke; rather, they are the very shades of terrorism's lasting fires' (Olson 2016, 23). The unmasking of Category III criminals as trauma victims exposes them as equally possessed by the dead of their past, both their abusers and their partners in suffering. Consequently, the acts of violence they commit later become attempts 'to express grief, vent rage, and alleviate survivor guilt' (13) in order to achieve closure of trauma that never happens.

The main characters in these films have an insatiable appetite for consumption, and while women are shown to consume luxury goods, men consume women. Motivated to a large extent by the 'repulsed fascination with the naked and open body' (Stringer 1999, 363), the films show men engaging in rampant and often sadistic sex with wives, girlfriends and prostitutes, alongside brutal scenes of rape and torture with strangers. In most of these scenes, the naked female body is objectified so it appears dehumanised and inanimate. The women are commonly unresponsive, unconscious, or simply dead, and the men who use them do not care. This makes every intercourse symbolically necrophilic. Lifeless female bodies, a collection of parts, often feature in the films alongside plastic mannequins, visually conveying objectification. In *Dr. Lamb* and *Diary of a Serial Killer*, female corpses are animated by ropes attached to their arms and legs, thus turning them into life-size marionettes. Dismembered body parts are used for sexual gratification. Through the act of ingestion, the cannibal 'achieves the ultimate connection with another human' (Brown 2013, 6). For these women, inertia is the only form of resistance, but it is not a state from which they easily recover. Even if their bodies survive the ordeal, their psyches have been consumed by the cannibal.

Gothic Geographies: Hong Kong as a Gothic Space

Not every Category III Gothic film is set in Hong Kong, but those that are paint a similar picture of the city. The settings are mainly in overpopulated tenement buildings and the housing estates of Kowloon and the New Territories. Williams (2005) argues that Lam Kor-Wan's mental state should be read in the context of Hong Kong's oppressive housing conditions (210). Lam lives in Mongkok, the most densely populated area in the city; in the 1990s, it was estimated as housing 165,000 people per square kilometre (demographia.com). The cramped apartment, which Lam shares with his family, doubles as his 'workshop' where he dismembers his victims' bodies while everyone is out. Moreover, in *The Rapist*, the rapist becomes emblematic of the district Tuen Mun, and Tom Hilditch describes it as 'Hong Kong minus the money. A dormitory town for shampoo boys, karaoke girls and building site labourers. A Hong Kong of stone-washed denim jeans, of knapsacks, tattoos, white socks, mainland haircuts and plastic shoes' (Hilditch 2011, para. 5). Hilditch is scathing in his description of the area:

> As you drive from Central to Tuen Mun the tourist emblems of Hong Kong disappear one by one. First go the syringe-skyscrapers, the five star hotels and polished shopping centres. Then you lose the designer shops, the boutique cafes, the cavernous restaurants and their blazing neon signs. Finally even the old style tenements, their colourful markets

and bustling streets fade away and you are left, as you complete the journey of between two and five hours, amid a clinical arrangement of brutal, sodium-lit, concrete tower blocks, shrivelled trees and broken playgrounds. (para. 1)

Tuen Mun in *The Rapist* is depicted through a combination of dimly-lit claustrophobic spaces and maze-like corridors and passages, surrounded by eerie empty parking lots (Figure 12.5). The rape scenarios are predictably similar: the women are followed as they walk through the desolate cityscape, attacked in an elevator, and then dragged to an unused staircase. The victims' lifeless bodies are pressed against the railings and ventilation grills, intensifying the atmosphere of restriction. Scenes shot from the perspective of the victims augment the feeling of claustrophobia as they play out the classic Gothic trope of live burial. *Red to Kill* adopts a similar aesthetic, but also includes a labyrinth of industrial-looking half-empty spaces hidden within a public housing estate, which is a dormitory and workshop for the wards of a special needs centre. The Gothic potential of this labyrinth is realised through a promise of a monster at its centre (Figure 12.6), but also because it allows for the manipulation of time and space that for Kavka constitutes the visual code of Gothic cinema. The lifeless bodies of the violated women are likened to the mannequins strewn around the building which the rapist also uses for sexual gratification. Both films combine lurid sexploitation with highly controlled understated imagery dominated by chiaroscuro lighting and shadow play, as well as shot composition that is organised around bars, diagonals and frames-within-frames. These elements of the neo-noir's visual style – which is popular within low-budget independently produced thrillers – are characteristic of the dark aesthetics used to depict Hong Kong in Category III films.

Cityscapes in these movies are often filmed at night and visually obscured by poor lighting, rain, smoke, steam and movement. Neo-noir Hong Kong is a city ablaze with neon light, but this explosion of colour is visible only through a blurred reflection in, for instance, the windshield of a moving car awash with rain, or the wet asphalt of the city streets. It is a city in motion, observed from a moving vehicle (*Taxi Hunter*, *Dr. Lamb*), or through the point of view of a distracted character lost in the crowd (*Run and Kill*, *The Rapist*). As we move through the city, the bright shop windows explode like blinding supernovas and disappear into darkness. By day, the technicolour mosaic of light is replaced with the drab reality of low-income housing, rubbish-infested alleyways and streets swarming with people. We see claustrophobic interiors with tight spaces, narrow staircases, and passages between towering buildings that block out the sun augment the sense of entrapment. Sparse windows let in only a limited amount of light because they are often barred with heavy metal grates mounted to protect the inhabitants against intruders. In the films, however, the

Figure 12.5 The interplay of caged spaces and shadows in *The Rapist* (Chuen-yee Cha, 1994)

Figure 12.6　Evil lurking within the labyrinthine spaces of *Red to Kill* (Hin Sing Tang, 1994)

bars and grates appear to cage the protagonists within and the metal frames are often used to immobilise the victims by preventing their escape.

A quintessentially Gothic city, Hong Kong in Category III films is much more than just a setting or location. It is an active force that denies its inhabitants full agency over the unfolding events. Individual acts of violence may be perceived as 'unorganized, random and chaotic' (Williams 2005, 206), but the threat of violence in this dystopian city is systemic. The limitations of space caused by Hong Kong's geographical features engender a cancerous form of architecture with the buildings sprouting ever-smaller units within to accommodate a growing number of people. Overcrowding and lack of privacy distort interpersonal relationships and contribute to social isolation. Sky-high tower blocks reach into the clouds, but the city is rarely shown from this perspective. Instead, we watch it through low and canted angles exaggerating the heaviness and roughness of urban infrastructure alongside long tracking shots that depict the city as a trap whose walls are closing in. In *The Underground Banker*, for instance, Tong's wife is burnt alive inside their apartment. The gangsters put a chain on the metal door grate (ironically installed for greater security) and trap the victim inside. Likewise, in *Run and Kill*, Ching Fung ties Cheung's mother to a window frame and then throws her out of a window. The elaborate execution of Cheung's daughter involves surrounding her with a spider's web of ropes soaked in gasoline and setting the contraption on fire. Window grates are repeatedly used in *Love to Kill* as part of a set-up for the sadistic play. Category III Hong Kong is a city of cages within cages sending out a clear message that there is no way out. The physical and psychological confinement of the films' characters evokes the spatial model of Gothic where the isolated self is forced to continue separately from outside life (Kosofsky-Sedgwick 1986, 12–13) (Figure 12.7).

The manipulation of space through shots, camera angles and composition adds to our sense of anxiety and constructs a hostile environment. Frequently shown through the distorted point of view of the killer, the space of the city appears to be fluid and responsive to the murderous design. Category III Hong Kong is Gotham City without Batman. The victims are rarely saved; their survival is a matter of chance. Its blue-collar monsters are the vengeful oppressed; their motivations and indifference to brutal consequences make them reminiscent of zombies. But they are all the more frightening because they are unmistakably human. Category III films are seldom classified as Gothic, perhaps because their internal hybridity makes them a genre of their own. But they invoke and develop the Gothic mode through their themes, characters, taboos and aesthetics within a significant B-movie tradition. These films turn to Gothic as a technique for registering the horrors of the corrupted city, broken by its relentless pursuit of capital, its lower-class inhabitants depicted as its waste product. They employ an abundance of familiar Gothic conventions, from oppressive landscapes and physical and psychological containment to obsession with taboos, disease and degeneration, and the return of the primitive. They bring to life a whole array of convincing Gothic monsters whose 'inner and outer identities are layered over each other to produce the effects of humanity, perversity, racial impurity, and degeneration' (Halberstam 1995, 24). But perhaps the most enduring Gothic motif in these films is that of the cannibal (the eater of human flesh, as well as its metaphorical extension – the rapist and the serial killer) as the personification of Hong Kong in the

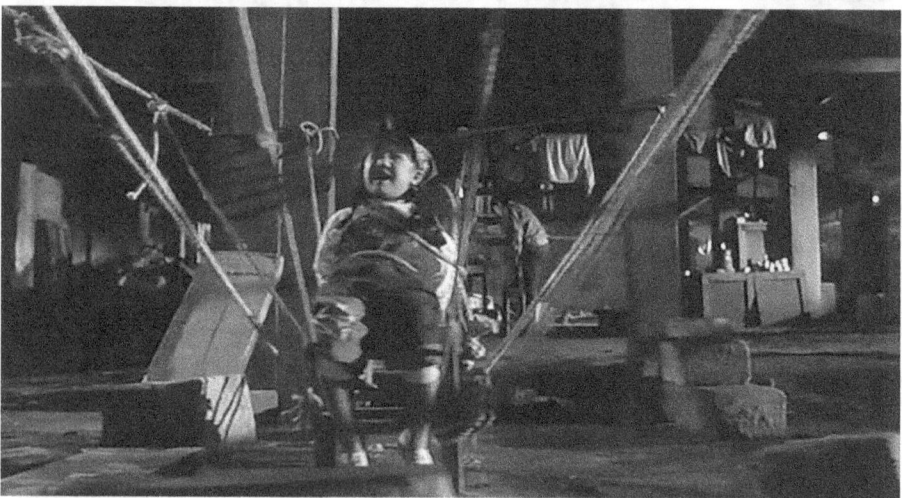

Figure 12.7 Spaces of entrapment and separation. Upper: *The Underground Banker* (Bosco Lam, 1994); lower: *Run and Kill* (Billy Tang, 1993)

1990s: the city consuming itself out of fear of being devoured by its 'barbaric' mother.

Bibliography

Bordwell, David (2011), *Planet Hong Kong: Popular Cinema and the Art of Entertainment* (Madison: Irvington Way Institute Press).
Botting, Fred (1997), *Gothic* (Routledge).
Bronfen, Elisabeth (2014), 'Cinema of the Gothic Extreme', in *The Cambridge*

Companion to Modern Gothic, ed. Jerrold E. Hogle (Cambridge: Cambridge University Press), 107–22.
Brottman, Mikita (1997), *Meat is Murder! An Illustrated Guide to Cannibal Culture* (London: Creation Books).
Brown, Jennifer (2013), *Cannibalism in Literature and Film* (Basingstoke: Palgrave Macmillan).
Halberstam, Judith (1995), *Skin Shows: Gothic Horror and the Technology of Monsters* (Durham, NC: Duke University Press).
Hilditch, Tom (2011), 'Tuen Muen Rapist', *Hong Kong Murders*, <hkmurder.wordpress.com/about/tuen-muen-rapist/> (last accessed 17 September 2016).
Hoover, Michael and Lisa Stokes (1998), 'A City on Fire: Hong Kong Cinema as Cultural Logic of Late Capitalism'. *Asian Cinemas*, 10/1, 25–41.
Kavka, Misha (2002), 'The Gothic on Screen'. *The Cambridge Companion to Gothic Fiction*, ed. Jerrold E. Hogle (Cambridge: Cambridge University Press), 209–28.
Kaye, Heidi (2004), 'Gothic Film', in *A Companion to the Gothic*, ed. David Punter (Oxford: Blackwell), 180–92.
Kosofsky-Sedgwick, Eve (1986), *The Coherence of Gothic Conventions* (London: Methuen).
Marx, Karl, *Capital*, Vol. 1, trans. Samuel Moore and Edward Aveling. Online edition *Marx/Engels Internet Archive*, <www.marxists.org/archive/marx/works/1867-c1> (last accessed 27 September 2016).
Movie Screening Ordinance Cap. 392. 10 November 1988, <www.legislation.gov.hk/blis_pdf.nsf/4f0db701c6c25d4a4825755c00352e35/5C214D8D7E17D6D4482575EF0001FA07/$FILE/CAP_392_e_b5.pdf> (last accessed 2 August 2016).
Punter, David (1998), *Gothic Pathologies: The Text, the Body and the Law* (Basingstoke: Palgrave Macmillan).
Stokes, Lisa Odham and Michael Hoover (2003), 'Enfant Terrible: The Terrorful, Wonderful World of Anthony Wong'. *Fear Without Frontiers: Horror Cinema Across the Globe*, ed. Steven Jay Schneider (Godalming: FAB Press), 45–59.
Stringer, Julian (1999), 'Category 3: Sex and Violence in Postmodern Hong Kong', in *Mythologies of Violence in Postmodern Media*, ed. Christopher Sharrett (Detroit: Wayne State University Press), 361–80.
Wester, Maisha (2015), 'Text as Gothic Murder Machine: The Cannibalism of Sawney Bean and Sweeney Todd', in *Technologies of the Gothic in Literature and Culture*, ed. Justin D. Edwards (London: Routledge), 154–65.
Williams, Tony (2005), 'Hong Kong Social Horror: Tragedy and Farce in Category 3', in *Horror International*, ed. Steven Jay Schneider and Tony Williams (Detroit: Wayne State University Press), 203–19.
Yueh-yu Yeh, Emilie and Neda Hei-tung Ng (2008), 'Magic, Medicine, Cannibalism: The China Demon in Hong Kong Horror', LEWI Working Paper No. 74, Hong Kong Baptist University, https://repository.hkbu.edu.hk/cgi/viewcontent.cgi?article=1039&context=lewi_wp (last accessed 17 January 2017).
Zheng Yi (1996), *Scarlet Memorial: Tales of Cannibalism in Modern China* (Boulder: Westview Press).

Filmography

Crime Story (*Cung on zo*). Directed by Kirk Wong, Golden Harvest, 1993.
Daughter of Darkness (*Mit moon cham on: Yit saat*). Directed by Kai-Ming Lai, Scholar Films, Martini Films, 1993.
Daughter of Darkness 2 (*Mit moon cham on 2: Che chung*). Directed by Kai-Ming Lai, Mandarin Star Films, 1994.

Diary of a Serial Killer (*Guang Zhou sha ren wang: Ren pi ri ji*). Directed by Otto Chan, Skylark Films, 1995.
Dr. Lamb (*Gou yeung yi sang*). Directed by Danny Lee, Grand River Film, 1992.
Ebola Syndrome (*Yi boh lai beng duk*). Directed by Herman Yau, Jing's Production, 1996.
Happy Together (*Chun gwong cha sit*). Directed by Kar-Wai Wong, Block 2 Pictures, Jet Tone Productions, Prenom H, Seowoo Film, 1997.
Henry: Portrait of a Serial Killer. Directed by John McNaughton, Maljack Productions, 1986.
Human Pork Chop (*Pang see: Song jun tin leung*). Directed by Benny Chan Chi Shun, Lee Sing Entertainment, 2001.
Love to Kill (*Nue zhi lian*). Directed by Siu-Hung Chung and Kirk Wong, Heroes United Films, 1993.
Men Behind the Sun (*Hei tai yang 731*). Directed by Tun Fei Mou, Sil Metropole Organization, 1988.
Red to Kill (*Yeuk saat*). Directed by Hin Sing Tang, Martini Film, 1994.
Run and Kill (*Wu syu*). Directed by Billy Tang, Come On Film, 1993.
Society. Directed by Brian Yuzna, Society Productions, Wild Street Pictures, 1989.
Taxi Hunter (*Di shi pan guan*). Directed by Herman Yau, Galaxy Films, 1993.
The Eight Immortals Restaurant: The Untold Story (*Bat sin fan dim: Yan yuk cha siu bau*). Directed by Danny Lee and Herman Yau, Heroes United Film, 1993.
The Rapist (*Tun Men se mo*). Directed by Chuen-yee Cha, Concept Link Productions, 1994.
The Silence of the Lambs. Directed by Jonathan Demme, Orion Pictures, 1991.
The Underground Banker (*Xiang Gang qi an: Xi xue gui li wang*). Directed by Bosco Lam, Win's Film Productions, 1994.
The Untold Story 2 (*Yan yuk cha siu bau II: Tin jue dei mit*). Directed by Yiu-Kuen Ng, Magnum Films, 1998.
We're Going to Eat You (*Di yu wu men*). Directed by Hark Tsui, Seasonal, 1980.
Young and Dangerous: The Prequel (*San goo waak chai ji siu nin gik dau pin*). Directed by Andrew Lau, Golden Harvest, 1998.

13. B IS FOR BHAYANAK: PAST, PRESENT AND PULP IN BOLLYWOOD GOTHIC

Tabish Khair

In terms of both turnover and global reception, 'Bollywood' cinema is dominated – as is the production of films not just in Bombay but also in other film hubs of India – by what Indians call 'masala' (spicy) films. This broadly translates into 'commercial cinema' in Western terms – though India also has a rich tradition of 'parallel (art) cinema' and 'middle cinema', both of which get obscured by masala films nationally and, increasingly, internationally. But within this predominance of masala films there lurks a double mystery: the term 'gothic' is seldom employed in Indian film criticism, and 'horror films' (a term far more freely employed) have never really caught on in India, except, for a while and solidly as B-films, in the 1970s and 1980s. Both terms – 'gothic' and 'horror', as explicated later in this chapter – are haunted by cultural differences when applied to Indian film or literature: they can be said to exist, ambivalently and inevitably, but at a tangent from their European versions.

The double mystery of the ghostly in/existence of both 'gothic' and 'horror' in Indian cinema needs to be examined in this light. It is by looking at this mystery that this chapter will explore how B-movie Gothic interrogates the histories and regions of 'India'. In short, I will argue that both the absence of a long tradition of horror *qua* horror and the fact that Indian films which will not be called 'horror films' in the West are called 'horror films' by astute scholars of Indian cinema point to the same thing: what is often called 'horror' cinema in India is closer to Gothic film, and, as is the case with major Gothic periods in Europe, the heydays of horror B-films tend to mark a passage of stylistic and political *transition*.

However, as noted, the term 'gothic' is seldom applied as a generic definition of Indian films, largely because of its European provenance and the apparent ease with which the past and present permeate each other even in 'non-gothic' India. When it is applied to Indian films, 'gothic' tends to be used simultaneously with 'horror': as in the title 'Dark tales from Bollywood: Indian Gothic horror cinema and the nation's Others' (Valanciunas 2015). While, as we shall see, there have been B-movie Indian adaptations of Western Gothic texts – most obviously Bram Stoker's *Dracula* – there has been no extensive use of the term 'gothic' in either Indian film criticism or Indian (as distinct from 'postcolonial') literary criticism. However, before I illustrate the matter more clearly, the term 'horror', in scare quotes when applied to Indian films (also dubbed subliminal-horror in the next section), can be read as 'gothic' too. The reasons for this will be clarified in the last section of the chapter, but let us start by looking first at the relative lack of horror *qua* horror films in India.

1.

It is not that 'horror' films are not made in India. Almost all the major film centres of India – and although Bombay, now Mumbai, is the most visible one *more* Indian films are produced in other cities – have made 'horror films' (variously defined or often left undefined), and many of them fit the designation 'B-film'. If one looks at the Bombay film industry primarily, as is necessarily the focus of this chapter, one can list dozens of supposed horror films, though most of the really successful ones are basically ghost films or psychological thrillers.

The first significant 'horror film' was Kamal Amrohi's *Mahal* (Palace/ Mansion, 1949), which was a major success and cemented the stardom of Madhubala, sometimes called India's Marilyn Monroe, and Ashok Kumar. It also provided the launch pad for perhaps the most successful singer of any film industry, the perennial Lata Mangeshkar. This was a ghost story placed in stereotypical feudal ('Mahal' means Mansion or Palace) settings. Another major 'hit', Biren Nag's *Bees Saal Baad* (Twenty Years Later), followed in 1962. Based on a Bengali hit thriller from 1951, which was itself a loose reworking of Sir Arthur Conan Doyle's *The Hound of the Baskervilles*, this was a psychological thriller. Between them, *Mahal* and *Bees Saal Baad* exemplify the trend whereby most so-called 'horror films' coming out of India until the 1970s were ghost stories or psychological thrillers. In that sense, it need hardly be stressed, they fit the 'gothic' definition far better than the 'horror' one.

They were not horror films, if one defines horror as a particular subgenre: 'Unlike terror fiction, horror sickens the mind, congeals the blood, and stymies the faculties with repulsive evidence of violence, contact with ghastly supernatural beings and presences, and a dread of impending doom' (Snodgrass 2005, 180). However, various factors, not least the omnipresence of the Indian Film Censor Board, which tends to ply the scissors on scenes of gratuitous violence and ordinary sex, unless hugely stylised, prevent me from adopting too narrow a definition of horror films in India. Aditi Sen notes that '[i]t is extremely difficult to define the horror genre in India. Unlike in Hollywood, horror took a long time to penetrate the Indian scene' (Sen 2011, 75). But she also goes on to argue that the definition 'horror' *can* be applied to early films, such as those listed above, which did *not* feature supernatural elements:

> [E]arly Bollywood blockbuster films, including Raj Khosla's *Woh Kaun Thi* ... Kamal Amrohi's *Mahal* ... Biren Nag's *Bees Saal Baad*, and Mehmood's *Bhoot Bangla* (The Haunted Bungalow) can all be categorized as horror even though their creators were not conscious of the genre. The films were just referred to as suspense thrillers with spooky elements and none of these old films had anything to do with the supernatural. The inexplicable spooky events always had a 'scientific' explanation. (Sen 2011, 77)

I do not dismiss Sen's reading of these early blockbusters as (in my words) *subliminal-horror* films. But to begin with, I will also not confuse horror films with ghost and other films, loosely associated with the genre. This is a matter I will return to, but it is important, at this point, to list other sub-generic trends which, like the ghost story and the psychological thriller, often verge on 'horror' and are read as 'horror films' by scholars (Vitali 2011).

Another trend that is often repeated in different Indian cinema traditions is that of the horror-fantasy genre, usually centring round myths of the snake-woman. Its most successful Bombay version was probably Rajkumar Kohli's *Nagin* (1976): this, one can argue, is a distinctively Indian horror-fantasy genre, as it plays on extant and powerful myths of the snake goddess (Haq 2015). Once again, to call the snake-woman sub-genre 'horror' would be misleading: while horror – in the literal sense of its etymology as making 'hairs stand on end' – might play a passing role, such stories and films include suspense and fear as well as desire and attraction. The snake – especially the cobra – is by no means only an object of 'evolutionary fear' in India (as simplistic 'literary Darwinism' would put it); it is also the object of cultural veneration, aesthetic adoration, religious devotion and transcendental desire, with strong erotic aspects, which far exceed the fascination with the snake in contemporary Western cultures. Here again what we encounter is an Indian version of the 'Gothic', which is never simply horrific.

I will have cause to return to this subliminal-horror genre in order to understand why the blockbusters mentioned by Sen are considered 'horror' by her, even though (as she is fully aware) they resist supernatural explanations, and why the horror genre *qua* horror took so long to arrive in India. Moreover, the genre has not had a really sustained tenure, especially if we refuse to equate it with subliminal-horror films, such as ghost stories, psychological thrillers and snake fantasies. The snake-woman sub-genre is also essential to a contextualised understanding of the B-movie Gothic in India. But more of that in the last section of this chapter.

2.

Valentina Vitali is right in noting that 'Indian cinemas have not produced horror films except for a short period, between the late 1970s and the early 1990s, when the genre saw a brief moment of glory' (Vitali 2011, 130). It is to Kohli and the Ramsay Brothers (whom Vitali correctly highlights as the main reason for the effulgence of the horror *qua* horror genre in the period) that one has to give the credit for producing Bombay's first successful horror films, which were both basically B-films and definitely *not* just ghost stories or psychological thrillers. Sen notes this too:

> The Ramsay Brothers undoubtedly introduced the horror genre in India. Although their first movie, *Do Gaz Zameen ke Neeche* (Two Yards Under the Ground), was neither the first monster flick nor the first movie dealing with the supernatural, the success of this film, and later the unprecedented success of *Purana Mandir* (The Old Temple), created a niche for monster flicks and the horror genre. (Sen 2011, 76)

Most discussions of the horror genre *qua* horror centre on the Ramsay Brothers, but a good point of departure into the horror B-film genre is Raj Kumar Kohli's *Jaani Dushman* (Inveterate Enemy, 1979). Sen lists this as among the 'films that were not consciously made as horror, but still had elements of the supernatural'.

Jaani Dushman is not just an example of that rare film which was not a ghost story, a psychological thriller or a snake fantasy; it was also a major commercial success, starring an established and respected actor (Sanjeev Kumar) – and in that sense not *just* a B-film. And yet, in its effects, its production values and its 'borrowings' from other (mostly Western) films, *Jaani Dushman* was nothing but a B-film. Actually, it might be relevant in this context to start off by quoting a letter from one Anthony Henriques, 'a reader of the Indian cinema magazine *Filmfare*', who had this to say in 1988: '[T]he Ramsay Brothers and the others who produce horror movies would be better advised to tap the rich vein of Indian ghost stories instead of relying on second-hand imitations of third grade foreign horror movies' (Valanciunas 2011, 47).

As a second-hand imitation of third grade foreign films, Kohli's *Jaani Dushman* can be viewed as a kind of Indian werewolf/vampire film – but with crucial differences. The film starts off sometime in the past, when an aristocratic and newly married husband discovers that his bride, all dressed in red, who has been the love of his life, has slipped off just before the wedding to meet her real lover. Enraged, the jilted groom turns into a werewolf-like monster and kills both the girl and her lover. But that is not the end of the matter. The aristocratic groom continues to terrorise the region, abducting newly married brides (dressed in red) and killing them. When the monstrous groom is finally cornered and killed, his spirit simply enters that of his killer – who continues to transform into the monster and kill new brides dressed in red. This monster – who is incarnated from one man to another, so to say – is superhumanly strong and dexterous, and cannot be killed by bullets. The horror continues.

As is obvious from this summary, the 'dushman' (enemy) in *Jaani Dushman* shares not just the characteristics of the werewolf/vampire (even though the make-up is not always too convincing) but also those of the two dominant 'horror' sub-genres: the transmigration of souls (ghost stories) and the psychological thriller, which, as Bharati Raja's *Red Rose* (1980) exemplifies, usually centres on some version of an amorous disappointment. Another element that has to be noticed – and which we will return to – is the setting of *Jaani Dushman*: it is not an urban setting but a rural or, actually, given its aristocratic backdrop, a semi-rural one.

In this too the horror B-films of the late 1970s and 1980s tend to differ from ghost stories and, particularly, psychological thrillers, which *could* have a modern or urban setting. On the other hand, horror B-films often have semi-rural or semi-urban settings, with the metropolis intruding, if it does, not as a space of safety or sanity but as a source of further decadence. This is not incidental. As Valanciunas states, '[c]heaply-made Ramsay horror films circulated at the margins of mainstream Bollywood; however, the films drew large audiences to the cinema halls in smaller urban centres and towns' (Valanciunas 2011, 47). Sen notes of Harinam Singh's *Shaitani Badla* (Devilish Revenge, 1993) – which depicts the revenge of a male servant raped and killed by a group of women having a 'kitty party' in a suburban Mumbai farmhouse – that it was 'a low-budget horror flick especially made for small towns' (Sen 2011, 76). All discussions of the success of Ramsay Brothers stress the fact that their horror films depended largely on small town audiences, which might partly explain their focus on the semi-rural and depiction of the metropolis as a source of decadence.

One of the things – apart from poor production values that, as Sen correctly notes, often provided for 'unintentional humour' (Sen 2011, 75) – shared by all

Ramsay Brothers films, *Jaani Dushman* and other Indian Horror B-films from the 1980s was a largely 'feudal' setting. Discussing a Dracula-inspired Ramsay Brothers film, *Bandh Darwaza* (The Closed Door, 1990), both Vitali and Valanciunas note the common Ramsay trope of a monstrous figure of feudal authority. This can be said of almost all Indian Horror films from the late 1970s to the early 1990s. They also often include stock associated characters and situations, such as abandoned caves, secret cults, evil or devious priests, skull-garland-wearing and martial servants, all of these imparting an 'Indian' setting in which one can find an eclectic mix of 'foreign' horror elements, particularly 'borrowed' from British 'Hammer Horror' films.

The feudal settings and hidden 'ancient' religious elements of these films need to be noted in the light of an important point raised in this book: that (non-Indian) B-movies such as *Night of the Living Dead* (1968), *The Texas Chainsaw Massacre* (1974) and *Rabid* (1977) resonate powerfully with the anti-Enlightenment and anti-capitalist politics of early Gothic texts. Critics have observed that the long decade of the 1980s, which marked the (relative) effulgence of Indian horror, was a 'transit period' between the angry young man type of films, associated mostly with the early stardom of Amitabh Bachchan, in the 1970s, and the glorified 'family dramas' that took over in the mid-1990s (Uberoi 2006). Actually, one can locate in these horror films an amalgamation of the violence and 'action' associated with the 1970s 'angry young man' films and the 'family' constructed, along with the construction of the 'Hindutva family' in political discourse, from the mid-1990s onwards.

The feudal family setting is not incidental in this regard, because the mid-1990s return to 'family dramas' was largely selective in its depiction of *Indian* families. I have pointed this out in my reading of two remakes of the Devdas story by Bankim Chandra: Bimal Roy's *Devdas* (1955) to Sanjay Leela Bhansali's *Devdas* (2002). The families in Bhansali's *Devdas* are remarkable for their affluence, with even servants dressing like left-leaning cultured middle-class people (Khair 2006). Dwyer and Patel have aptly noted the tendency in film criticism to neglect discussing some aspects of *mise-en-scène*, such as setting and costume (Dwyer and Patel 2002, 42), and the difference of 'visuality' along these lines in the two remakes of *Devdas* definitely speaks volumes. Though the story revolves around a romance between a man of a higher class and caste and a woman of a lower class and caste, the differences are hardly visible in Bhansali's *Devdas*, which is a visual extravaganza set in opulent houses, while they are quite visible in Roy's *Devdas*. In general, the *Indian* family that 'returns' in the successful 'family dramas' of Bollywood (and TV) in the mid- and late 1990s is a glorified construction – in keeping with Hindutva myths of 'shining India' – and this is a trend that has continued up until now in both films and TV shows.

From this perspective, the feudal family of Horror B-films in the 1980s provides an indication of Indian anxieties about the past *and* the growing

Hindutva-dominated resurgence of a certain kind of conservative (and affluent) 'family values'. It is perhaps revealing that the monstrosity in such films is both placed in the past – a hidden 'Indian' past of secret cults, devilish beings and terrible crimes – and also depends for its cinematic and visual 'translation' on borrowed foreign elements. I would not like to make too much of the foreign elements, except as cinematic possibility and plagiarism. For instance, I am not convinced by all of Vitali's arguments about the distinctive use of the Dracula story in *Bandh Darwaza* – partly because, in common Indian parlance, at least in North India where I grew up in the 1970s and 1980s, the word 'Dracula' was used generically to signify something like a 'vampire' and various stories and anecdotes featured a 'Dracula' who was far more generic than anything imagined by Bram Stoker. And yet the 'foreign' elements in such films do suggest not just a feeling of fearful ambivalence and horrific inevitability towards one's own (hidden) past but also fearful ambivalence towards and horrific inevitability about borrowings from 'foreign' spaces. All these resonate with anxieties about the times, and can again be found, with the 'native' elements tinsel-glorified to the fullest extent possible, in both the ascending narratives of Hindutva and those of 'family dramas' from the mid-1990s onwards.

This returns us to the success of Horror B-films, especially those made by the Ramsay Brothers, in the small towns of India. These small – or taluk – towns occupy a space that has been largely ignored, until recently, in Indian and postcolonial literary criticism, which has moved from a Gandhian celebration of Indian villages to a postcolonial and post-Rushdie celebration of metropolitan spaces. This has ignored, at least from the 1940s up until 2016, the largest growing space in India: those of small 'taluk' towns. However, just as the rise of the Bharatiya Janata Party (BJP) and, later, the current BJP Prime Minister Narendra Modi can only be understood by acknowledging how different taluk towns are (Khair 2015) – discursively and materially – from both metropolises and villages, the popularity of B-movie horror in the 1980s can only be understood by looking at taluk towns.

In that sense, B-movie Horror in India explored discursive territories that lay beyond the horizons of A-movie productions, even when they were 'masala' films. The fact that so many early 'horror' films were just 'subliminal-horror' – either being ghost stories, which fitted into established and mainstream beliefs, or given a 'scientific' explanation – is an index of this. A-films could be credulous, but only within the confines of established discourses of religion: for instances, ghosts, or snake-goddess myths, or, as has been the case with another 'ghost-story-like' sub-genre such as the Subhash Ghai blockbuster *Karz* (1980), that of the transmigration of souls. *Or* they could be credulous only to the extent that they finally matched up, or pretended to do so, to establish categories of 'educated' rational discourse – and hence the periodic 'scientific explanations'.

Part of this had to do with the relative cultural prestige of A-films and the people associated with them, and part of it had to do with their audiences. However, the taluk town audience occupies a space that is not just that of rural 'credulity' or metropolitan 'reason', rural 'tradition' or metropolitan 'modernity'. It is this amalgamation, seen not just as possibility (as is done in metropolitan discourses of hybridity, etc.) but also as threat and danger, which explains the success of Horror B-films in Indian taluk towns. The feudal setting in contemporary times, the semi-rural or semi-urban context, the eclectic mix of 'Indian' and 'foreign' elements and anxieties about both, even the return to a mythologised Indian 'family' – all these can be understood better in the context of the space occupied by taluk town audiences, a space between, opposed to and partaking of both the village and the metropolis. One can even argue that the heyday of horror B-films coincided with the decades when taluk towns were coming into their own – but had not assumed the political clout they have today. The 1970s and 1980s were also the decades that marked the beginning of a trickle of people from these taluk towns to Indian metropolises and abroad, a trickle that became a torrent in the 1990s – a 'monster' that moved out of its lair in taluk towns and finally, from the 1990s onwards, came to impact on national culture and politics, through a complex process that is still going on, and of which the rise of Modi as well as of other regional leaders to national prominence is an aspect.

3.

What I wish to propose is that the heydays of horror B-films were a transit period in more than one way – not just a transit period from 'angry young men' films to 'family dramas' but also a transit period in which taluk town sensibilities exerted themselves, in rich confusion, first in small taluk towns and then, with internal migration and growing confidence, nationally, and perhaps, as the reception of Modi in the West shows, internationally. Hence, while horror *qua* horror films continue to be made, they are no longer as visible, and Indian films have reverted to subliminal horror – such as stories of ghosts and/or the transmigration of souls – or to glossier versions of 'mythologicals' (which were an early staple of Indian films too). Both these movements depict the consolidation of a certain mainstream – loosely Brahminical – ethos, which is also reflected in the policies of BJP and Hindutva parties. Epics based on the *Ramayana*, etc. or the story of some saint and films about the transmigration of souls are thoroughly mainstream and acceptable in the pan-Indian context. The sort of febrile approach towards everything – village or town, tradition or modernity, 'Indian' or 'foreign' – unconsciously depicted in, say, Ramsay Brothers films is largely missing, or has been turned into a resounding triumphalism on the behalf of 'Indian' elements in many of these recent films.

This also brings us to a matter lurking in the backdrop of our discussion: why the early horror films that succeeded tended to be ghost stories, horror fantasies around snake myths, or psychological thrillers of some sort, sometimes given a slightly supernatural touch (blood dripping on a rose, etc., as in *Red Rose*). Apart from the socio-economic explanation highlighted above, why did horror *qua* horror have so short a lease in Indian cinema? And why, while horror *qua* horror has not disappeared, are we again largely back to subliminal-horror films or outright 'mythologicals' and related religious fantasies, some in the shape of 'family dramas'?

To answer this, one has to look at the concept of 'horror' – literally translated as 'bhayanak' – over much of India. Indian aesthetics is heavily influenced by the *Natyashastra* of Bharata, probably composed around the first century BC, and commented on in major works since then. Devy notes that '[t]radition considers the *Natyashastra* as an additional Veda, so important has it been in the history of Indian literary theory' (Devy 2002, 3). The sixth and seventh chapters of the *Natyashastra* explicate the concept of the Bhava-Rasa theory of Bharata, a definitive aesthetics in Indian traditions, whose terms and ideas have seeped into popular discourse too.

Without going into the details, which are highly intricate, one needs to note, in our context, that Bharata arranges the Rasa – roughly 'essence', but also used in contemporary Hindi to mean 'juice' – into eight categories, each connected to a corresponding Bhava (roughly, 'emotional/mental states'). Put simply, and with some inevitable simplification, Bharata classifies the Rasa under eight categories (*ashtarasa*) and provides the corresponding Bhava which gives rise to the Rasa. These are known as *Sthayi Bhava* or, roughly, 'stable emotions'. They are: *rati* (love), *hasa* (mirth), *shoka* (grief), *krodha* (anger), *utsaha* (heroism), *bhaya* (fear), *jugupsa* (disgust) and *vismaya* (wonder). The corresponding eight Rasa are *sringara* (amorous), *hasya* (humorous), *karuna* (pathetic), *raudra* (furious), *vira* (valorous), *bhayanaka* (horrific), *bibhatsa* (repugnant) and *adbhuta* (wondrous) (Pande 1996). The discussion gets much more complicated and nuanced in *Natyashastra*, but we can stop here and focus on the word 'bhayanak', which passes for 'horrific' and 'horrible/terrible' in ordinary spoken Hindi (and associated languages) today. Bhayanak is the state arising from 'bhaya' (fear).

Horror films in India – B or A, subliminal or specific – are viewed by their audiences as dealing with something 'bhayanak'. However, the notion of bhayanak is not the same as that of 'horror' in the West, at least in the sense quoted at the start of this chapter: 'horror sickens the mind, congeals the blood, and stymies the faculties with repulsive evidence of violence, contact with ghastly supernatural beings and presences, and a dread of impending doom'. As the notion of 'bhayanak' is an aesthetic one that shares in all human and divine possibilities, it is not merely a negative notion: it is, actually, closer to that of the 'sublime' in Western philosophy. As such, Bollywood pulp films that want to promote narrowly 'horrific' effects often fail: the aspect of 'horror', so to say, does not exist in its reductive purity for many Indians.

It is in this sense that one can understand why Sen, as noted earlier, stresses that the films I called 'subliminal-horror' are horror films, though she also notes that they lack 'supernatural elements'. She is right: they are in some ways 'horror' films too, because they cater to audience expectations of the *bhayanak rasa* which does spell 'horror' in India.

This also helps us understand why those Bollywood pulp films that use 'horror' to suggest the sublime of the Gothic, and other elements associated with the Gothic in the West, meet with a better response. But even then, these elements have to be mediated through Indian cultural images. The 'nagin' (snake-woman), the ghost, the transmigrated soul, even the Jekyll–Hyde murderer, these are all characters that share more of the sublime than the narrowly horrific, for they are not simply 'sickening' and extraneous to normal experience and even divinity. They are an exaggerated aspect of it.

One of the interesting things about the *bhayanak* genre in Indian films is that narrowly horror films, such as many of those made by the Ramsay Brothers, have not been 'musical' hits. On the other hand, subliminal-horror – or generically *bhayanak*, whether B or A – films have often been huge musical hits. This was the case with the early *Mahal*, *Nagin* and *Karz* (the story of a man who is murdered by his wife and her companion and is reincarnated again to discover and avenge the crime), among others.

Even though music is essential to all 'masala' films, the correspondence of great songs with subliminal-horror blockbusters is, I think, a good illustration of how these films have a gothic tenor. A similar effect cannot be achieved in horror *qua* horror films without a great reduction of its horrific efficacy. (One can see this in many B-films, including those by Ramsay Brothers.) In this sense, I would suggest that the 'subliminal' in subliminal-horror be taken not just as indicating 'what is below the threshold of consciousness', but also as bearing an echo of the 'sublime' as in the Gothic. The vast categories of what I have dubbed subliminal-horror in India can bear, and even exult in, loud – and sometimes excellent – music, because they are basically about the 'sublime', which is not just horrific, but also awe-inspiring and vastly beautiful. In that sense, one can argue that the Indian 'horror' genre, broadly defined, is and will continue to be dominated by something akin to what in Western terms can be called B-film Gothic. The *bhayanak rasa* sometimes includes horror *qua* horror films, but mostly it demands a *version* of the Indian Gothic.

Finally, the question remains: would we not be better off using the term 'gothic', rather than 'horror' in scare quotes or a transitional description like 'subliminal-horror?' I doubt it, for the term 'gothic' is just as difficult to apply without scare quotes in India. For instance, while 'bhayanak' in Indian aesthetics is *like* the 'sublime' in Western philosophy, it is not exactly the same.

Let us look at this very briefly, with the help of Anne Carson's poetic paraphrase of the sublime in Longinus: 'Threat provides the Sublime with its essential structure, an alternation of danger and salvation, which other aesthetic experiences (e.g. beauty) do not share' (Carson 2006, 48). Here, what is immediately revealed is the basic Manicheanism that finally undergirds most Western notions, even those which resist it, like that of the 'sublime'. Danger and salvation, for instance, are not necessarily alternative experiences in the Indian aesthetic and philosophical traditions that I have alluded to: they are part of the same thing. The 'bhayanak' is part not just of human responses, but even of human existence, along with the other 'rasa': in that sense, it is not just horrific, nor can it be reduced to a generic description, like 'gothic'. In short, *scare quotes* are necessary not just when describing horror films in India, but also when talking of Gothic B-films from India.

BIBLIOGRAPHY

Carson, Anne (2006), *Decreation* (London: Jonathan Cape).
Devy, G. N. (ed.), (2002), *Indian Literary Criticism: Theory and Interpretation* (Hyderabad: Orient Longman).
Dwyer, Rachel and Patel, Divia (2002), *Cinema India: The Visual Culture of Hindi Film* (Delhi: Oxford University Press).
Haq, Kaiser (2015), *The Triumph of the Snake Goddess* (Cambridge, MA: Harvard University Press).
Khair, Tabish (2006), 'The Ironies of Bollywood', *16-9*, Copenhagen, <http://www.16-9.dk/2009-04/pdf/16-9_april2009_side11_inenglish.pdf> (last accessed 1 April 2016).
Khair, Tabish (2015), 'India 2015: Magic, Modi, and Arundhati Roy', 50th Anniversary Editorial, *The Journal of Commonwealth Literature*, September, 50, 259-66.
Pande, Anupa (1996), *A Historical and Cultural Study of the Natya Sastra of Bharata* (Jodhpur: Kusumanjali Publications).
Sen, Aditi (2011), 'I Wasn't Born with Enough Middle Fingers': How Low-Budget Horror Films Defy Sexual Morality and Heteronormality in Bollywood', *Acta Orientalia Vilnensia*, 12/2, 75-89.
Snodgrass, Mary Ellen (2005), *Encyclopedia of Gothic Literature* (New York: Facts on File).
Uberoi, Patricia (2006), *Freedom and Destiny: Gender, Family and Popular Culture in India* (New Delhi: Oxford University Press).
Valanciunas, Deimantas (2011), 'Indian Horror: The Western Monstrosity and the Fears of the Nation in Ramsay Brothers' Bandh Darwaza', *Acta Orientalia Vilnensia*, 12/2, 47-60.
Valanciunas, Deimantas (2015), 'Dark Tales from Bollywood: Indian Gothic Horror Cinema and the Nation's Others', conference programme, <http://code.sfu.ca/iga2015/programme/august1.html> (last accessed 8 April 2016).
Vitali, Valentina (2011), 'The Hindi Horror Film: Notes on the Realism of a Marginal Genre', in Felicia Chan, Angelina Karpovich and Xin Zhang (eds), *Genre in Asian Film and Television* (London: Palgrave Macmillan), 130-48.

Filmography

Mahal (Kamal Amrohi 1949)
Bees Saal Baad (Biren Nag 1962)
Devdas (Bimal Roy 1955)
Nagin (Rajkumar Kohli 1976)
Jaani Dushman (Rajkumar Kohli 1979)
Red Rose (Bharati Raja 1980)
Karz (Subhash Ghai 1980)
Bandh Darwaza (Ramsay Brothers 1990)
Shaitani Badla (Harinam Singh 1993)
Devdas (Sanjay Leela Bhansali 2002)

NOTES ON THE CONTRIBUTORS

Katarzyna Ancuta is a lecturer in the Faculty of Liberal Arts, King Mongkut's Institute of Technology, Ladkrabang, Thailand. Her research interests oscillate around the interdisciplinary contexts of contemporary Gothic/Horror, currently with a strong Asian focus. Her recent publications include contributions to *A New Companion to the Gothic* (2012), *Globalgothic* (2013), *The Cambridge Companion to the Modern Gothic* (2014) and *Ghost Movies in Southeast Asia and Beyond* (2016), as well as two co-edited special journal issues on Thai (2014) and Southeast Asian (2015) horror film.

Tuğçe Bıçakçı Syed is a Ph.D. candidate in the Department of English and Creative Writing at Lancaster University, where she completed her MA in Contemporary Literary Studies. Her research theorises the expression 'Turkish Gothic' in relation to work on Globalgothic, focusing on the representations of national identity, collective memory and social anxiety in Turkish Gothic narratives from 1923 to the present. Her other areas of interest include Islamic Gothic, folklore, vampire fiction and Gothic Sci-Fi, as well as contemporary Gothic in film and TV.

Claudia Böhme is a lecturer and post-doc. researcher in Media Anthropology in the Department of Sociology and Anthropology, University of Trier. She has worked as a lecturer and researcher in the Department of Anthropology and African Studies at the University in Mainz and at the Institute of African

Studies, University of Leipzig. Her Ph.D. '*White Elephant* – The Negotiation of Culture in the Tanzanian Video Film Industry' has developed out of several years of field research in the video film sector in Tanzania and she has acted in several Tanzanian TV serials and movies. Her research has been published in *Global Nollywood* (2013), *Trance Mediums & New Media* (2014), *Bongo Media Worlds* (2014), *Cultural Entrepreneurship in Africa* (2016), *Africa Today* and the *Journal of African Cinemas*. She is co-editor of the online journal *Swahili Forum*.

John Edgar Browning (Ph.D., SUNY-Buffalo) is a Marion L. Brittain Postdoctoral Fellow at the Georgia Institute of Technology. He is internationally recognised for his horror, vampire and Dracula scholarship, with over fourteen published or forthcoming books that include *Speaking of Monsters: A Teratological Anthology* (2012), *The Forgotten Writings of Bram Stoker* (2012) and *Zombie Talk: Culture, History, Politics* (2015), as well as over sixty published or forthcoming articles, book chapters and reviews on similar topics.

Justin D. Edwards is Chair of Gothic Studies at the University of Stirling. He is the author or co-author of several books, including *Grotesque* (2013), *Mobility at Large* (2012), *Postcolonial Literature* (2008), *Gothic Canada: Reading the Spectre of a National Literature* (2005), *Gothic Passages: Racial Ambiguity and the American Gothic* (2003) and *Exotic Journeys: Exploring the Erotics of U.S. Travel Literature* (2001). He is also the editor or coeditor of *Other Routes: 1500 Years of African and Asian Travel Writing* (2006), *Downtown Canada: Writing Canadian Cities* (2005), *Postcolonial Travel Writing: Critical Explorations* (2010), *Gothic in Contemporary Literature and Popular Culture: Pop Goth* (2012) and *Technologies of the Gothic in Literature and Culture: Technogothics* (2015).

Michael Fuchs is an Assistant Professor (non-TT) in American Studies at the University of Graz, Austria. He has co-edited three books (most recently *ConFiguring America: Iconic Figures, Visuality, and the American Identity*, 2013) and authored more than twenty published and forthcoming journal articles and book chapters on horror films, adult cinema, video games, American television and contemporary American literature. Currently, he is co-editing three new books and working on three monographs. One of these monographs is on animal monsters in horror cinema.

Johan Höglund is Associate Professor in the Department of Languages, Linnaeus University, and Director of the Linnaeus University Centre for Concurrences in Colonial and Postcolonial Studies. He has published extensively on the connection between popular culture and empire, including the monograph *The American Imperial Gothic: Popular Culture, Empire, Violence* (2014) and the edited collections *Animal Horror Cinema: Genre, History and Criticism* (2015), with Katarina Gregersdotter and Nicklas Hållén, and *Transnational and Postcolonial Vampires: Dark Blood* (2012), with Tabish Khair.

Enrique Ajuria Ibarra is Assistant Professor at Universidad de las Américas Puebla, Mexico. He has previously published several articles and book chapters on Mexican horror cinema. He is currently preparing a book on the relationship between travel, Gothic and the horror film, and co-editing a collection of essays on Latin American Gothic.

Tabish Khair is an Indian English author and Associate Professor in the Department of English, University of Aarhus, Denmark. His creative writing books include *The Bus Stopped* (2004), which was shortlisted for the Encore Award (UK), and *The Thing About Thugs* (2010), which has been shortlisted for a number of prizes, including the DSC Prize for South Asian Literature and the Man Asian Literary Prize. His academic books include *Babu Fictions: Alienation in Contemporary Indian English Novels* (2001), *Other Routes: 1500 Years of Asian and African Travel Writing* (2005) and *The Gothic, Postcolonialism and Otherness: Ghosts from Elsewhere* (2009).

Jay McRoy is Professor of English and Cinema Studies at the University of Wisconsin – Parkside. He is the author of *Nightmare Japan: Contemporary Japanese Horror Cinema* (2007), as well as over thirty articles on world cinema and visual aesthetics. His is also the editor of *Japanese Horror Cinema* (Edinburgh University Press, 2005) and co-editor (with Richard Hand) of *Monstrous Adaptations: Generic and Thematic Mutations in Horror Film* (2007). His current research interests include experimental cinema, digital aesthetics, and the intersections between trauma theory and representations of apocalypse in world cinema.

Xavier Aldana Reyes is Senior Lecturer in English at Manchester Metropolitan University; he is also a founder member of the Manchester Centre for Gothic Studies and editor of the University of Wales's forthcoming Horror Studies book series. He is the author of *Body Gothic: Corporeal Transgression in Contemporary Literature and Horror Film* (2014) and *Horror Film and Affect: Towards a Corporeal Model of Viewership* (2016), and co-editor, with Linnie Blake, of *Digital Horror: Haunted Technologies, Network Panic and the Found Footage Phenomenon* (2015). His work has appeared in international peer-reviewed journals such as *Horror Studies*, *Gothic Studies*, *The Bulletin of Hispanic Studies*, *Actual / Virtual* and *The Journal for Cultural and Religious*

Theory. He recently completed the monograph *Spanish Gothic: National Identity, Collaboration and Cultural Adaptation* (2017) and is editing the collection *Horror: A Literary History* for the British Library.

Daniel Serravalle de Sá is Associate Professor at the Federal University of Santa Catarina, Brazil. His research interests include popular culture and the relationship between literature and cinema. In recent years, he has written about the Gothic and its manifestations in different cultural contexts. He is the author of the book *Gótico Tropical: o sublime e o demoníaco em O Guarani* (2010) and has published chapters in the books *World Film Locations: São Paulo* (2013), *Directory of World Cinema: Brazil* (2013) and *Tropical Gothic in Literature and Culture: The Americas* (2016).

Maisha Wester is Associate Professor in the Department of African American and African Diaspora Studies at the University of Indiana. She has published numerous essays and book chapters on African American Gothic literature as well as horror cinema. Her book *African American Gothic: Screams from Shadowed Places* was published in 2012.

INDEX

Note: *italic* page numbers refer to illustrations, n refers to notes

abasyuka, 164
Abdülhamit II, Sultan, 140
abjection, 54
addiction, 34–46
Africa Magic (satellite programme), 161
African and Asian film, 12–13, 156–220
African Cinema, 159
African video movies, 159–61
African-American film, 10, 48
Afro-Caribbean zombies, 64
Akira Kurosawa, 174
Alaric de Marnac, 102–5
Las alegres vampiras de Vögel / Vampires of Vögel (1975), 100
Alien (1979), 25
alienation, 19, 35–7, 76
Allen, James, 35
Alucarda, la hija de las tinieblas / Alucarda, Daughter of Darkness (1977), 50–63, *53*, *60*
Alucardos, retrato de un vampiro / Alucardos, Portrait of a Vampire (2010), 10, 50–63, *60*
American Gothic film, 16–81
American International Pictures, 58
Amrohi, Kamal, 210, 211

Ancuta, Katarzyna, 12, 184
Anderson, Paul W. S., 65
anime, 12, 173
'Annabel Lee' (story), 2
anti-capitalism, 214
Antichrist (2013), 125
anti-Enlightenment, 123, 214
Apel, Dora, 35
Appadurai, Arjun, 161
Aragão, Rodrigo, 11, 64–80
Aranda, Vicente, 99
Arctic setting, 19, 21
Argento, Dario, 6
Arslan, Savaş, 143
Atlas Film, 144
Austrian ultra-low-budget movies, 12
Austro-trash, 108–21
avant-garde, 57–8
Avenging Consciousness (1915), 2
Aya Stefanos'taki Rus Abidesinin Yıkılışı / The Demolition of the Russian Monument at St Stephan (1914), 140–1

Bachchan, Amitabh, 214
Bacon, Simon, 56

225

INDEX

Badham, John, 100
Badley, Linda, 163
Baiestorf, Petter, 11, 64–80
Balmain, Colette, 174
Bandh Darwaza / The Closed Door (1990), 214, 215
Banzi, Mussa, 13, 157, 159, 162–6
Barber, Karin, 159
Bardem, Juan Antonio, 98
Barrot, Pierre, 160
Bataille, Georges, 176
Bava, Mario, 58
BBC Television, 85
Beardsley, Aubrey, 174
Bécquer, Gustavo Adolfo, 103–4
Bees Saal Baad / Twenty Years Later (1962), 210–11
Beez, Jigal, 164
being-in-the-world, 22
Bergman, Ingmar, 125–6
Berlin Film Festival, 144
Bhansali, Sanjay Leela, 214
Bharatiya Janata Party (BJP), 215–16
Bhava-Rasa theory, 217
'bhayanak', 12, 209–19
Bhoot Bangla / The Haunted Bungalow (1965), 211
Bıçakçı, Tuğçe, 11
Binnaz (1919), 141
Black Americans and zombies, 64
The Black Cat (1934), 5
Black Sunday (1960), 89
black-and-white film stock, 25, 28, 85, 147
Blackness, 39, 42, 48
Blacula, 33–4
Blacula (1972), 99
Blatty, William Peter, 144–6
Blaxploitation, 32–49, 99–100
Blind Dead, 103–4, *104*
The Blob (1958), 10, 26–30, *28*
'Blobs', 17–31
Blödaren / The Bleeder (1983), 126
Blood Couple a.k.a. *Double Passion*, 46
Blood for Dracula (1974), 100
Blood from the Mummy's Tomb (1971), 91–2
Blood Runs Cold (2011), 11–12, 124–5, 127, 131
Blouin, Michael Joseph, 174
B-movies, definition of, 4
body Gothic, 127
Body Gothic, 112
body horror films, 27–30, 57–8
Böhme, Claudia, 13

Bollywood, 12
Bollywood Gothic, 209–19
Bong, Joon-ho, 8
Bordwell, David, 187
'borrowings', 212, 214
El bosque del lobo / The Ancines Woods (1970), 102
Botting, Fred, 4, 53–4
Boyle, Danny, 65
'Boys Do Get Bruised', 47
Bray Studios, 85–7
Brazil, 11, 65–80
Bride of Frankenstein (1935), 5, 83
Brides of Dracula (1960), 90
Brioni, Simone, 8
British Board of Film Censors (BBFC), 87–9
Brodén, Daniel, 123
Bronfen, Elisabeth, 188
Bronk, Katarzyna, 56
Brost, Johannes, 131
Brown, Todd, 62n
The Brown Coat (2008), 162
Browning, John, 11
Browning, Tod, 62n
Browning, Todd, 5, 99, 161
Buddhism, 174–5
Buenos Aires Rojo Sangre festival, 72
Buñuel, Luis, 58
Burton, Tim, 184
Busanghaeng / Train to Busan (2016), 9
Bwawa la Shetani / Swamps of the Devil (2007), 162–3, 166–7
Byron, Glennis, 2

Cade Bambara, Toni, 34
caged spaces and shadows, *203*
Caleb Williams (book), 76
Campbell, John W., 21–2
Canadian film, 162
candomblé religion, 76, 77
Canibal-Mabuse, 67
Cannes Festival, 46
cannibal exploitation films, 7
Cannibal Holocaust (1980), 7–8
cannibalism, 11, 64–5, 191, *198*
  and the oppressed, 194–201
Capital (book), 196
capitalism, 36–7, 46–8, 196–8
Carmilla (story), 54–5, 92, 99
Carrie (1976), 9
Carroll, Noel, 3–4
Carson, Anne, 219
The Castle of Otranto (story), 64, 151
category III films, Hong Kong, 12, 186–208

226

INDEX

Catholicism, 7, 53, 58, 62n, 103
censorship, 126
Chan, Jackie, 186
Chandra, Bankim, 214
Cheonnyeon ho/ The Thousand Year-Old Fox (1969), 8
China, 189, 192–4, 196–7
Chinese cinema, 9
Chinese Civil War, 8
Christianity, 35–6, 44–5, 103–4
Church, David, 60–1
Çığlık / The Scream (1949), 140, 143–4, *143*, *145*, 152
Cinapse.co, 134
'cine bizarro', 95
'cine de terror', 95
'cine negro', 95
Cinema Marginal, 66
cityscapes, 202
class politics, 108–21
Clover, Carol J., 134
Cohen, Jeffrey, 43
colonialism, 8, 124
comedy, 111–13, 213–14
Communism, 8, 187, 189, 192–4, 197
Complying with Colonialism: Gender, Race and Ethnicity in the Nordic Region, 122
El conde Drácula / Count Dracula (1970), 97, 99
'conscious cinema', 34
Cooper, Ian, 91
copyright, 139
Corman, Roger, 58, 90
'costumbrismo', 102
counterfeiting, 55–6
Craven, Wes, 127
Crazy as Hell (2002), 10
Crime Story (1993), 186
Critics' Choice award, 46
Cronenberg, David, 27
Cronon, William, 116
Cross of the Devil (1975), 103
'La cruz del diablo' / 'The Devil's Cross' (1975), 103
cult cinema, 50–63
cultural memory, 56
Cultural Revolution, 196–7
Culture, Health, and Religion at the Millennium: Sweden Unparadised, 136
Culture and Crisis: The Case of Germany and Sweden, 123
The Curse of Frankenstein (1957), 84, 86–9, *87*

The Curse of the Mummy's Tomb (1964), 91
Cushing, Peter, 86–7, 90, 92, 102

Da Sweet Blood of Jesus (2014), 47
Dante, Joe, 65
'dark ecology', 68–72
Dark Ecology, 66
'The Dark Old Spaceship', 23
'Dark tales from Bollywood: Indian Gothic horror cinema and the nation's Others', 210
Darkness Falls (2003), 9
Daughter of Darkness 2 (1994), 187
Daughter of Darkness (1993), 12, 187, 192–4, 200
Daughter of Horror (1955), 28
Davenport-Hines, Richard, 172
David, Marlo, 40
Davies, Ann, 105
Dawn of the Dead (1978), 65, 78
de la Iglesia, Eloy, 98
De Luxe color, 28
Una de miedo / A Horror Film (1935), 99
La de monstruos / A Monster Film segment (1935), 99
de Ossorio, Amando, 102, 103–4, *104*
de Rais, Gilles, 104–5
Dead Snow (2009), 65
Def By Temptation (1990), 10, 32, 47
Deliverance (1972), 130
Demirağ, Turgut, 144
Demirhan, Metin, 144
Demker, Marie, 136
Deodato, Ruggero, 7–8
Devdas (1955), 214
Devdas (2002), 214
Devdas story, 214
The Devils (1971), 54, 62n
'The Devious Landscape of Scandinavian Horror', 125
Devy, G. N., 217
Diary of a Serial Killer (1993), 187, 195, 198–9, 201
Diawara, Manthia, 35
Dilunga, Haji, 162, 167–9
Das Ding aus der Mur (2012), 12, 108–21
Das Ding aus der Mur: Zero (2015), 12, 108–21, *111*, *113*
disabled bodies, 60–1, 62n
Do Gaz Zameen ke Neeche / Two Yards Under the Ground (1972), 212
Dönmez-Colin, Gönül, 141
Don't Torture a Duckling (1972), 7

227

döppelgangers, 2, 83–94
Down Place, 85, 87
Doyle, Sir Arthur Conan, 210
Dr Jekyll and Mr Hyde (1931), 83
Dr. Lamb (1992), 187, 189, *190*, 194, 199–202
Dracula (1931), 5, 83, 124, 161
Dracula (1958), 86–9, 99
Dracula (1979), 100
Dracula (character), 38, *88*, 164–5
Dracula (novel), 3, 64, 151
   Gothic atmosphere, 148
   and Indian film, 210, 215
   and Japanese film, 173
   and Turkish film, 144
Dracula A.D. 1972 (1972), 90, 92
Dracula Has Risen from the Grave (1968), 90, 91
Dracula: Prince of Darkness (1966), 90
Dracula's Daughter (1936), 83
Drakula İstanbul'da / Dracula in Istanbul (1953), 140, 141, 144, 146, 150–2
'drive-in' pictures, 58
Du Maurier, Daphne, 5
Dunsany, Lord, 174
Dünyayi Kutaran Adam / The Man Who Saved the World (1982), 142
Dwyer, Rachel, 214
dynamics as spectacle, 3
dystopian visions, 198–9

Eastmancolor, 87–9
Ebola Syndrome (1996), 187, 190–1, *192*, 194
Ebusuud, Shaykh Al-Islam Mehmed, 149
ecoGothic, 66–72
ecological disasters, 64–80
ecological sustainability, 12
Ecology without Nature, 66
Edelstein, David, 127
Edison Studios, 2
editing, 73
'Edo Gothic', 174–5
Edwards, Justin D, 10
The Eight Immortals Restaurant: The Untold Story (1993), 12, 186
El Santo, 61n
Elliot, Kamilla, 151
emigrant myth, 127–31
Emigrant novels, 128–31
Empire and the Gothic, 123
Enlightenment, 173
environmental politics, 113–16
Erksan, Metin, 144–6

Ertuğrul, Muhsin, 141
El espanto surge de la tumba / Horror Rises from the Tomb (1973), 104–5
Espírito Santo, 72
ethnicity, 72–7
'Euro-horror', 95
European Gothic film, 82–156
Eve's Bayou (1997), 47–8
Evil Dead (1981), 73, 126
The Evil of Frankenstein (1964), 90
evisceration special effects, 70
execution, *53*, *181*
exorcism, 52, 54
The Exorcist (1973), 54, 140, 144–6
'exploitation cinema', 76, 95, 187–8
El extrano amor de los vampiros / Night of the Walking Dead (1975), 100

The Fall of the House of Usher (1960), 5
'family dramas', 214–15
fantaterror, 11, 95–107
Fear Without Frontiers: Horror Cinema Across the Globe, 6
The Fearless Vampire Killers (1967), 99
Fellini, Federico, 58
female ghosts, 9
female transformation, *71*
female vampires, 165–6
feudal family, 214–15
feudal settings, 214
Field, Audrey, 87–9
filamu ya kutisha (frightening film), 13, 157–71
Film Censorship Board, 161
Filmfare magazine, 212–13
'final girl', 134
Fisher, Terence, 99, 100–1
flesh-eating zombies, 64–5
The Fly (1986), 27
folklore
   Anatolian, 148–52
   European, 103
   Nordic, 132
   South Korean, 8–9
   Tanzanian, 13, 163
   Turkish, 11, 140, 146
Forbes, Robertson, John, 90
foreign bodies, 10
forests, 66–72
Foucault, Michael, 119
Franco, Francisco, 11, 96
Franco, Jess, 58
Franco, Jesús, 96, 97, 99
Francoism, 100

INDEX

Frankenstein (1910), 2
Frankenstein (1931), 5, 21, 83, 99, 124
Frankenstein (novel), 19–21, 64, 173
Frankenstein and the Monster from Hell (1974), 90
Frankenstein Created Woman (1967), 90
Frankenstein Must Be Destroyed (1969), 90
Frankenstein's Bloody Terror (1968), 101, 105
Freaks (1932), 62n
Freud, Sigmund, 112
Friday the 13th (1980), 164
Friedkin, William, 54, 140, 144–6
Frightmares: A History of British Horror Cinema, 91
From Beyond (1986), 27
Fuchs, Michael, 12
Fulci, Lucio, 7–8, 9, 65, 67

Ganja and Hess (1973), 10, 32–49, 35, 37
García Maroto, Eduardo, 99
García Riera, Emilio, 52
Las garras de Lorelei / The Loreley's Grasp (1974), 101
Gatiss, Mark, 86
gaze, 40–1
Gelder, Ken, 56–7
Gen Takahashi, 13, 172–85, 177, 178, 180–1, 183
Gerard, Emily, 148
German Expressionism, 2, 99
German silent horror, 58
Germany, 162
Germany, West, 99
ghosting process, 55–6
ghosts, female, 9
Giallo, 7
Gilling, John, 103
Ginger Snaps (2000), 9
The Girl with the Dragon Tattoo (2011), 134, 136
Girolami, Marino, 65
Glaser, Ed, 142
global warming, 72–7
globalisation, 78
glocal myths, 96–101
GMC, 162
Go Ohara, 13, 172–85, 180, 181, 183
Godwin, William, 76
Goksung / The Wailing (2016), 8
Golden Bear Award, 144
Gordon, Stuart, 27
Gore, Al, 113
gore effects, 180–1

Görünmeyen Adam İstanbul'da / The Invisible Man in Istanbul (1955), 141
Goth (2008), 13
Goth: A Novel of Horror / Gosu: Risutokatto Jiken, (novel), 175–6
'Goth' fashion, 183–4
Goth: Love and Death (2008), 172–85, 177, 179
Goth: Wristcut Incident (novel), 175–6
Gothic, definition of, 2–9
'Gothic' (goshikku), 172–3
Gothic & Lolita Psycho (2010), 172–85, 180, 181, 183
Gothic citations, 52–7
'Gothic horror' film, definition of, 4, 6–8
Gothic Lolitas (Gusu-Loli), 12–13, 172–85
Gothic romances, 53
El gran amor del conde Drácula / Count Dracula's Great Love (1973), 100, 105
Grand Guignol, 84
Grau, Jorge, 96
Graz, 108–11, 110, 113–19
 Nuclear Power Plant (NPP), 113–14
Great Depression 1930s, 83, 141
Greene, Doyle, 57–9, 61–2n
Griffith, D. W., 2
Grosz, Elisabeth, 109
Gunn, Bill, 10, 32–49
Gustavsson, Tommu, 126
Gutiérrez, Vicente, 55
Guzmán, Ulises, 10, 50–63
Gwoemul / The Host (2006), 8

'H' category, 161
'H' certificate, 83
hadithi ya kutisha stories, 162
Halberstam, Judith, 173
Hallab, Mary Y., 112
Halloween (1978), 134
Halperin, Victor, 64
Hammer Film Productions
 B-movies, 83–94
 Gothic formulas, 96
 Gothic movies, 11
 influence of, 58, 99, 105, 214
 inspired by Hollywood B-movies, 5
 mummies, 100–1
Hantke, Steffen, 6
Hanyeo / The Housemaid (1969), 8–9
Happy Together (1997), 187
Hark, Tsui, 196
Harrow, Kenneth, 160–1
haunted houses, 11, 23
Hawks, Howard, 19

229

INDEX

Hehn, David, 108–21
Heidegger, Martin, 18, 22
Henriques, Anthony, 212–13
Henry: The Portrait of the Serial Killer (1986), 189
Heumann, Joseph K., 119–20
Las hijas de Dracula / Vampyres (1974), 99
Hilditch, Tom, 201–2
The Hills Have Eyes (1977), 127, 130
Hindi films, 12
Hindutva, 214–16
Hinton, James E., 42
Hisakatsu Kuroki, 179
Hitchcock, Alfred, 2, 5, 7
HIV/AIDS, 165, 168–9
Hogle, Jerrold E., 55
Hoglund, Johan, 11–12
Hollywood v. Hard Core: How the Struggles Over Censorship Created the Modern Film Industry, 91–2
'Hollywood Vampire Zombie' film collection, 161
The Holy Mountain (1973), 57, 62n
Homecoming (2004), 65
Hong Kong
   Category III films, 12, 186–208
   Gothic film, 161, 186–208
   as a Gothic space, 201–6
   handover, 187, 189, 192–4, *195*
Hong Kong Film Award, 186
Hooper, Tobe, 127
horror, definition of, 3–4
Horror and the Horror Film, 6
Horror Film: Creating and Marketing Fear, 6
Horror International, 6
Horror of Dracula (1958), 84, 86–9, 88
The Horror of Frankenstein (1970), 90
horror-fantasy genre, 211
hortlak, 11, 148–51
Hostel (2005), 127
The Hound of the Baskervilles (story), 210
Hughes, William, 67, 109, 123
Human Pork Chop (2001), 187, 189–90, *198*
Hüseyin Rahmi Gürpınar, 141
Hutchings, Peter, 89–90
hybridity, 186–7
   accent, 146–52
Hyperobjects, 66

I Spit on Your Grave (1978), 126
I Walked with a Zombie (1943), 64
Ibarra, Enrique Ajuria, 10

Imagery of Lynching, 35
imperialism, 8
İnanç, Çetin, 142
India, 161, 209–19
Indian Film Censor Board, 211
Islam, 146, 151
Islamicisation, 11
'It', 17–31
It Came from Beneath the Sea (1955), 23
It Came from Outer Space (1953), 10, 23
It! The Terror from Beyond Space (1958), 10, 23–5
The Italian (novel), 151
Italy, 5–8, 89, 99
cannibal films, 196

Jaani Dushman (1979), 12, 212–14
Jackson, Peter, 73
Japanese cinema, 5, 9, 12–13, 172–85
Japanese occupation of South Korea, 8
Jaws (1975), 118
Jekyll and Hyde (1913), 2
Jensen, Lars, 122
The Jewel of Seven Stars (story), 92
J-horror, 6
Jodorowsky, Alejandro, 57–8, 62n
Jones, Duane, 42
Jumbe, Shariff, 162–3, 166–7
Jungfrukallan / The Virgin Spring (1960), 125
Ju-On series (2000–16), 8
Justine (story), 54–5

kaidan (ghost stories), 173
Kanibaru Sinema, 66
Kapico, 162
Kariakoo, 162
Karnstein Trilogy (1970s), 92, 99
Karz (1980), 12, 215, 218
Kataude mashin garu / The Machine Girl (2008), 180
katuni za miujuza (miracle comics), 164
Kaufman, Lloyd, 119
Kavka, Misha, 2–3, 188, 202
Kawin, Bruce, 6
Kaye, Heidi, 2, 188
Kaziki Voyvoda / Vlad the Impaler (novel), 144
Kendi Oiwa, 175
Kenji Mizoguchi, 174
Keskinen, Suvi, 122
Khair, Tabish, 12
Khosla, Raj, 211
Kijiti, Bob, 165

230

INDEX

Kilink İstanbul'da / *Killing in Istanbul* (1967), 142
Kilink Uçan Adama Karşi / *Killing vs. Superman* (1967), 142
Kim Ki-young, 8–9
Kineto Shindô, 174
King of the Zombies (1941), 64
Klimovsky, León, 98, 100
Klotman, Phyllis, 35
Kneale, Nigel, 85
Knights Templar, 102–4
Kohli, Rajkumar, 211–13
Kolóğlu, Sohban, 144
Komeda, Kryzyszyof, 149, 152
Konuralp, Sadi, 146
Körkarlen / *The Phantom Carriage* (1921), 125
kosupure (cosplay), 184
Koven, Mikel J., 7
Kristeva, Julia, 54, 58
Kristina från Duvemåla (musical), 130
Kubrik, Stanley, 125
Kumar, Ashok, 210
Kumonosu-jô / *Throne of Blood* (1959), 174

Laemmle, Carl, 2
Lagerlöf, Selma, 125
Laguna, Sonny, 124
Lâle Film studios, 146
Larsmo, Ola, 130–1
Larsson, Stieg, 136
Latidos de pánico / *Panic Heartbeats* (1983), 105
Lau, Andrew, 186–7
The Laughing Dead, 112
Le Fanu, Sheridan, 54, 55, 92, 99
Lee, Christopher, 86–90, 87, 88, 92, 97, 99, 102
Lee, Spike, 47
Leffler, Yvonne, 125, 136
The Legend of the 7 Golden Vampires (1974), 90
Lemmon, Kasi, 47–8
lesbians, 93, 99
Lewis, Jon, 91–2
Lewis, Matthew, 151
lighting, 3, 42, 52, 202–4
Liljeblad, David, 124
Loftsdóttir, Kristín, 122
London International Festival of Science Fiction and Fantastic Film, 72
Longinus, 219
López Eguiluz, Enrique, 11, 96

López Moctezuma, Juan, 10, 50–63, 62n
Lorde, Audre, 48
Love to Kill (1993), 187, 199–200, 205
Lovecraft, H. P., 3, 10, 21–3, 102–3, 177
Lowenstein, Adam, 127
'Lullaby' (song), 152
Lust for a Vampire (1971), 92, 93
lynching, 35

Madhubala, 210
Madness (2010), 11–12, 124–5, 127–31, 129, 136–7
Mahal (1949), 210–11, 218
make-up, 72–3, 87
Malachi, 134
Malenka, la sobrina del vampiro / *Fangs of the Living Dead* (1969), 99
manga, 12, 173, 175
Mangeshkar, Lata, 210
mangroves, 64–80, 75, 77
Mangue Negro (2009), 11, 64–80
Manifesto Canibal, 66
La mansion de la locura / *The Mansion of Madness* (1973), 57–8
Mar Negro / *Dark Sea* (2013), 72
La marca del hombre lobo / *Frankenstein's Bloody Terror* (1967), 11, 96
El mariscal del infierno / *Devil's Possessed* (1974), 105
'Martian Gothic', 85
Marx, Karl, 196
masala films, 12, 209, 215, 218
Mask, Mia, 48
Mbembe, Achille, 160
McRoy, Jay, 12–13
Mehmood, 211
Meiji Restoration (1868–1912), 174
Men, Women and Chain Saws: Gender in the Modern Horror Film, 134
Men Behind the Sun (1988), 12, 187
Mexican horror wrestler films, 61-2n
Mexico, 9–10, 50–63, 100
mexploitation cinema, 59, 61-2n
mganga (the healer), 163–7
Mil gritos tiene la noche / *Pieces* (1982), 95
Millennium Trilogy (novels), 136
Miller, Cindy, 112
'mirroring effect,' 4
mise-en-scène
   cinematic apparatus, 182
   Egyptian, 100–2
   Gothic, 3, 87
   intimacy, 178
   original, 163

231

INDEX

mise-en-scène (cont.)
   past, 36, 52
   visual resemblance, 21
   'visuality', 214
   voyeurism, 7
'El miserere' / 'The miserere' (story), 103–4
misogynist imagery, 7
Moberg, Vilhelm, 128–31
mockumentary, 10
modernity, 58
Modi, Narendra, 215–16
Molina, Jacinto, 95, 98, 101, 103
The Monk (story), 151
Monseigneur Bertrand, 140
Monsiváis, Carlos, 55
monsters, 10, 19–26, 158
monstrous bodies, 111–13
monstrous transformations, 188–94
Los monstruos del terror / Assignment Terror (1970), 98–9
montage, 50
'Ele monte de las ánimas' / 'The Forest of the Souls in Purgatory' (story), 103
Mortgart, James, 152
Morton, Timothy, 66–7
Motion Picture Association of America (MPAA), 91–2
Movie Screening Ordinance Cap. 392, 186
mummies, 83–94, 100–1
The Mummy (1932), 83
The Mummy (1959), 89
The Mummy's Shroud (1967), 91
Mürebbiye / The Governess (1919), 141
Murray, Robin L., 119–20
Muslims, Turkey, 140–1
'mythologicals', 216–17

Na, Hong-jin, 8
Nag, Biren, 210–11
Nagin (1976), 211, 218
Naoyuki Tomomatsu, 180
Naschy, Paul, 95, 97, 101
national Gothic myths, 104
national monsters, 102–5
natural disasters, 77–9
naturalism, 189
Natyashastra, 217
Naum, Magdalena, 122
Neda Hei-tung Ng, 197
Negras, Fábulas, 72
Newman, Kim, 92
Niger, 160
Nigerian Gothic horror films, 161–2

Night of the Living Dead (1968), 64–5, 78, 92, 101, 124, 214
No profanar el sueño de los muertos / The Living Dead at Manchester Morgue (1974), 101
Noboru Iguchi, 180
Nobuo Nakagawa, 174
La noche de los brujos / Night of the Sorcerers (1974), 99
La noche del terror ciego / Tombs of the Blind Dead (1972), 97, 102–4, *104*
A Noite do Chupacabras / The Night of the Chupacabras (2011), 72
Nollywood films, 157, 160–1
Nordic Crime, 123
Nordic Exceptionalism, 123
Nordic Gothic B-movies, 11–12
Nordic history, 122–5
Nordic Horror film, 125–7
Nordic Noir, 123, 125, 136
Nordin, James M., 122
North Korea, 8
Nosferatu, eine Symphonie des Grauens / Nosferatu (1922), 46, 99, 124
La novia ensangrentada / The Blood Spattered Bride (1972), 99
'Nsyuka', 13, 164–5
Nsyuka (2003), 157, 162, 164–5
Nyby, Christian, 19

O'Bannon, Dan, 65
Olson, Daniel, 200
Ölüler Konuşmaz Ki / The Dead Don't Talk (1970), 11, 139–56, *147*
On the Postcolony, 160
Onibaba (1964), 174
onryō (wronged or suffering woman), 175
La orgía de los muertos / Terror of the Living Dead (1973), 101
La orgia nocturna de los vampiros / The Vampires' Night Orgy (1974), 100
Oscar, John P., 168
'othering', 191
Otherness, 19–26, 43–4, 57–61, 174
Otsuichi, 175
Ottoman Empire, 149–50
Özkaracalar, Kaya, 146–7
Ozombie (2012), 65

Pánico en el transiberiano / Horror Express (1972), 102–3
El pantano de los cuervos / The Swamp of the Ravens (1974), 101
'paracinematic reading', 112–13, *113*

INDEX

Park, Ki-hyeong, 6, 9
Parker, John, 28
parodies, 65, 99–100, 118
Patel, Divia, 214
Persona (1966), 125
'Philosophy of Composition', 163
The Philosophy of Horror, 3
The Picture of Dorian Gray (book), 3
Pinheiro, David, 11
Pirie, David, 89–90
The Pit and the Pendulum (1961), 5
Pitt, Ingrid, 99
Plan 9 from Outer Space (1959), 2
El pobrecito Draculín / Poor Dracula Junior (1977), 100
Poe, Edgar Allan, 2, 5, 57, 90, 163
Polanski, Roman, 92, 149
Popobawa (2007), 159, 167–9
Porto dos mortos (2008), 11
portraits, 151, 152
poverty, *190*
POVs, 73, 74
Predator (1987), 163, 165, 167
Predator 2 (1990), 167
Prince, Stephen, 109
Psycho (1960), 2, 7
Psycho Gothic Lolita (2011), 13
psychopaths, 172–85
Punter, David, 109
Purana Mandie / The Old Temple (1984), 212

qua horror films, 209–10, 212, 216–18
Quatermass 2 (1957), 85
The Quatermass Xperiment (1955), 85, 86
Queen's Award to Industry, 91

Rabid (1977), 214
racial isolation, *35*
racial politics, 10, 32–49
racist violence, 32–49, *35*
Radcliffe, Ann, 151
Raimi, Sam, 73
Raja, Bharati, 213
Ramsay Brothers, 212–16, 218
Randolph Hearst, William, 174
The Rapist (1994), 187, 200–2, *203*
Rasa, 217
The Raven (1935), 5
Rebecca (1938), 5
red colour, 84, 87
Red Rose (1980), 213, 217
Red to Kill (1994), 187, 194, 200, 202, *204*

La Residencia / The House That Screamed (1969), 11, 95–6
Resident Evil (2002), 9, 65
The Return of the Living Dead (1985), 65
The Revenge of Frankenstein (1958), 87–8, 90
'revenge of nature' films, 78
Revisitando Zombio / Revisiting Zombio (2009), 71–2
Reyes, Xavier Aldana, 4, 7–8, 11, 112, 127
Rigby, Jonathan, 84
Rivero, Gómez, 104
Romasanta, Manuel Blanco, 102
Romero, George, 9, 64–5, 101
Romero, Tina, 55, 61
Rosemary's Baby (1968), 92, 149
Rouch, Jean, 160
Roy, Bimal, 214
Run and Kill (1993), 187, 193–4, *195*, 200, 202, 205, *205*
Russell, Ken, 54, 62n
Rymdinvasion i Lappland / Invasion of the Animal People, Terror in the Midnight Sun (1959), 126

Sá, Daniel Serravalle de, 11
Saami, 122
Sade, Marquis de, 54–5
La saga de los Drácula / The Dracula Saga (1972), 100
Salander, Lisbeth, 136
Sampi, 122
Saner Film Production Company, 144–6
Sangster, Jimmy, 92
The Satanic Rites of Dracula (1973), 90, 92
Saw (2004), 127
Scandinavian Colonialism and the Rise of Modernity: Small Time Agents in a Global Arena, 122
Scarlet Memorial: Tales of Cannibalism in Modern China, 196–7
Scars of Dracula (1970), 90, 92
Schauerroman, 162
Schneider, Jay, 6
sci-fi, 2, 85
Scognamillo, Giovanni, 143–4
Sconce, Jeffery, 112–13, *113*
Scott, Ridley, 25
Scott, Robert A., 65–6
Sen, Aditi, 211–14, 218
Seoul Station (2016), 9
serial killers, 102, 177, 186
Serrador, Narciso Ibáñez, 11, 96
sexploitation films, 46

233

INDEX

sexuality, 32–49, 53–4, 60, 76, 88–9, 92, 99
Seyfi, Ali Rıza, 144
Şeytan / The Devil (1974), 140, 144–6, 151–2
Shaitani Badla / Devilish Revenge (1993), 213
'shaky cam', 73
shape-shifters, 23, 69
'sharing' of the body, 27
Shelley, Mary, 2, 5, 19–21, 64, 86, 90, 173
she-wolf film, 101
The Shining (1980), 125
Shintoism, 174–5
Shumileta / Queen of the Devils (2000s), 165–6
Sigurdson, Ola, 136
The Silence of the Lambs (1991), 199
silent German horror, 58
Sime, Sidney, 174
Singh, Harinam, 213
Sjöström, Victor, 125
Det Sjunde Inseglet / The Seventh Seal (1957), 125
Smith, Andrew, 67, 109, 123
Smith, Robert, 146
snake-woman, 211, 218
'social realism', 141
Society (1989), 194–5
socio-economic horror, 188–94
Son of Frankenstein (1939), 83
South America, 5
South Korea, 5–6, 8–9
Souza, César 'Coffin', 66
Soviet-Japanese War, 8
spaces of entrapment and separation, 205
Spain, 11, 95–107, *104*
special effects, amateurish, *113*
spectacle horror, 127, 182
'splatstick', 12, 119–20
splatter action, 166–7
Steps Entertainment Ltd, 162
stereotypes, 182
Stevenson, Robert Louis, 2
Stockholm Syndrome Film, 11–12, 122–38
Stoker, Bram
  copyright, 86
  Gothic atmosphere, 148
  Gothic novel, 3, 64
  Hammer Film Productions, 92–3
  Hollywood film, 5
  hortlak, 151
  Indian film, 210, 215
  Japanese film, 173

popular source material, 90
Spanish film, 97, 99
Turkish film, 144
Strayer, Kirsten, 58
Stringer, Julian, 186–8
Sturgeon, Theodore, 10, 17–18
sublime, 217–19
subliminal-horror films, 211–12, 215–16, 218–19
Sugar Hill (1974), 33
Süper Adam İstanbul'da / Superman in Istanbul (1972), 142
Süper Adam Kadınlar Arasında / Superman Among Women (1972), 142
Süper Adam / Superman (1971), 142
Superman, 142
Süpermen Dönüyor / Superman Returns (1979), 142
Süpermenler / Supermen (1979), 142
surrealism, 51–2, 57–8, 99
Suspira (1977), 6
Susuz Yaz / Dry Summer (1964), 144
Swahili theatre, 161
Swamp Thing (1982), 17
Swede Hollow (novel), 130–1
Sweden, 11–12, 136–7
'The System of Prof. Tarr and Dr. Fether' (story), 57

Tales from the Crypt (TV series), 47
Tales from the Hood (1995), 32, 47
Tamba, Sultan, 162
Tamba Arts Group, 162, 165
Tanzania, 13, 157–71
Tarzan İstanbul'da / Tarzan in Istanbul (1952), 141
Taste the Blood of Dracula (1970), 90
Taxi Hunter (1993), 187, 194, 199, 202
teenage youth, 90
'Tell-Tale Heart' (story), 2
The Terror Experiment (2010), 65
'Terrorist Dismembered Killing' film collection, 161–2
'Terrorist Ghost Killing' film collection, 161
The Texas Chain Saw Massacre (1974), 112, 124, 126–7, 134, 136, 214
theatricality, 182–3
The Thing from Another World (1951), 19–23, *20*
'Things', 17–31
Thompson, Katrina Daly, 168
3D film, 101
Tiananmen Square massacre, 189, 193

Tiempos duros para Drácula / Hard Times for Dracula (1976), 100
Tierney, Dolores, 59
time
  beings out of, 17–31
  B-movie Things, 19–26
  human, 24
Tôkaidô Yotsuya kaidan / Ghost Story of Yotsuya (1959), 174
Tokyo zankoku keisatsu / Tokyo Gore Police (2008), 180
El topo (1971), 57, 62n
torture, *53*
torture porn, 127
Tourneur, Jacques, 64
Trädgårdh, Lars, 122–3
Transylvanian Superstitions, 148
'trash', 108–21, 159–61
'traumagothic', 200
Tres eran tres / Three Were Three (1958), 99
Troma films, 119–20
true crimes, 187–8
Tsunami Arts Group, 166
Tsuyoshi Kazuno, 179
La tumba de la isla maldita / Hannah, Queen of the Vampires (1973), 99
La tumba de los muertos vivientes / Oasis of the Zombies (1982), 101
Turkey, 11, 139–56
  Atatürk's reforms, 146
  Muslims, 140–1
Turkey, Republic of, 141
Turkification, 139–40, 143–6
Turkish Star Wars, 142
Turkish War of Independence, 141
Turksploitation, 139, 142–6
28 Days Later (2002), 9, 65
The Two Faces of Dr. Jekyll (1960), 89

ubusyuka, 164
Üç Supermen Olimpiyatlarda / Three Supermen in the Olympics (1984), 142
Uçan Daireler İstanbul'da / Flying Saucers in Istanbul (1955), 141
udigrudi, 66
Ugetsu Monogatari (1953), 174
ultra-violent films, 7–8
The Underground Banker (1994), 187, 195, 199, 205, *205*
'unhuman', 18–19
'unintentional humour', 213–14
Universal Horror, 97, 99
Universal International, 92

Universal Pictures, 5, 86–8, 90, 105
Universal Studios, 2, 58, 96
'The Unnamable' (story), 21–3
The Untold Story (1993), 187, 191, *192*, 195, *198*, 199
The Untold Story 2 (1998), 187, 191, 194, 200
Usiku wa machungu – Mikononi mwa Popobawa / Night of Bitterness – In the Hands of Popobawa (book), 168

Valanciunas, Deimantas, 213–14
Valenti, Jack, 91–2
'Vampire and Corpse' film collection, 161
Vampire Girl Vs. Frankenstein Girl / Kyuketsu Shojo tai Shojo Furanken (2009), 180
A Vampire in Brooklyn (1995), 10
The Vampire Lovers (1970), 99
'Vampire Zombie Brutal War' film collection, 161
vampires, 2, 10, 34–46, 50–63, 83–94
  female, 165–6
Un vampiro para dos / A Vampire for Two (1965), 99
Vampyros Lesbos (1971), 99
Van Riper, Bowdoin, 112
Vargtimmen / The Hour of the Wolf (1968), 125
La venganza de la momia / The Vengeance of the Mummy (1975), 100–1
'vernacular cinema', 7
Vietnam war, 8
visual codes, 188, 202
visual effects, 141
Vitali, Valentina, 212, 214–15
von Trier, Lars, 125
voodoo, 64
voyeurism, 7

Walpole, Horace, 3, 64, 151
Wanachi Video Production, 157, 162
Wanyakyusa, 164
wazimamoto, 166
We Are Going to Eat You (1980), 196
We Are Monsters (2014), 124–5, 127, 131
Weinstock, Jeffrey, 56
welfare state, 122–5, 135–6
Wells, Paul, 57–8
Wendl, Tobias, 163
Werewolf of London (1935), 83
werewolfs, 101
West Germany, 99
Wester, Maisha, 10, 197

INDEX

Whale, James, 5, 21, 99
White, Luise, 166
White Elephant, 157, 159
White Zombie (1932), 64
Whiteness and Postcolonialism in the Nordic Region: Exceptionalism, Migrant Others and National Identities, 122
Who Goes There? (novel), 21–2
Wiklund, Tommy, 124
Wilde, Oscar, 3
Williams, Tony, 6, 189, 196, 201
Wirkola, Tommy, 65
Wither / Vittra (2012), 11–12, 122–38, *133*
Without Sanctuary (book), 35
Witoszek, Nina, 122–3
Woh Kaun Thi (1964), 211
Wong, Anthony, 186, *192*, 195
Wong Kar-Wai, 187
Wood, Edward D., 2
Wood, Robin, 112, 126–7, 158
World War I, 141
World War II, 174, 187
World War Z (2013), 9
The Wrong Turn (2003), 162

X certificate, 86–7
X the Unknown (1956), 85

Yalınkılıç, Yavuz, 11, 146–52
Yarbrough, Jean, 64
Yeh, Emilie Yueh-yu, 197
Yeogogoedam / Whispering Corridors (1998), 6, 9
Yeon, Sang-ho, 9
Yeşilçam, 141, 144
Yıldız Palace, Istanbul, 140
Yip, Veronica, 186
Yoshihiro Nishimura, 180
Young and Dangerous: The Prequel (1998), 187
Young Frankenstein (1974), 100
young women as animalistic threats, 8–9
YouTube, 108
Yubari International Fantastic Film Festival, 72
Yuzna, Brian, 194–5

Zanzibar, 168
Zaramo people, 163
Zheng Yi, 196–7
Zola, Emile, 189
zombBie-movies, 65, 67–80
Zombie 2 (1979), 7–8, 9, 65
Zombie Holocaust (1980), 65
zombies
 Afro-Caribbean, 64
 Black Americans and, 64
 Brazil, 11
 colonialism, 8
 environmental disasters, 64–80, 69, 74, 77
 flesh-eating, 64–5
 iconography, 2
 South Korea, 9
 Spain, 101
zombification, 65
Zombio (1990), 11, 64–80